Becoming Religious in a
Secular Age

Becoming Religious in a Secular Age

MARK ELMORE

UNIVERSITY OF CALIFORNIA PRESS

University of California Press, one of the most
distinguished university presses in the United States,
enriches lives around the world by advancing scholarship
in the humanities, social sciences, and natural sciences. Its
activities are supported by the UC Press Foundation and
by philanthropic contributions from individuals and
institutions. For more information, visit www.ucpress.edu.

University of California Press
Oakland, California

Library of Congress Cataloging-in-Publication Data

Names: Elmore, Mark, author.
Title: Becoming religious in a secular age /
   Mark Elmore.
Description: Oakland, California : University of
   California Press, [2016] | "2016 | Includes
   bibliographical references and index.
Identifiers: LCCN 2016000006 | ISBN 9780520290532 (cloth :
   alk. paper) | ISBN 9780520290549 (pbk. : alk. paper) |
   ISBN 9780520964648 (ebook)
Subjects: LCSH: Himachal Pradesh (India)—Religion—
   20th century. | Himachal Pradesh (India)—Religion—
   21st century.
Classification: LCC BL2016.H56 E46 2016 | DDC
   200.954/52—dc23
LC record available at http://lccn.loc.gov/2016000006

Manufactured in the United States of America

25 24 23 22 21 20 19 18 17 16
10 9 8 7 6 5 4 3 2 1

Contents

Illustrations

What Is This Thing Called Religion?

THE SACRED WAS EVERYWHERE, UNTIL IT WASN'T

When I discovered Mircea Eliade's theory of religion as an enthusias-
tic, if impetuous, undergraduate at the University of California, Santa
Barbara, I felt as though I had found the skeleton key that could unlock
the mysteries of cultural difference, revealing a world of infinite variety
unified by an undeniable unity. Amid the bewildering chaos of the
world's people and the seemingly infinite permutations of time, Eliade
showed me an undeniable pattern. Whether looking around campus,
remembering the Quechuan people I encountered during my high
school study abroad program, or even considering the primitivist
visions of radical environmentalists, I saw worlds of meaning founded
by the eruption of the sacred, dividing the world into sacred and profane and giving structure to the passage of time. I saw my confused
peers floating in the homogenous space of unfounded worlds. Everywhere I looked, I saw hierophanies. I used Eliade's theory to interpret
everything, from national parks to yogic postures, (shamefully) seduc-
ing those around me with the smarmy elegance of a magician who can
turn anything into the same thing.

Comforted by this vision of amniotic simplicity, I traveled to India
in the year before starting graduate school. With an innocence that now

Figure 1. Child and drummers at Bushahar festival. Photo by author.

seems both endearing and idiotic, I refused to bring a guidebook, a camera, or even a map. I was determined to have a "true" experience. I decided that I would take only third class trains and local buses and would reject the company of other travelers. I took little more than an old backpack, some hiking boots, one change of clothes, and my intellectual baggage. Arriving in India that first time, I thought myself to be a seasoned traveler wise to the patterns of human life. I wasn't expecting a spiritual paradise or a Gandhian fantasy of social equality, but I was arrogant enough to think that I carried no expectations.

I couldn't have been more wrong. The fierce reality of daily life in South Asia eviscerated romantic veils I didn't even know I had. I began to suspect that many of the things that had once resonated with the ring of truth were little more than echoes in the dark. Eliade's theories felt about as useful as my heavy hiking boots in the hundred-degree heat of the Delhi summer.

Those first months in South Asia fundamentally unsettled me in ways that I am only now—twenty years later—coming to understand. I had been ripped open by a world that defied description. Like Eliade, I had been seduced by the oldest of temptresses: a theory of unification. Boarding my flight home in Delhi, I let myself be soothed by the thought that I would never return. Again, how wrong I was. I would end up spending three of the next ten years in India.

Still reeling from my experiences, I began my graduate work in the study of religion, enrolling in Sam Gill's class Approaches to the Academic Study of Religion. A trickster of the highest order, Gill performed magic that every first-year graduate student should be lucky enough to endure. He destroyed me. He stoked the fire that my experiences in South Asia had kindled. And yet, of all the gifts I have received during my incredibly lucky life, there are few more precious to me than the experience of taking Gill's course.

The class was a revolution of the highest order. Among other things, I came to understand just how pernicious my Eliadean seduction had been. I learned not only that the cross-cultural connections that

Eliade's theories enabled were echoes of my own desires but also, and more importantly, why they were this way. Eliade's theories were inextricably tied to European colonization. To put it simply, the reason why religion across cultures looked so similar is because "religion" was *our* concept. It was as if I had a viewfinder installed permanently inside of my glasses. No matter where I was, I saw hierophanies everywhere I looked. Yet this was not because I was truly seeing what was there in the world, a truth that might testify to our unified humanity and thereby speak for the truth of religion itself. I was not discovering the perfect correspondence between map and territory. I had experienced a hall of mirrors reflecting the map, and in the process of seeking correspondence, I ignored the territory.

These personal experiences mirrored a change within the discipline of religious studies. The classical University of Chicago training in the history of religions had become suspect. Eliade continued to be a touchstone for the field, but now he was a punching bag and not a theoretical foundation. The myth of secularization, which underpinned so much research in the second half of the twentieth century, was quickly unraveling, and the field of postcolonial studies was coming of age.

As I contemplated my next project, I knew that I wanted to work on the emergence of religion as a category of understanding and organization in the South Asian context. There have been numerous important contributions to this field in the last decade, and by the time I was ready to begin working on my project, many of the foundational questions about the emergence of religion and secularity in South Asia—especially as related to communalism and violence—had already been amply addressed. These studies revealed how contemporary forms of religious identification (Hindu, Muslim, Sikh, etc.) relied on colonial formations of knowledge. They ably addressed the historical roots of these formations (in colonial and precolonial forms), but I couldn't help feeling like something was missing. While communalism was an adequate theory to understand the emergence and perpetuation of religious violence, it couldn't explain much else. Although I accepted that

Orientalism and colonial power structures certainly shaped the formation of these traditions, I often found it difficult to believe that these traditions could be reduced to such power relations.

This sentiment is a common one among historians of religions and those trained in the history of Sanskrit literature, as I am, yet most of these scholars reject arguments of postcolonial theory or of the invention of tradition, on the grounds of historicist assumptions. They see the roots of traditions (regional, theological, devotional, administrative, etc.) in precolonial formations. I too see these roots, but I reject the idea that discovering a precursor to a particular historical formation succeeds in explaining that formation. A pernicious holdover from the nineteenth century, this historical one-upmanship is commonly accepted as academic research. It is an origin story—a form of myth making that is officially sanctioned by contemporary academic practices. Historical research is imperative. I reject the belief that we have understood a phenomenon when we have discerned its earliest roots. Roots are important, but so are the trunk, the branches, and the leaves.

THE CONTOURS OF BECOMING RELIGIOUS

Becoming religious is a biography of the idea of Himachali religion. It is a coming-of-age tale that narrates the arrival and maturation of the idea that Himachal has a religion of its own. This story is, however, very different from the common tale of a triumphant will or narratives of foresight and self-congratulation. It is a story of becoming, the outcome of which was neither foreseen nor inevitable, one that, while having come to maturity, is far from complete.

The process of becoming religious as I describe it here is inextricably tied to the particular historical and cultural conditions in which it developed in the Western Himalayas in the second half of the twentieth century. Nonetheless, I believe it has a number of important insights to offer the study of religion more broadly. The story I tell in this book is not simply about understanding a particular tradition in its historical and geographic context, or about the simple imagination of a Western cultural construct in a non-Western context, or about recovering alternative social imaginaries. It is about something simultaneously more common and much more fundamental. It is about transformations in the very nature of what is real, about what is known and knowable, and about the ways that people should act. Said another way, the process of becoming religious, as I develop it here, operates on ontological, epistemological, and ethical registers. Becoming religious transforms the very nature of the world, the means by which it is known, and the ways one can relate to it.

In exploring this story, my goal is to show how certain individuals within a particular socio-historical context come to understand themselves as religious and how this understanding shapes their mode of being in the world. This is a story about the general mystery of becoming. It is not a story about disclosure or about origin and imitation. It is about how to think about religion. It would seem that this is a question as old as it is ordinary. The range of approaches for responding to it has long been established, the main questions framed, the schools delineated. This is certainly true. But if all of this is already settled, why is it that religion is, as Justice Potter Stewart described pornography, "impossible to define but immediately recognizable"?

This too is an old question. Or rather, it is a more like a truism than a question. And so I question it: is it difficult to define but recognizable because we have yet to discover the definition? I think not. Well, then, what does recognition consist of? What is it that is being recognized and rings true?

There is a kind of trick in that recognition passes so quickly from observation to assessment—the immediacy of recognition. The immediacy of recognizing religion gives off a flare of authenticity. We recognize religion like we recognize an old friend—it is something obvious and indisputable. As such, religion appears as natural to us as the color of trees or the sweet smell of sandalwood.

This line of thought is also far from revolutionary. Once, the great theorists of religion debated its origins, its function, and its phenomenology. Looking beneath the superficial glean of recognition, they showed how religion was really neurosis or the social.[1] As the heady days of early social science began to fade, the resonances once heard in Freud's dark theories of masochism and Eliade's optimistic philosophy of unification began to ring not of truth but of self-delusion, fascism, and barely disguised imperialism.

It is into this morass that *Becoming Religious* dives. While no self-respecting scholar of religion assumes that religion is a natural category to be explained, diagnosed, or destroyed, scholars across the disciplines (to say nothing of popular discourse) continue to labor under precisely this semiconscious delusion.

Since at least the time of Wilfred Cantwell Smith, scholars of religion have been self-conscious about religion's construction. They have recognized that religion has a history—that it is not the name all beings have given to how they grapple with life's big questions. These social constructions of religion are certainly important contributions and have revealed many things.

And yet no matter how seductive such constructions have been (consider, for example, that British colonialists inculcated Christian ideals via literary study rather than missionization), I have always felt somehow dissatisfied with these explanations. But it was not until I taught a class on theory and method in the study of religion that I began to put things together. As my students went through Kant, Feuerbach, Freud, and Weber, I had to work to help them read beyond the question of whether or not the theories were "right." For most students, they obviously were *not* right. Then, I asked them not whether they agreed with Freud, but why Freud thought he was right. As the course progressed and we examined scholars from more recent times, the problem reversed. The students no longer struggled to understand how Marx could reduce religion to such a small thing. They immediately recognized "religion as a cultural system" and spirituality as the thin veneer worn by corporate capitalism to produce consumers from even the most discerning people. It was during these classes that my unsettled intuitions began to take shape as coherent thoughts. I had long come to understand the value of reading Freud even though his conclusions seemed transparent. Simply put, what unsettled me was what I heard in Freud's formulation and that of Timothy Fitzgerald and Russell McCutcheon. In a word, it was arrogance. Fitzgerald was no less certain that religion "cannot reasonably be taken to be a valid analytical category"[2] than Freud was that "religion is an illusion."

But what was there to learn from this? That men are arrogant? Certainly, but that is not a very illuminating conclusion. It was only when I was rewriting *Becoming Religious* and beginning to grapple with a similar arrogance that I saw in the simple historicist narratives of religion's past. So many scholars seemed to argue over when religion *really* began and whether an indigenous religion could exist if religion itself was part of colonial projects. They suggest that, now that we have finally discovered the origin of religion in the development of secularism or in the changing strategies of colonial reform, we can be done with it. Even if we now know that religion will not disappear into the glow of development, at least we know when and where it started.

But as I tried to reconcile all of these ideas with all of the work I had done in the Western Himalayas, I found that virtually none of it was helpful. Clearly, religion was important in the everyday lives of people in Himachal, but examining its origins in colonial projects, in the indigenous reforms of the Bengal Renaissance, or through the paradigms of Hindu fundamentalism provided only the thinnest of insights. It is from this unsettled place of irreconcilability that I began to think about the question of religion anew.

WHAT IS YOUR RELIGION?

Longhaired and wild-eyed, the deity's medium lurches back and forth, "playing" (*khelnā*)[3] with the deity's power inside him. Having just returned from a week-long tour of neighboring villages where he answered questions, expelled demons, and healed sick children, the

Figure 2. Gūr "playing" during a festival. Photo by author.

deity was elated to be back with the people who sung his songs, knew his true name, and shared his home. During the rite, which lasted several hours, I collected his songs and stories, learning about his origins (*devbāni*), genealogical connections (*vaṃśāvalī*), and miraculous powers (*pratyaskṣa*).

When the rite was over, everyone settled down with steaming bowls of stew made from freshly sacrificed goat. As we ate, a young boy, Vijay, approached me with a confidence I had only seen in minor government officials or adolescent boys. I grew anxious, fearing a rebuke for some unintended slip in etiquette or (perhaps worse) an invitation to his room to become a pawn in his quest for social capital. But his mission was neither so self-assured nor so selfish. Having listened to my questions and watched my frantic scribbling all afternoon, he felt the need to communicate the essential thing I seemed not to understand. In the lyrical, Pahāṛī-inflected Hindi of the region, he said: "This is our religion" (*devīdevatā sanskṛti*).[4]

I starred blankly at him, frozen in the uncanniness of the moment. Of course this was his religion. Wasn't that obvious? Yet if this statement was only the truism I thought it to be, then why did he act as if it were a revelation? Why, moreover, did everyone around me respond to the boy as if he had revealed something powerful? The experience was unsettling. I longed to share the revelatory awe of my companions, but I could not, and that failure haunted me for years. I returned to Himachal several times after that. I read deeply into the archive of its vernacular history. But as my knowledge of Himachal grew, I became increasingly convinced that I would not know anything until I could understand the power of Vijay's statement.

I became a father in the intervening years. I found myself enraptured with the power and creativity of my son's developing mind, and I invested all my energy in him. I thought I had given up on Vijay when, out of the banality of daily life, insight came to me in the Safeway parking lot.

I was helping my son out of the car when he pointed to the store and said: "This is a supermarket." The wonder in his eyes and the joy of recognition in his face brought with it one of the great pleasures of father-hood. Just for a moment, he had lifted the veil from my tired eyes: I could see the store as he had—for the first time. It *was* a supermarket. And in that moment, the uncanniness of Vijay's statement that had so bedeviled me unraveled in a kaleidoscope of recognition. I saw the unadulterated pleasure of recognition in my son's face. He had unified a concept with an object of his experience. In his joy, I was finally able to understand the power and pleasure of recognition that animated Vijay's statement. It was only my calloused ears that had been deaf.

In both content and function, *Becoming Religious* is a narrative of rec-ognition. The core narrative—which traces how Himachalis recognized their own beliefs and practices as religious—is energized with stories of my own struggle to understand the lived worlds of contemporary Himachal people, which narrate my own process of relating to religion. In bringing my own voice to the text, I hope to invite the reader to imag-ine religion not as an object, as an identity one wears like a set of clothes, or even as something that can even be embraced or rejected but rather as an intimate, dynamic process that has no end. Framing my work in this way, I hope that my readers will generate a series of recognitions, or at least questions. I hope to enable them to see how much is at stake when they respond to the question, "What is your religion?" Or when, in cas-ual conversation, they mention that they are spiritual but not religious. Moreover, I hope to reveal the constant and ongoing persistence of this question and the impossibility of avoiding it.

PART 1. POWER: HOW HIMACHAL DISCOVERED ITSELF AND ITS RELIGION

Watch a newborn baby nurse in the first days of its life. The elegant grace of the process is spellbinding. So few things appear as immediate and natural that explaining the causal link between a child's needs and a mother's breast seems to be a task fit only for pedants or dullards. And yet this ingeniously designed system has humble origins. Breast milk shares its parentage with the mucus that gathers in my nasal passage to fight viruses or bacteria that attack my body when I'm sick. The milk begins not as a response to the needs of a child but as a byproduct of the duct system's production of the antibacterial enzyme lysozyme, which is present in all bodily secretions and fundamental to our basic survival.

Like the feathers of birds and the swim bladders of sharks, this is an example of what Darwin called pre-adaptation and what contemporary biologists call exaptation.[5] Exaptation refers to a biological process of transmission that occurs when a trait that evolved for one reason under particular environmental conditions is subjected to a new environment in which that trait offers a great adaptive advantage.

This concept is tremendously helpful in illustrating the conditions that enable the emergence of religion in Himachal Pradesh and the postcolonial world more broadly. Exaptation is the process that enables the possibility of becoming religious in a secular age. More than a metaphor, it suggests much about the pages to come, and the chapters 1 and 2 take their orientation directly from it. They explain radically shifting conditions following India's independence that enabled and directed the emergence of Himachali religion—a set of conditions predicated on the arrival of secular governance, innumerable projects of developmental modernization, organizational efforts, regional unification and organization, and the application of modern legal forms. In short, the very possibility of Himachali religion is dependent on the establishment of all those things that were once thought to destroy religion.

These first two chapters offer a genealogy of the religion that was the subject of Vijay's assertion, "This is our religion." His association of religion with a set of communal activities that occurred as a local deity returned home was predicated on the aggregation and identification of particular people ("our"), the division of certain beliefs and practices from others ("this"), and the differentiation of an operative category of faith that could be recognized in the practices of a group ("religion").

Part 1 explore how the modernization projects of the 1950s and 1960s that aimed at economic reform, political organization, and rural electrification set the dominant conditions within which Himachali religion could emerge. It shows how the arrival of secularity provided the environment for religion's emergence. Despite the colonial-era myth that India was preeminently a religious space and the consensus of historians that religion's emergence in relation to national secularism was largely worked out by the second half of the nineteenth century (if not during the Bengal renaissance), religion didn't arrive in the Western Himalayas until the second half of the twentieth century.

This section explains how religion emerged as a second-order effect of the process of becoming "sufficiently developed." In the years that followed the Indian Independence Act, the new country's constitutional assembly articulated the foundational structure of the Indian state. States were created under the evolving federalist system of governance, and they were allocated differing degrees of autonomy from the political center. Large and powerful states such as Uttar Pradesh and Bengal were given enormous latitude in formulating the character of their states. Other regions were given somewhat less autonomy, and some were judged (for a multiplicity of reasons) to be incapable of independent administration. The region that would later be called Himachal Pradesh was one of these states. The assembly vote on this question was, however, not unanimous, and a special covenant was established between the assembly and prominent leaders from Himachal. The assembly promised that, as soon as the region was "sufficiently developed," it would attain its true "area" and "status." That is, Himachal would integrate large regions of the foothills currently under the control of Delhi and Punjab and would attain all the independent rights accorded to the largest states in the nation.

However, the attainment of full statehood did not turn on Himachal becoming sufficiently developed. Ironically, Himachali leaders won the fight for statehood by capitalizing on Indira Gandhi's reelection strategy for the 1971 elections. Despite the fact that Himachal attained statehood as a token of political patronage, enormous energy at both urban and rural levels was expended during the two decades between the covenant and its realization in trying to decipher what it meant to be sufficiently developed and how it could be achieved.

Two strands of thought dominate most contemporary reflection on relations between religion and secularity in South Asia. Though it takes many forms, the first of these is predicated on the idea that India has always been a preeminently religious place.[6] The other, which dominates the thinking of South Asian historians, assumes that the appearance and development of religion in relation to national secularism was largely complete by the second half of the nineteenth century.[7]

The cultural history of the Western Himalayas offers a stark counterpoint to both these positions. While this history—the empirical ground of this book—calls into question much of the contemporary debate on religion and secularism in South Asia, the position developed here is directed less at South Asian historians and more specifically at the emergence of the category of religion.

Seen in this light, part I of *Becoming Religious* can be understood as a comment on the problem of origins within the academic study of religion—as manifested both in early social scientific theories of religion and more contemporary accounts of the "creation" of various traditions. As such, it is a redirection of historicist or essentialist concerns toward the forms of emergence suggested by evolutionary biologists.

This attention to exaptation is more than word play. The idea of exaptation offers us a unique ability to reaffirm the importance of beginnings that fixates Timothy Fitzgerald as much as it did Freud, while avoiding the cultural imperialism and historical teleology of Herbert Spenser, the psycho-infantilization of Karl Marx, and the fantastic, fictional origin stories of Sigmund Freud's *Moses and Monotheism*. Perhaps more importantly, it offers a theoretically defensible and historically rigorous solution to Russell McCutcheon's critique of sui generis religion and the many reductive misreadings of Talal Asad, who confused his *Genealogy* with liberation or conspiracy.[8]

PART 2. KNOWLEDGE: MAKING AND MANAGING
HIMACHALI RELIGION

"What is your religion?" It's a common question that elicits an immediate, almost unconscious response: "I am Catholic." "I am Hindu." "I am Pagan." "I am atheist." "I am spiritual, not religious." The ease with which we answer this question conceals a secret history that is both personal and social. For anyone reading this book, religion is a question we have already responded to. We deploy ready-made answers without skipping a beat, and, for the most part, our answers feel natural. They belong to us. And yet, because these responses come so naturally to us, it is incredibly difficult for us to peek behind them—to understand how and why we developed them or to contemplate how they shape our understanding of ourselves, of our relations with others, and of our relations to truth. These unthinking responses hide the particular sedimented history of our making—the contingencies that stand in as natural, the random that dissimulates itself as necessary.

To understand in the abstract that one's proclivities and dispositions are a complex product of personal and social history is simple enough. Getting behind them to understand how they have shaped the very horizon of our experience is something else altogether. This study offers such an opportunity. Imagine, for a moment, encountering a group of people who have never responded to "religion" because it simply didn't exist. For the vast majority of people living in the Western Himalayas, this was the case well into the second half of the twentieth century. Of course, there were lots of things that one might categorize as religious—local deities, rites of possession, calendric festivals—but there was simply no need or desire to frame or interpret these things as religion. The concept—not simply the word—was unavailable and unnecessary. From the 1960s onward, however, Himachalis found themselves asking, "What is our religion?" Seen from the present, the response, like Vijay's, is clear and immediate: *devīdevatā saṇskṛti*. But it would take decades of intellectual, political, rhetorical, and ethical negotiations to arrive at that answer. At present, deciding what is and is not legitimately religious, how one should live a religious life, and how one should relate to religious tradition are all issues that Himachalis have responded to and continue to respond to.

Chapters 3 and 4 show how religion made its entrance in the Western Himalayas as an implicit product of the quest for statehood and the land reforms of the 1950s. However, while Himachalis had become a people by this point, religion had not yet become the object of explicit reflection and reform. It was neither the object of intellectual elaboration nor the object of bureaucratic administration. Instead, there was only the "minor" issue of who could manage lands once managed by village deities. As the need to establish that the region was sufficiently developed grew ever stronger and the apparatus of the state grew more sophisticated, Himachali religion emerged as, simultaneously, an explicit object of intellectual curiosity subject to the desires and demands of the archive, an object in need of translation, and an object of governmental organization.

Part 2 takes up the subsequent transformations: the development of a vernacular science of religion and the emergence of the political, regional, intellectual, and ethical negotiations necessary to situate Himachali religion in relation to its others (the economy, secular governance, identity, etc.). The chapters of part 2 explore how new modes of knowledge production, new forms of public discourse, new forms of expertise, and new styles of governance are instrumental to the process of becoming religious in the modern world.

Chapter 3 explores the emergence and development of Himachal's vernacular science of religion, a discourse that has come to define the shape and scope of Himachali religion. Struggling to articulate their argument for recognition as an autonomous state, early Himachali leaders realized that literacy rates, kilometers of roads, and village electrification metrics alone were not sufficient justifications for establishing statehood. As India came of age as an independent nation, this need to see beyond metrics of development became a national, and not simply a regional, concern. As its mission, the first major independent census endeavored to "invest the dry bones of village statistics with flesh-and-blood accounts of social structure and social change," and like other regions across India, Himachal began a series of "village surveys." Contracted by the census bureau, these surveys employed educated villagers to construct reviews of the history and culture of their villages. It would be difficult to overestimate the impact of this work. While the surveys themselves did not become widespread authoritative texts, the idea that one could write the history of one's own village took root quickly. Soon, farmers, pharmacists, and shopkeepers alike were all working to preserve and articulate what they called "our religious culture" (*devīdevatā saṇskṛti*).

The transformation of laypeople into vernacular historians reveals an edifying paradox. Written in a simple, standardized Hindi intelligible to the entire literate public, the histories they produced are not arcana of elite, idle academics but rather neighborly addresses offered by writers who believed that they were heeding a "calling" to reveal Himachal to itself. Ironically, it is the selflessness of responding to a calling beyond the taints of economic exchange that gave these writers their "expertise," and enabled their texts to shape the texture of daily life in the region.

This paradox facilitates a twofold empowerment. As the authors of the texts were not remunerated for their efforts, the works are imagined as being free of dubious authorial motivations. Freed of subjective machinations, they were seen not as stories told about the past but rather as the revelations of truths previously obscured. To use the term to which this discourse strived to live up to, they are objective knowledge. In the process of becoming religious, the second primary movement—after the establishment of an object—is this object's ascension to the status of objectivity and the forms of normalization and archival control such objectivity entails. In Himachal at least, it is not, as René Girard would have it, that "the secret heart of the sacred is violence," but that the secret heart of the sacred is objectivity.[9]

Guaranteed by the objectivity of scientific knowledge, itself possible only through the expertise of vernacular historians, *devīdevatā saṇskṛti* emerges as something the state can (and must) relate to. It must mark, manage, and maintain the porous boundaries between itself and its others. And yet this is much more than a state project to delimit its sphere of influence, as if it were creating religion ex nihilo.

In chapter 4, I explore the complicated acts of translation involved in the interpretive labor of religion. I show how the reification of religion (essential to the process of becoming religious) depends on a complicated series of cross-domain translations (of metaphoric translations and extensions) that use the domains of "religion" and "governance" as mutually supportive metaphors. That is, the meaning and scope of both religion and governance takes shape as individuals translate back and forth between the domains of religion and government. They become intelligible in the process of being related to and differentiated from that which they are not. They each become objects within the scope of that which they are not. State officials draw boundaries around that which is legitimately religious and that which falls under the control of the state. Villagers use metaphors of understanding originating within the hall of the secretariat building to elucidate the unseen activities of their deities.

PART 3. ETHICS: BECOMING RELIGIOUS AND THE MYSTERIES OF BEING

The final puzzle piece that lies at the heart of *Becoming Religious* was revealed to me late—perhaps too late. I had always been uneasy with the triumphalist narrations of Himachal's ascension to statehood and the transparent associations made between divinity and the state. At the same time, I had written a book that I described as the biography of an idea, and I was uncomfortable with the implicit assumptions of such a narrative. It suggested that Himachali religion had become a thing, that it had come of age, and that I could now delimit its content and structure like any other object.

Something about this always unsettled me. I orbited the issue for the first few years of my professional academic life, writing two different drafts from the same ethnographic work at the heart of *Becoming Religious*. Inevitably, the results were always the same. I would arrive at the last chapter, and the voices from my fieldwork would begin to haunt me. Each time I would try to draw the narrative to a close, the voice of an elderly villager or an earnest young woman would rise up to contest it, demanding to be heard. Sometimes these voices were tiny; sometimes they bellowed. The results were always the same. I would try to weave their voices into the narrative I had constructed, and this weaving inevitably turned into the unraveling of that which I had woven previously.[10]

This could have continued for years. I could have pretended not to hear the voices and sent the manuscript off. Instead, with the manuscript's second incarnation half-unraveled, a personal disaster ripped my life up at the roots and shook me vigorously for a couple of years. During that time, I realized, to my despair, that there was an incredible symmetry between my autobiography and the biography of Himachali religion I was narrating. Both were narratives of triumph. I had achieved all the dreams that had driven me from the vague longings of a fifteen-year-old boy alone on a public bus in an unknown Ecuadorian village to the mythical tenure-track job. The Himachali religion that farmers and pharmacists had sought for decades to describe and define was now safely ensconced in the hearts and minds of Himachalis. It was only when the beautiful rooms of my personal life began to crumble that I recognized those voices that inevitably unraveled my narratives.

Tumbling amid the flotsam my life had become, I was teaching a class on existentialism when I stumbled on phrase in Cheryl Strayed's book *Tiny Beautiful Things:* "the great mystery of becoming." I remembered a famous passage from a speech by Yashwant Singh Parmar, in which he says that, since its birth, Himachal Pradesh has been "in a state of becoming rather than being."[11] Having spent too much time in graduate school with Heidegger's *Being and Time,* I couldn't help but notice such a phrase. Yet after much reflection, I dismissed it as one more verbal eccentricity from one of Himachal's loquacious intelligentsia.

Strayed's narrative, which brought together several apparently accidental events from her life into a process of becoming, broke me open. It was only then that I understood that what I had previously seen as an ending was, in fact, a beginning. The shift from being to becoming may seem small, but it changes everything. What was once a tragedy marking the disappearance of a realized dream became something else entirely, a fresh glimmer of hope reborn.

A story narrating the biography of Himachali religion was not a story about the maturation of an object; it was an adventure, a process, "a becoming" that, to quote a favorite passage from Nietzsche, knew "no satiety, no disgust, no weariness" and was "without goal, unless the joy of the circle is itself a goal."[12]

The final section of this book describes life after the maturation of Himachali religion. At this point in the process, Himachal's religious culture had become a naturalized object—an object one cannot avoid and which one must consciously relate to. In this way, religion became an object that requires some type of response analogous to other "natural" objects like one's own body, mortality, or disease.

The naturalization of religion does not mark the end of "becoming" and the arrival of "being." Rather, it marks the beginning of a full-throated debate about the nature, scope, and function of religion. Having become an object, religion is now an opening where self-definition and self-understanding take place. It is no longer only a placeholder in the restructuring of the state as it was in part 1. It is more than an object of academic reflection and governmental management as it was in part 2. As an object separated from its others (state, economy, politics, etc.), defined and organized by a science of religion, and regulated and managed by the state, it emerges as an ethical force and an object of desire. At this moment, becoming religious enters its "ethical mode." The question is no longer *whether* one can relate to religion or whether it is

Figure 3. Road to Sangla Valley. Photo by author.

known or knowable but rather *how* one relates to religion and how it does or should inform one's thoughts and actions.

That is, Himachalis have *become* religious much in that same way that we in the West must be *understood* as "religious." This is very different from the self-identified category that one gives when asked about religion by census takers or new friends at parties. In this sense, claiming that one is secular, agnostic, or spiritual is no different than claiming that one is Christian, Muslim, or Hindu. All of these individuals have established a relationship to whatever they consider to be religion. We live in a time when it is impossible *not* to be religious. We must assume a relation to religion, even (or perhaps especially) when we define ourselves as areligious. This does not erase the enormous and powerful difference between the various forms of becoming religious. Rather, it recognizes that the question of religion is no longer an ontological or an epistemological question. It is an ethical one. The question has become how, in taking a particular position in relation to religion, one situates oneself.

In the final weeks of editing this manuscript, I remembered an essay from my first graduate class with Sam Gill. At the time, he was just finishing the essay, which would be published in a collected volume.[13] We read it in class, and in many ways it was a distillation of everything he was attempting to show us. Now, more than ten years later, it is hard for me not to laugh as I recognize that my own words are a reflection of Sam Gill's approach to the study of religion as play, *sub specie ludi*. Perhaps, like the deities of Himachal Pradesh, my understanding was there all along. Or perhaps it was only revealed in becoming. Analogously, there is nothing that you do not already know in *Becoming Religious*, but it hides the most important of all secrets.

A GLIMPSE OF THE WESTERN HIMALAYAS

The narrative that follows is meant to be neither comprehensive nor authoritative. It is a story designed to orient the reader—a strategic essentialism. The precolonial pasts of the Western Himalayas are spottily documented. The majority of our information comes from inscriptions (mostly from Chamba), architecture, traveler's accounts (Chinese, Mughal, French, etc.), scattered references in Sanskrit literature (mostly from the epics and the Purāṇas), and local texts (genealogical rolls, Sāñchā texts, pilgrimage registers, land holding registers, merchant ledgers, etc.). The picture that emerges is that the Western Himalayas were fairly isolated from the plains to the south, the Tibetan plateau to the northeast, and Kashmir to the northwest (although there was limited trade and travel between the regions). There were, of course, occasional points of contact, as foothill states paid tribute to Mughal or Sikh rulers, Buddhist monks traveled the valleys of the Satluj or the Beas, and wandering ascetics inevitably passed through the area in their peregrinations.

For much of this time, there were three larger state formations in the Western Himalayas: Chamba, Kullu, and Kangra. However, the size and

Figure 4. The mall in Shimla. Photo by author.

power of these states fluctuated greatly over time. When the great Chinese traveler Hsuan-tsang visited India from 629 to 645, he reported that nearly the entire region was controlled from Kullu and that it was filled with Buddhist monasteries and universities. At other times, Kangra appears to have controlled large tracts of land, and at still others, each of these larger polities was fractured into many tiny principalities.

What is clear is that the boundaries of these small states were continually shifting, that war was a constant feature of the interactions between communities, and that the region continued to experience new migrations. This is evidenced by the many families whose histories tell of being forced from Rajasthan or the Gangetic Plain. This instability was equally true as the British moved westward in the late eighteenth and early nineteenth century. At that time, the Gurkhas controlled much of the land of Kinnaur, Garhwal, and Bushahar. Raja Sansar Chand was attempting to take land from Kahlur and Chamba. The British arrived into this matrix of conflicting relations, warring families, and hill battles and used it to their benefit. Their system of spies allowed them to gain detailed knowledge of the local rivalries. They took advantage of threatened kings and used their small but knowledgeable armies to push back the Gurkhas and control what would become known as the Shimla hill states. The British defeat of the Gurkhas in 1815 marked the arrival of a new game in town.

With the arrival of the British to the Western Himalayas, many things changed, though the changes were neither unified, systematic, nor simultaneous. Many of the areas taken from the Gurkhas were administered as princely states. They were relatively independent, and legal and administrative matters were attended to internally. Their interactions with colonial officials were limited, though they increased later in the nineteenth century. One resounding change that colonialism initiated in this area was the solidification of state boundaries. The once porous and often contested boundaries between states were fixed, and all interstate disputes were settled by British courts.

In 1846, the British defeated the Sikhs and took over the hill regions that the Sikhs had controlled since 1805. These regions, which included Kanga, Kullu, and Lahaul, were administered centrally as part of Punjab and received different treatment than the Shimla hill states and Chamba. The land settlement processes were more extensive and more carefully constructed than those in other regions, and they were used as granaries and produce fields to support the growth of Shimla.

Arguably the most important development in the Western Himalayas during the colonial period was the growth of Shimla from an empty hillside to the administrative center of the world's largest empire in a matter of decades. I will address the growth of Shimla more specifically later, but for now it is important to understand that the city quickly came to dominate not only the colonial imaginary but also the administration of the Western Himalayas. Increasingly, it was recognized as the hub through which information and commerce in the hills proceeded. The growth of Shimla was a product of colonial will. There was no reason why this city should have become the center of Western Himalayan politics and economics. It is perched on the side of a steep

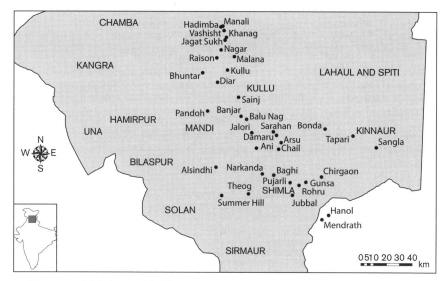

Figure 5. GPS-located fieldwork sites.

hill, has limited water resources and little to no arable land, and is difficult to access from every direction. However, from the 1830s onward, Shimla's size and importance increased steadily. The infrastructure laid by the British to accommodate its overheated administrators provided the basis for the modern state of Himachal Pradesh.

Shimla did not immediately become the center of Himachal Pradesh. The Western Himalayas came rather late to the struggle for independence. It was not until the late 1940s that there was a significant nationalist presence outside of Shimla. Even in Shimla, nationalist sentiment was relatively weak. The brunt of the anticolonial movement in Himachal was pushed forward by the Congress-backed Praja Mandal movements that marched in Dhami, Suket, Bushahar, and other areas. The development of regional consciousness was, however, not as tied to the nationalist cause as it was in many other areas. Though the Praja Mandal movements were backed by Congress and inspired by Gandhian principles (notably Satyagraha), they were more concerned with issues of local corruption and princely misrule than questions of national integration.

When independence did come to India, the hills were not a primary concern for leaders like Nehru, Patel, or Sitaramayya. There were many other problems needing immediate attention. Though the hills remained largely unaffected by the violence that plagued the rest of the subcontinent, the formation of the state of Himachal Pradesh did not come quickly. The biggest political problem in the Western Himalayas following independence was the princes. How were they to be integrated into India? Would they leave? Would they retain control of their land? Would they receive compensation from the state? As archival documents from the All India States People's Conference (AISPC) show, most of the mergers proceeded smoothly. However, in places like Bilaspur, where the raja resisted calls to integrate, mergers were more difficult. The raja of Bilaspur claimed cultural and political independence and struggled to retain autonomy, often through violent means. A letter from S. R. Chandel, president of the Bilaspur Praja Mandal, to the members of the AISPC summarizes many of these problems and the type of struggle of the Mandal workers: "The ruler [of Bilaspur] is an autocrat with no vestige of a restraint on his personal will and actions. Feudalism of the worst type has been crushing the people for centuries. People's sense of revolt against even blatant injustice and naked tyranny has become dull."[14] After applying pressure from a number of angles, the Mandal workers succeeded in forcing the raja to merge with India. During the struggles for the integration of Bilaspur into the Indian union and many other similar struggles across the Western Himalayas, a group of elites emerged who worked for the expulsion of princely rule. From this group, a region-wide organization was formed, and it was this group of leaders that most forcefully pushed for the formation of Himachal Pradesh. Without a doubt, the most important leader to emerge from this group was Y. S. Parmar, the architect of modern Himachal and its first chief minister. Well educated and passionate, Parmar became the primary spokesman for the state as he forced himself into the Praja Mandal struggles and fought for Himachali recognition for more than two decades.

These decades were the most important for the foundation of the state of Himachal Pradesh. This was a tumultuous time in the Western Himalayas. Political allegiances were being redrawn, administrative and information networks were growing, land holdings were being redefined, new courts were created, new ministries were formed, and new elite classes were forged. In the period immediately following India's independence from the British Raj, the Western Himalayas retained their heterogeneous character. The Shimla hill states, in combination with Chamba and several other small pieces of land, were consolidated and designated as a chief commissioner's province, which was recognized as a "Part C" state when the Indian Constitution came into force on January 26, 1950. However, this recognition was felt by many, including Parmar, to be lacking both geographically and politically. It did not include many princely states. This perceived gap began a twenty-year struggle to enlarge the geographic territory of the state and its political power within the Indian federalist system. As a Part C state, Himachal Pradesh was granted a legislative assembly that began to form ministries and write legislation, including the land reforms of the early 1950s, the Panchayati Raj Act of 1951, the Ex-Communication Act of 1955, and the Compulsory Primary Education Act of 1953.

The geographic area of the state grew rapidly with the steady inclusion of new princely states and the accession of districts previously held by other municipalities. However, in 1956, a majority decision by the States Reorganization Committee in 1956 recommended that Himachal be merged with Punjab. Himachal provided water and power for Punjab's growing agricultural sector and its population, so there was an enormous amount of pressure, particularly from Punjab, on central authorities to merge the areas into one municipality. The desire was so great that in legislative lore it is said that Y. S. Parmar was offered the chief minister post if he would agree to the unification. He refused the post and, in concert with other Himachali leaders, rejected the merger. Instead, Himachal Pradesh became a union territory administered by a lieutenant governor. Its legislative assembly was dissolved, and most of the control that had the region had enjoyed in the early 1950s was revoked. Slowly, through processes of lobbying and economic expansion, the leaders of Himachal worked to regain what they had lost. In 1963, the Legislative Assembly was returned, and in 1966, with linguistic reorganization, the state's borders were redrawn, redistributing land between Himachal and Punjab. The state was more than double its earlier size. It now included Kangra, Kullu, and Lahaul, as well as the administrative and economic center of the Western Himalayas, Shimla. However, it was not until January 25, 1971, that Indira Gandhi—for reasons that are an endless source of speculation—granted Himachal the full statehood it now enjoys.

After Himachal received statehood, Y. S. Parmar took the position of chief minister and T. S. Negi became Speaker of the House. At this point, things began to change rapidly. A wide range of ministries was established in these first few years of statehood. The Department of Tourism, the Department of Language and Culture, the Department of Information, and the Department Education, among others, were all created during this period. The structures that would reshape relations with New Delhi and help construct "the state" in everyday consciousness were developed. The state that took shape was decidedly influenced by Parmar's vision, which I will examine in more detail later. His vision, which saw economic development as a panacea, was premised on the assumption that, if the economic "backwardness" of the region could be modernized, then its people, with their ignorance and superstitions, would be modernized in the process.

In addition to facing considerable economic and administrative challenges, Parmar's cabinet had to deal with a decidedly diverse populace, much of which the elites, who spent their time in Shimla, Chandigarh, and Delhi, knew nothing about. To combat this ignorance, Parmar initiated a process of learning about and cataloging the state he was administering, using the Department of Language and Culture; the Academy of Art, Language and Culture; tourism officers; and the extensive census village surveys. The information collected and archived during this undertaking has become the backbone of Himachali public culture. The networks of reporters and distribution means have helped forge a Himachali imaginary that is foundational for the formation of the strong sense of identity now associated with Himachal and which undergirds the authority of the working state.

Like most places in India, Himachal is changing rapidly. The state is working hard to sell off many of its assets. The Department of Tourism is selling its less profitable hotels and rest houses with the goal of eventually privatizing all of its holdings. The Department of Agriculture is privatizing many of its processing plants. Cable television distributed from Shimla is combining local news coverage with Hindi films and broadcasting their signal to the remotest regions of the state. The last five years have seen the number of vernacular daily newspapers triple, and coverage has become more localized and more thorough. Before, few dailies carried information about Shimla; now, readers in Rampur and Brahmaur can expect at least a couple stories every day about their region. Furthermore, the quality and availability of education have increased rapidly in the state. Whereas literacy rates were in the teens in the 1951 census, they are now among the highest in the country.

Moreover, tourism in the state continues to rise. With prolonged tensions in neighboring Kashmir and Himachal's well-established tourism market, Himachal continues to draw tourists from across the subcontinent. The number of foreign tourists coming to state is also increasing. With the Dalai Lama's residence in Dharamsala, several large Buddhist monasteries throughout the state, and a very popular global-trance-culture travel circuit stop in Manali, Himachal pulls tourists from across the globe.

Economically, the state has profited handsomely from two sectors. The first, which is tied to its tumultuous early history and the construction of the Bhakra Dam, is the development of hydroelectricity. The region's steep mountains are now being crisscrossed with tunnels and water diversion schemes that generate electricity and revenue for the state. While many of the early hydroelectricity projects were undertaken by the Indian central government—which means that much of the revenue generated from these projects are flowing to the central government—most of the newer developments are held jointly by state and private companies. The second is the export of apples. Apples are big business in Himachal, as evidenced by the growth not only of production but also of the area under cultivation. From 1950 to 1951, only about 400 hectares were under cultivation. From 2001 to 2002, 92,820 hectares were devoted to apple production. Himachal's foothills are covered with apple trees, and the signs of the success of these farmers are everywhere—from modern farming equipment and new roads to $500 PDAs that can be seen in chai shops four hours from the nearest road.

However, as Himachal has changed, the social modernization that Parmar envisioned has not proceeded according to plan. Much to the chagrin of elites in Shimla, the rural population continues to perform animal sacrifices, visit mediums (*maśāni*) to speak to the dead, and rely on forms of possession (*khelnā*) to make practical decisions. What is more, the functioning of state ministries continues to rely on the idea that the state itself is the land of gods or that it is blessed by a particular divinity. Thus, the economic advancement of the last three decades, the ascendancy of an independent economy tied to world markets, and the Western-educated population has not dispelled the importance of local traditions and in particular the role of local deities. In fact, all of this has helped to provide the space within which local deities have grown more important.

Thus, as I trace the broad shifts in the production and reproduction of authority in the Western Himalayas, particularly in the movement from local authority to centralized authority, I will be attentive to the ways that this transformation has articulated the relationship between religion and the state—the ways that, despite the desires of people like Parmar for enlightenment, local deities cling as tenaciously to their communities as their communities do to them. While changing the rules of the game—the ways that people relate to their gods, the ways they understand and think about sovereignty, and the place of the deity in their material lives—the growth of the postcolonial state has not completely eradicated older forms of religion. Rather, religion and the state have become intimately intertwined in a new way, one that does not rely on older patterns of king-deity sovereignty or the brute force of arms.

PART ONE

Power

How Himachal Discovered Itself and Its Religion

Becoming Sufficiently Developed in Himachal Pradesh, or How Religion Became a Problem

On March 18, 1948, the great Indian nationalist Sardar Patel cut deep into the buoyant hopes of early Himachali politicians when he informed them that the region of Himachal Pradesh was not ready for self-governance or autonomous statehood. The disappointment of this judgment was mitigated by Sardar Patel's assurance that the region would attain its "proper status and area" once it was "sufficiently developed." For more than two decades (1948–1971), the struggle for statehood precipitated by Patel's promise defined the activities and aspirations of Himachal's emerging intelligentsia. By improving literacy rates, bringing electricity to villages, and promoting pilgrimage sites, they sought to prove that the hilly areas were at least as developed, modern, and secular as any of India's new states. The requirement that the region become "sufficiently developed" jumpstarted a serious and far-reaching discussion on the meaning, scope, and content of development and its role in the attainment of modernization. What did it mean to be "sufficiently developed"? Moreover, what was Himachal's "proper" status and area? Did Himachal need to attain a certain literacy rate, a specific degree of industrialization, a particular percentage of fiscal independence, a greater cultural harmony with the rest of India, or some combination of these factors? No sphere of life was exempted from the need

Figure 6. Sign in Malana. Photo by author.

for development. Roads were built. Schools were opened. Hydroelectricity was harnessed. Cultural practices were scrutinized. Communications networks were developed.

Therefore, it is more than a little ironic that, in the heady years of reform following Patel's covenant, Prime Minister Nehru himself came to Himachal to inaugurate the Bhakra-Nangal dam project—a project that for him (and for much of the nation) represented the ingenuity and audacity of India's developmental progress. For Nehru, it was a landmark achievement that stood as "a symbol of the nation's will to march forward with strength, determination, and courage." He argued that there was no "greater and holier place" than the dam. In his words, it was the "biggest temple and mosque and gurdwara" that man could possibly construct.[1]

Yet amid all of Nehru's and the nation's intoxicated self-congratulation that accompanied the inauguration of this unprecedented development project, no one seemed to have noticed that Himachal had become a colony within a country that had been decolonized less than a year before. Like the British before them, the new Indian national government exercised parental grace as it extracted the natural and human resources of the region, thereby consigning it to continued dependence. Although the dam flooded tens of thousands of homes, fields, and temples, Himachal has to this day received almost no benefit from the massive project. Despite paying an enormous environmental and human cost, the state receives less than 2 percent of the power generated from the project (for which it pays current market prices) and none of the stored water. The hydroelectric power generated was transported to the plains and distributed to large companies such as the nearby National Fertilizers Limited. The stored water was passed freely on to Punjab and Rajasthan. Nehru, echoing the feelings of a generation of optimistic nationalists, described the Bhakra Nangal Project as "something tremendous, something stupendous, something which shakes you up when you see it. Bhakra, the new temple of resurgent India, is the symbol of India's progress." If it was a symbol of India's progress, a harbinger of resurgent India, then the people of Himachal Pradesh needed to be very, very afraid. If they were not careful, they would continue to pay a very high price for the nation's forthcoming prosperity.

BECOMING RELIGIOUS WHILE BECOMING DEVELOPED

It was against this backdrop of becoming "sufficiently developed" that the people of the region gradually came to understand themselves as being religious. The political mobilization that accompanied the push to recognize Himachal Pradesh as a constitutionally autonomous state was the decisive force in forging a unified Himachali identity. This identity simply did not exist before the emergence of this political mobilization. Identity was largely confined to local forms of identification, which were based on family, village, or local princely state. The emergence of "Himachali" as a marker of identity was essential for the emergence of all other modifiers (Himachali religion, Himachali politics, Himachali character, Himachali literature, etc.)

Much of the argument of this book turns on my assertion that the creation of two new categories—the Himachali and the Himachali religion—was decisive for the formation of contemporary ways of being in Himachal. On the surface, this may seem to be a simple argument, but in the early twentieth century, it was clear neither that such categories would become important nor what they might consist of. When the British arrived in the Western Himalayas to beat back the advancing Gurkha army, the territorial entity now recognized as Himachal was a ramshackle assortment of tiny principalities with competing alliances to larger regional powers (those of Kashmir, Punjab, Mughal, Nepal, Tibet, etc.). Since these principalities were separated by glacier-covered mountains, raging rivers, and linguistic barriers and subject to ever-shifting alliances with neighboring powers, there was simply no need for a transregional alliance or the adjectival forms that would accompany such an alliance.

It is clear that, before the arrival of Europeans in the Western Himalayas, a category that would link the various peoples of the hills into a singular unit was not necessary. The people living in Kangra and Kullu, who occasionally killed one another, had no need (administrative, promotional, defensive, or otherwise) to discuss a category of person that would include all people living in the region. The situation was very different for the British men and women who began to populate the Western Himalayas in the early nineteenth century. For these folks, coming up with a classification for the particular type of people inhabiting these hills was necessary for a couple of reasons. First, these settlers obviously saw themselves as being very different from the "natives" who carried them up the mountains and brought and prepared their food. There is nothing interesting or surprising about this. Yet what is surprising is that they also made a series of important distinctions between those who inhabited the hills and those who lived in the plains of North India, the most significant of which was that the hill dwellers were more peaceful and healthy than their counterparts on the plains. In the tumult that followed the chaos of the Indian Rebellion of 1857, the character of the hill people became a critical rationale for the official relocation of the Raj's summer capital to Shimla. A letter sent by Viceroy John Lawrence to Secretary of State Charles Wood in 1864 sums up Shimla's many strategic advantages: "This place, of all hill Stations, seems to me the best for the Supreme Government. Here you are with one foot, I may say, in the Punjab, and another in the North-West Provinces. Here you are among a docile population and yet near enough to influence Oude. Around you, in a word, are all the warlike races of India, all those on whose character and power our hold in India, exclusive of our own countrymen, depends."[2]

The people of the hills were seen as isolated from the corrupting influence of power and politics so pervasive in the plains. Raised in the "invigorating air" of the mountains, they were perceived as having risen above the languor and lethargy of others in the subcontinent. This quality of docility—although how true it was is more than a little debatable—is one of the more important facets of self-constructed identities in modern Himachal.

The way that Shimla's British residents imagined the people they lived among was inflected by two interrelated theories of distance, one geographic and the other cultural.[3] This cultural and geographic distance gave Pahāṛīs[4] a special place within the colonial imaginary. They were simultaneously lauded and infantilized. They were not believed to require any of the moral recalibration that was thought to be necessary to "civilize" as the Indians who lived on the plains. Envisioned as having the same moral capabilities as the Brits while remaining innocent of so many human vices, they needed only protection. Both the physical isolation and the noble innocence of Pahāṛīs were critical for how these people "became religious" in the second half of the twentieth century.

The first and most pervasive of these theories of distance equated the hills with health, vigor, and moral character. This theory was predicated on a climatological understanding of the relationship between heat and civilization that was pervasive under colonial rule. It was famously summed up in Montesquieu's *The Spirit of the Laws:* "The heat of the climate may be so excessive as to deprive the body of all vigor and strength. Then the faintness is communicated to the mind; there is no curiosity, no enterprise, no generosity of sentiment; the inclinations are all passive; indolence constitutes the utmost happiness; scarcely any punishment is so severe as mental employment; and slavery is more supportable than the force and vigor of mind necessary for human conduct.... The Indians are naturally a pusillanimous people; even the children of Europeans born in India lose the courage peculiar to their own climate."[5]

The British saw a sharp contrast between the peaceful and industrious people of the Western Himalayas and the indolent people of the plains. The British seemed to recognize themselves in the hill people, although they considered the hill folk more innocent than themselves. With this as a sort of cultural prerequisite at work, it is less than surprising that Shimla was an attractive place. My assertion is that the British occupation of Shimla, particularly by British women and children (who lived in the city year round, whereas the mostly male government officials were only there in the summer), helped to produce a new understanding of religious life in the hills that came to define both the future political struggle and the public forms that evolved in the postcolonial state. We have already seen that colonial officials often noted the "passive" nature of hill people when they were arguing that the Raj should move his offices to Shimla each summer. This "passivity" continued to be an important descriptor of villagers. In official letters, reports, diaries, and plays, the "Paharees" were applauded for their excellent physical and moral character. For example, Fanny Parks, after an excoriating remark about the "disgusting" marriage practices of the hills, closed one particularly telling section with: "I am told that honesty was the distinguishing characteristic in former times of the Paharis, but intercourse with civilized Europeans has greatly demoralized the mountaineers."[6] This quote points us in an important direction. Just as the hills were closer to the natural state of things—"natural" here being defined by its relationship to a British archetype—the people were understood as being closer to a state of nature. While the usual quips about the "backward" character of the Pahāṛīs punctuate the colonial archive, more often than not, it is this idyllic caricature of the hill people living close to the state of nature that pervades these writings.

This imagination was predicated on two interrelated theories of distance: one geographic, the other cultural.[7] The first and most pervasive of these theories equated the hills with health, vigor, and moral character. This perception drove the British to the hills in the first place, and it underpins much of the ideology that supported the colonial conquests of "the South." The belief was that, because the British were from a cooler climate, they were more civilized and not as culturally or morally debased as people from the south. According to many, as one moved from the plains to the hills, the character, temperament, and honesty of the native populations improved considerably.

James Fraser, one of the earliest British visitors to the Western Himalayas, suggested: "The farther removed from the plains, the heat, and the more accessible parts of the country, the higher does the highlander rise in activity of mind and body."[8] When he made this remark, Fraser was on a tour securing control from the Gurkhas. He was contrasting the differences between the people of the lower hills (Sirmaur and Nahan) with those of the upper hills (Bushahar and Jubbal), a distinction that continues to hold for many in the region.[9] The people of the hills were understood to be closer to the natural state of being; they were uncorrupted by the sins and indolence of the heat of the plains. They were, moreover, largely free of the corruption of civilization.

Pahāṛī women are often described as beautiful, pure, and much "freer" than British or Indian women. For example, George Powell Thomas, sounding like a tourist visiting the interior regions of Himachal, wrote: "I have seen some beautiful and sinless little hill girls of grace and air so innocent, so pure, so cherub-like, that it seemed impossible that they should become sensual—impossible that they

Figure 7. Lohri festival near the Tibetan border. Photo by author.

should have within them the seeds of lasciviousness and guilt."[10] Yet, as we will see below, it wasn't only the male colonialists that found the beauty and purity of Pahāṛī women more than a "curiosity."[11] English women's representations of Pahāṛī women made the strongest long-term impressions.

COLONIAL REFLECTIONS: IMPERIAL WIVES AND THEIR "PAHAREE" NEIGHBORS

In the introduction to her collection of Shimla village tales, Alice Elizabeth Dracott states that she edited out a number of local women's stories because they "were grotesquely unfit for publication." However, Dracott did not believe that this meant that Pahāṛī women were debased and depraved. Rather, she continued to subscribe to the myth that Pahāṛī women, though pretty and sexualized, were not tainted: "The typical Paharee woman is, as a rule, extremely good looking and a born flirt; she has a pleasant, gay manner, and can always see a joke."[12]

This was also an opinion held by more than a few men. Yet, again, it is not simply that the people of the hills understood themselves in these terms—as simple and openly embracing sensuality with a libertine quality. William Howard Russell, a correspondent for the *Times* in the late 1800s, described an amusing incident, the humor of which appears to have been somewhat lost on him. He travels to a fair, where he is met by the raja of Bushahar. After verbally abusing the "horror" that is the seven-faced *rāth* (chariot) of the deity being celebrated, Russell proceeds to tell us the real reason why he and his friends traveled to the fair and why they would go home disappointed: "We were most anxious to see the ladies, of whose beauty we had heard so much. The Rājāh said he would get them to dance for us. He sent out his orders; but we saw that wherever his messengers went there was an immediate dispersal of the women, who began to file off in charming groups through the woods, and to mount the hills, or descend the valleys to their homes. It was evident that we were unpopular."[13]

The sexual and moral purity of the people of the hills was employed most powerfully by the British as an index of difference against which to measure the hill people against the people of the plains. That is to say, from the time Pahāṛī people were defined as a group, they were defined in contrast to the Indians of the plains. In general, Pahāṛī communities were understood as being communal and free of the artificial distinctions of caste and class. The British often took undue advantage of this collective harmony. For instance, one of the rationales the British used to support the extension of the system of *begār* (forced labor) was the claim that this labor was part of Pahāṛī culture, the evidence being that, whenever anything needed to be built, the community would do the work together for the welfare of all. It was this myth of communal simplicity and equality that, ironically, allowed the British to exploit the Pahāṛī population. *Begār* was, according to this understanding, a system of equality in which villagers worked together to foster community growth.

These attitudes toward the inhabitants of the hills helped forge a communal identity among those individuals who were carrying British luggage, pulling rickshaws, typing records, and even just tilling their fields in the villages. It is in the minds of the British and in their speech, in their need to address a "man of the hills," that the notion of a Pahāṛī people has its origins.

As we trace the manner in which the basic characteristic of the Pahāṛī were articulated, we will become attuned to how the encounters between Shimla and the various hill states created the need for and, in turn, the particular character of Pahāṛī religion and culture. Much of what will emerge is implicit in the words of Emily Eden, the sister of Governor-General George Eden, who lived in Shimla in the 1830s and shaped how the city would emerge in the British public imagination. She stated: "I always wonder how ignorant of the ways of the world the inhabitants of these solitary valleys can be and how such ignorance feels. No 'craft boys,' no fashions, no politics, and, I suppose, a primitive religion that satisfies them. There are temples of great age in all these places, I imagine half of these people must be a sort of vulgar Adams and Eves—not so refined, but nearly as innocent."[14] In this example, as in others above, we see the emergence of some of the primary elements of what I call the metanarrative of Himachali culture: the belief that the inhabitants of Himachal are "pure," that they are in touch with the natural religions of the hills, and that they are honest and very different from both the Hindus of the plains and the corrupted, yet civilized, British.

The beginnings of a Himachali identity lie in the increasing interaction between the capital at Shimla and its rural base in surrounding communities. From the very beginning, in the nineteenth century, the town and its growth depended on labor from neighboring communities and foodstuffs from the fertile valleys of Kangra and Mandi. Therefore, Shimla quickly assumed a special role in the imaginary of the Western Himalaya. It was a place where one could seek one's fortune and where opportunity abounded. It was also a place where one could lose one's soul. Many communities continue to sing songs about this time. However, it was not until very late in the colonial period that communities began to organize themselves. Before this, the only voices coming from

Shimla's surrounding communities were those of princes, who were either demanding space in Shimla's influential public sphere or refusing to follow the city's protocols.

STRUGGLING TO BECOME SUFFICIENTLY DEVELOPED

The constitutional establishment of Himachal Pradesh as a province with limited sovereign status on August 15, 1948, was riven with a deep paradox that immediately drew into focus the divisions that marked the Western Himalayas. While political activists had been working for more than two decades to unite nascent local political leadership in a common fight against colonial and princely exploitation, the pronouncement of a constitutional entity brought the realization that these goals did not necessarily correspond to a group of people who identified themselves with this administrative abstraction. There were no media circulating in the region to unite the people, no shared languages, few joint festivals, and even fewer roads connecting the villages. As the entity was constituted, there arose a gap between the desires of the Himachali leaders and their political situation. In the space of this gap, I argue, political leaders employed the "desire of the people" as a means of simultaneously uniting the regions of the Western Himalayas and pushing forward their own political agenda of territorial ascension and political recognition.

Those involved in the early formulation of the state argued that Himachal Pradesh should be given the status of an autonomous state in India's "family of states" and, moreover, that the state should include all the hill areas of the lower Western Himalayas.[15] By contrast, major nationalist leaders felt the area was "insufficiently developed." One of India's most important founding fathers, Sardal Patel, announced Himachal's struggle in 1948 with a sentence that would haunt Himachalis for decades: "In the final stage, after this area is sufficiently developed in its resources and administration, it is proposed that its Constitution should be similar to that of any other Province."[16] This statement was taken by the Himachali politician Dr. Yashwant Singh Parmar and some of the early leaders of the Vidhān Sabhā (legislative assembly) as a mandate for reform.

From this point, Himachal's new administration, its earliest projects, and the public statements of its leaders were fixated on the achievement of statehood. In pursuit of this goal, they relied heavily on some of the core elements of Indian democracy. In their rhetoric, they employed the term "the people," and the "desire of the people" became a central motivating force in the struggle for Himachal statehood. Around this desire, a sense of identity slowly coalesced, and the Himachali subject was born.

The most important consequence of the articulation of a desire for state recognition was the construction and delineation of the people who constituted the state. It was not that these people did not exist before but rather that they did not exist as a unified public. As we saw in Dracott's writing, by the turn of the century, the British had begun to speak of the people of the hills as "Paharees," yet the political function of this nomination was not active. It was something the British used to name a people that they could barely see. Parmar provocatively articulated this conundrum as an ontological question: "Ever since its birth on August 15, 1948, Himachal Pradesh had been in a State of Becoming [rather] than Being. It has been enlarging, its Constitutional changes. Behind this process for the attainment of proper shape and status for Himachal had been the determined desire of the hill People for the search of a distinct identity for themselves and for their Pradesh in the Indian Union."[17]

After 1948, it became common to refer to "the people" in public and administrative spaces, such as in speeches and editorials, on the radio, and in internal government reports. In this case, the words of H. L. Vaidya are instructive. Writing about the insecurity of the post-1948 period, using the language of the 1938 Ludhiana All-India State's conference, Vaidya said: "A wave swept over hill areas and from every corner, from every shade of opinion came a unanimous voice for integration of all hill areas for the formation of a composite Himachal Pradesh having same language, culture, and problems."[18] This period saw the rapid emergence of "the people of the hills" as a distinct category, as a group to be distinguished from the Punjabis on the plains and the nationalists in Delhi. The strategic use of "the people" cannot be overestimated. Parmar states this best in a discussion of economic development and social change in his reworked doctoral dissertation: "The constitution of Himachal Pradesh, as the first entirely hilly province of India, gave the hill people a new personality. Having found an identity, they started identifying their ills. Heart-searching started all over."[19] But what was that identity? Of what did it consist? Where were its boundaries?

Much of the strategic usage of the term "the people" emerged in the extended public debate over the size and status of the state. In 1956, the States Reorganization Committee recommended the merger of Himachal with Punjab.[20] The recommendations of the committee were part of a broader effort on the part of the central government to limit the growth of regionalism, particularly on the basis of language, in the emerging nation-state.[21] Broadly, these recommendations were instrumental in the creation of the violent linguistic struggles that characterized Indian politics for more than a decade.

A union with Punjab was arguably the greatest fear of the emerging Himachali politicians.[22] At the time, the capital of Punjab was Shimla, a city that politicians such as Parmar claimed should be integrated into Himachal Pradesh. Moreover, in the early decades of national independence, Punjab had financed and facilitated, with the help of national development funds, the construction of major hydroelectricity projects that radically transformed the environment of the hills while the profits and benefits were siphoned off to the plains.[23] Many of Himachal's new political elites felt that the Punjabi administration would reinstate past colonization and subjugation.[24]

Language was always a tricky issue for Himachal. While the region's leaders sometimes articulated their desires along linguistic lines, Hindi had already replaced local dialects in administrative offices, and the

language of the hills (Pahāṛī) was widely considered a family of dialects rather than a language. As a result, leaders pursued another
approach to the problem of grounding regional unity. They compared
the cultural and religious traditions of the Himalayas with those of the
plains, particularly those of Punjab. Himachal was not Punjab.[25] In this
argument, which has become immensely important, Himachal and
Punjab are first distinguished on geographic grounds, which fostered
arguments about cultural and religious differences.[26]

As should be already clear, Himachali elites had much to fear from
Punjab. Distinguishing themselves culturally and politically was a central component of their political labor. Nowhere is this clearer than in
the debates conducted in the Vidhān Sabhā after the publication of the
States Reorganization Report, which recommended a merger with
Punjab. In that report, it was suggested that the hills and the plains
were intimately related—culturally and economically—and that a
merger would benefit both parties. I will not get into the legitimacy of
this statement and the factions that shaped it. I will use legislative
responses in the Vidhān Sabhā as a means of showing how clearly
Himachali leaders distinguished their region from Punjab and the way
that the proposed merger brought together competing factions within
Himachal's political leadership. Shri Hardayal Singh, a member of the
Legislative Assembly (MLA) from Kangra, was clear both in expressing his perception of the difference and in condemning it:

> The links between the people of the plains and hilly areas are such that
> people from hilly areas are afraid of those from the plains.... I regret to say
> that the poor people of Himachal Pradesh have been sacrificed like goats.
> No justice has been imparted to them and the Government of India took
> the decision under the reassure of communal forces of Punjab.... All this it
> to please the Punjabi communalists and not due to our wishes and they say
> our sentiments have been respected. I would call it adding insult to injury.
> The demand was that Himachal Pradesh be made a separate hilly State.[27]

For most MLAs, the committee's findings were disastrous. These individuals felt like pawns in a larger game. Himachal was tapped for its soil,

its water, its hydroelectric potential,[28] and the manipulation of communal relations. Himachalis, a nominally Hindu population, were brought into the debate as statistical buffers. On the assembly floor, Kashmir Singh blamed Himachal's difficulties on one of Himachal's greatest adversities: "The communalists who control the papers of Punjab desire that Himachal Pradesh should be merged with Punjab. Why do they desire so? What are their arguments? To it they reply that they desire that pure Hindus should be populated in their area and when Himachal is merged with Punjab the percentage of Hindu population will increase."[29] The effect of the report was important, as it united groups that were once powerfully divided. Factions from Kangra now worked alongside those from Bushahar and Kinnaur. As the specter of Punjab appeared, the longstanding disputes between the different factions from the hills seemed to dissolve, and everyone joined together to oppose the threat. United, they sought to further ground their claims to independence.

Many latched onto Himachal's topography as a means of distinguishing the region from Punjab.[30] Historically, Himachal had avoided the invasions of foreign conquerors and resisted being integrated into larger empires. Accordingly, and also because of the enormous geographic barriers of the mountains, it developed relatively independently. This led to the creation of a rich cultural heritage not shared by the people of the plains, and for leaders in this period, as for the vernacular ethnohistorians later, this heritage united the people of the hills. They were not united because they shared lineages, festivals, or other appellations. They were united because they were located in the hills and they were not from Punjab. As was announced at the festival inaugurating Himachali statehood, "the story of Himachal Pradesh, its formation and its enlargement in stages, has its base in the faith of its people, in the destiny of their Pradesh for which they are capable of making any sacrifice.... Merger would have meant strangulation of Himachal's efforts for development and annihilation of its rich cultural heritage. Threats and temptations could not deter the Pradesh leadership from carrying on a relentless struggle for maintenance of Himachal's identity."[31]

This distinction allowed the spokespeople for Himachali statehood to argue that the region had one culture and one religion. Earlier, the *White Paper on Indian States,* published in 1950, had argued: "The people of these hills want to have one State, as was put before the Government of India, in which these people, that is the western Pahārī speaking people with one culture, with one economy and one tradition, would be able to stand on their own."[32] This perception of unity was instrumental in the fight for statehood, and it proved to be even more influential in post-1971 Himachal. As Himachal's leaders emerged from the success of the Praja Mandal movement and the push for state recognition, the idea of a united religious culture of Himachal first took shape. The man that gave it much of its shape was Yashwant Singh Parmar.

Parmar was born on August 4, 1906, in the village of Chanalag in the princely state of Sirmaur. As he was the son of a prominent local family, his education was extensive. After primary school, he traveled to Lahore, where he attended the Forman Christian College, one of the foremost schools in Punjab. From there, he moved on to Punjab University, also in Lahore, where he received his first BA. He then proceeded to Canning College in Lucknow, where he received another BA, this time in law, followed by an MA and a PhD in sociology in 1942.

Parmar served in the courts of Sirmaur for more than ten years. He was a magistrate for the Sirmaur court from 1930 to 1937 and a district and session judge from 1937 to 1940. He also participated in a number of public groups. He served on several cricket boards and was an active member of the Theosophical Society, Dehra Dun. These active engagements with social groups inevitably led him to become involved with the Praja Mandals that were forming across the region. After several years of working on mobilization and protests for the movement, he was appointed president of its region-wide chapter, and this is where his path to the position of Himachal's chief minister began. During this time, he also began speaking of his desire to unify the region, a desire that dominated the second half of his life.

On January 25, 1971, newspapers across India congratulated Parmar and the citizens of Himachal on the achievement of statehood. Quotes like the following were common: "Dr. Parmar must be the happiest man today with his long cherished dream of Himachal Pradesh attaining Statehood becoming a reality."[33] From his earliest activities with the Praja Mandal groups, Parmar's primary goals were to unify Himachal and see it attain full statehood. His work faced its greatest threat in 1956, when the States Reorganization Committee recommended, on a 2–3 vote, that Himachal Pradesh be merged with Punjab. Parmar resisted strongly—though he had been offered the position of chief minister of Punjab—and he lobbied Nehru to retain Himachal's independence, arguing, "No price is big enough for keeping Himachal separate."[34]

It is important to keep in mind that this driving desire was written boldly across the landscape of his actions. It influenced his political moves, led him to project his desires onto the people of Himachal, and drew him steadily through a prolonged and difficult period. His press secretary summed it up: "Enlargement of the State by integrating contiguous hilly areas of Punjab and getting statehood for the hill people which provided a recognition to the Hillman at national level. Those were his dreams. There were very few people in this world who realize their dreams in their own lifetime and Yashwant Singh Parmar was the one, as he was the foliage of the hill soil."[35]

I argue that a number of things were needed to make Parmar's dream possible. First, he needed to speak the language of democracy, to speak of the desires of the people, and to locate himself as the mouthpiece of the people's desire. This allowed him to understand and project himself as a medium of the people. Though he spent much of his time in Delhi and was not known as being a man who "walked among the people," he presented himself as such, playing on the motivating power of democracy. Second, he had to articulate Himachal's uniqueness and unity. Third, he had to "modernize" the state. When the initial Himachal was formed in 1948, Sardar Patel outlined instructions that

Parmar and other Himachali leaders took as a mandate: "In the final stage, after this area is sufficiently developed in its resources and administration, it is proposed that its Constitution should be similar to that of any other province."[36] Following this, Parmar took it upon himself to develop Himachal economically and culturally so that it could move from being "backward" to taking its rightful place among the modern states.

One of the things that sets Parmar apart from other early Himachali leaders, like Krishna Nand Swami and even T. S. Negi, is that he believed himself to be speaking on behalf of all Himachalis. While many likely did not agree with what he was saying, the taint of regionalism was largely absent from his locutions. For decades, people have talked about Parmar as the champion of Himachali independence. Folk songs and editorials have been written about it and documentaries have been produced.[37] Although it is clear that the narrative of unification is undoubtedly important for Himachali identity, it is not clear that Parmar was actually speaking on behalf of the desire of the people. In fact, for much of the period associated with the initial struggle, he had never even been to most of the areas in Himachal Pradesh. Since we have little access to non-elite discourses from this time, I confine my discussion to elite discourses and the ways that this type of speech was legitimated and made part of everyday speech. Much of the educated populace believed that the backward people of the hills needed a spokesperson to communicate their desires— someone like Parmar, who could tell them what they wanted, since they couldn't articulate it for themselves. The hill people were believed to be mired in ignorance. Though some put it more eloquently, Vaidya got right to the heart of the issue: "The matter of the fact is that the dumb driven hill people required a person to translate their desires and aspirations to convince the authorities regarding the validity of the claim if the hill people. So, looking to the undivided devotion of this great son of the soil towards their cause, they reposed their full confidence in him. Hence, it is a common saying that Himachal and Dr. Parmar are synonymous."[38]

What is important in this respect is the need to speak to and from the heart, and Parmar spoke most powerfully when he spoke of desires. For Parmar, the hill people were a subaltern class par excellence. They had been held back by colonial and princely authorities and isolated by a lack of roads, education, and adequate administration. In his speeches, Parmar situated himself as the savior who had arrived to remove the veils of ignorance and silence. He would not only grant Himachal its statehood but also grant Himachalis their identity. Himachalis were then able to recognize their long-cherished desires. They revealed hidden histories and centuries-old struggles: "A wave of enthusiasm ran throughout the enlarged Pradesh [after the integration of Kangra, Kullu, etc.] on this historic event, in which the people saw the culmination of their long-cherished desire to come together."[39] But before we can get to the processes by which these narratives were uncovered, let us look at how Parmar conceived of the region's uniqueness.

In order to articulate the demand for statehood, Parmar had to make a strong argument for the cultural difference between the mountains and the plains. Since the early nineteenth century, the hills had been administered from the plains. Moreover, during the colonial period, Hindi had replaced most of the diverse languages of the region. So what held Himachal together as a state? On what basis could Parmar express the need to preserve the autonomy of the Himalayas? His strategy was to assert the cultural differences between the people of the plains of the Punjab and the people of the Western Himalayas:

> The social and cultural lives of these [Pahāṛī] people, their folk-songs, folk-dances, their fairs and festivals are peculiar to those hills and distinguish them from the people of the plains. The Government of Punjab itself in its publication—The Resurgent Punjab—published by the Public Relations Department, 1956 at page 25—has acknowledged "the hill people have a prepossessing appearance. Its charm is heightened by their unsophisticated manner. Shy and reserved before an outsider they surrender themselves without restrain to anyone who shows warmth to them. Truthfulness and honest are their most striking traits. A man's word is accepted with as little hesitation as his bond. Their dress is at once elegant and simple."[40]

In this quote, Parmar uses a Punjabi tourism advertisement against the government that created it. What is most interesting about the quote is that it is precisely the backwardness, the simplicity, and the unsophisticated manner of the hill people that are noted as making them unique. As Parmar would intone thousands of times, the people of Himachal had been cut off from the world for centuries. They developed on their own, untouched by the influences of the plains.[41] There is a deep ambiguity that runs through the heart of his discussion here, and it continues to haunt the state to this day. That is, what made Himachal different is that it had not developed in the same way as the plains. It had remained simple, honest, and unsophisticated. However, to usher in modern statehood and the citizenship that would entail, Himachal had to become "sufficiently developed."

At the very heart of Parmar's agenda was his plan for Himachal. In fact, his plan was to plan.[42] In his view, Himachal's economic and cultural problems were due to its isolation. It had very little infrastructure, means of communication, or organization. There were only two roads in the region, literacy rates were below 5 percent, and there was no form of production other than subsistence farming. Thus, just as Nehru set forth his Five-Year Plans for India, Parmar presented annual plans for Himachal and gave annual budget speeches.[43] He felt that the combination of hard work and planning could bring about the development that Patel had called for: "Standing on the threshold of Statehood today, Himachal Pradesh which came into being only 22 years ago by the integration of nearly 30 hilly states, has shown what can be achieved through thoughtful planning, sustained effort and dedication to work by the hard-working people who had to suffer centuries of neglect."[44]

For Parmar, economic planning took many forms over the decades, including construction, agriculture, tourism, and power. At the beginning, his primary goal was to bring the people of Himachal together through a system of road and bus networks.[45] He felt that the people had suffered because they were unconnected and that road construction was the key to development throughout the Himalayas: "Road construction is the most important development programme in the Himalayan region. The entire progress of this region depends on the development of roads"[46] Everything else would follow. Once roads were built cash crops could get to market, people could receive newspapers, tourism could develop, and people could interact with one another and share their common—though up to that point hidden—histories and cultures. Parmar believed in a form of economic determinism: "This hard reality [the lack of roads in Himachal] shows the extent of the backwardness of the hilly regions in comparison with the rest of the country. And roads being the only lifeline of the people of the hilly regions, any shortcomings in development of this vital field has varying degrees of repercussions on the other aspects of social and economic development."[47] Roads would usher in the full force of modernity.

Parmar believed that planning and development would transform the backwardness of the region. Himachal's religious and cultural conservatism could be turned around. Nowhere is this view clearer than in his discussion of modernization's effects on polyandry. The following an anecdote, connected to the second printing of Parmar's *Polyandry in the Himalayas*, circulates in closed circles these days. This text was released with great fanfare. It was published by one of India's most progressive Congress leaders and hailed by Indira Gandhi as a "commendable effort" and "valuable contribution." S. C. Dube was even more generous in his praise, calling it "admirable," "a major contribution," and an "important book." However, two younger MLAs were upset by the book. Not coincidentally, they were both women. Lata Thakur and the now-powerful Vidya Stokes were punishing in their critiques of Parmar. They asserted that he did not really understand Himachali women, that he was using the book for gross political gain, and that the book would have a negative effect on the women of the state. The criticism was consistent and intense. Thakur, a charismatic younger woman from Spiti, was particularly scathing in her criticism of Parmar. Then tragedy struck. Thakur, who was at the height of her political career, was killed in a car accident. When this story is told—I heard it several times myself in the halls of the legislative assembly—it is in hushed tones, in the way that someone tells a joke without having to say the punch line. Whatever the cause of her death, the criticism immediately ceased. Parmar's book was reworded and a second printing was issued.

What was it about the book that so upset Stokes and Thakur? Not having spoken to either of them about it, I can only speculate from their public comments. In short, Parmar's book reduced polyandry to a form of delayed development: patriarchy-in-waiting. Similar to his belief that road development would bring the blessing of modernity to Himachal, Parmar considered polyandry to be a social form that had developed because of Himachal's isolation and difficult economic conditions. He believed polyandry to be a product of the utility of a woman: "She is so much in demand because of her social and economic utility that a husband cannot do without her and cannot dispense with her services."[48] In fact, as if summarizing his historicist view of women, he asserted: "Her utility, her resourcefulness in domestic life, her refreshing company and the affectionate care of children have always proved to be a great asset to her partner in life and have, to a considerable extent, determined her status at different stages of civilization."[49] Therefore, Parmar contended, polyandry belonged to a stage of civilization that was tied to forms of economic dependence that modern development would be able to overcome.

Much of the book insinuated that it was Parmar who would advance Himachal to its next "stage of civilization," although he never directly stated this. In the final chapter, which was added after the debacle described above, he listed all of the changes that he had brought about through planning and development: literacy rates had increased by 25 percent, more than 2400 kilometers of roads were constructed, and the horticulture sector was expanded. He proudly wrote: "The unification of hill states under one administration set into motion various social, economic, and political forces which acting independently as also interacting helped to move the wheels of change faster than what could be ever imagined before."[50]

While religion receives little explicit attention in Parmar's writings or in his overarching articulations of the rationale for state formation, this was not because it was unimportant. It was because he believed that modernization—access to communication networks and central planning—would render religion unimportant in public life. He sought to displace older forms of social life with communication networks, modern industry, and central planning. As we saw above with polyandry, economic determinism guided Parmar's policy. Himachal's quest for statehood would be achieved through planning and modernization.

STUMBLING TOWARD THE FUTURE

Parmar's top-down approach was neither the only one at work in the hilly region nor the only one in the ranks of the state apparatus. In fact, there was a deep division between people like Parmar who were tied to economic determinism and people who were tied to cultural determinism. Those in the latter group believed that the state took shape not because of modern forms of planning that brought its backward people into the light of self-reflection but because of the specific beliefs and practices of the people who lived in the region. Ironically, land reforms made it possible to even separate these two developmental logics. These two issues are inextricably bound. The creation of an administrative and bureaucratic state recognized and legislated at the national level is tied to the formulation and dissemination of a united social and cultural identity. More exactly, the discourse on religion that emerged in and through the process of state recognition was integral to the perception that these historically divided regions were united. While it is generally believed that it was language that reorganized India, in Himachal, language actually played second fiddle to the more powerful discourse on religion and culture. Once religion was freed from the entanglements that land reforms severed, it became an object of study and cultivation, which in turn became the very seed stock for becoming religious.

CHAPTER TWO

God Is a Beggar

Land Reforms Create Religion as a Separate Sphere

GODS IN THE WAKE OF GOOD INTENTIONS

The previous chapter showed how Himachali identity was forged from the reforms that sought to produce a region that was "sufficiently developed" enough to determine its own future. These reforms had many effects, but none was more important for the emergence of Himachali religion than the land reforms initiated in the years between Sardar Patel's promise and Indira Gandhi's announcement of Himachali statehood. The two following scenes suggest the spectrum of transformations inaugurated by the land reforms.

Scene one: Lying on the ground, drooling and with his legs spread, a local villager was passed out drunk in front of the three-tiered Haḍimbā temple near Manali. People ignored him as they gathered to enter the shrine. Waiting in line were Israeli tourists with trance-tribe satchels and shell-encrusted leather purses, Bengali housewives with swollen feet, and excited boys from Chandigarh who were more interested in watching scantily clad Spanish women than seeing Haḍimbā. To the side of the temple, between the refurbished granary (*koṭhī*) and the well-appointed government office, sat a man with a multicolored hat and a swollen belly. He was the temple's *gūr*, Haḍimbā's medium and authoritative voice, the traditional center of Western Himalayan temple rites.[1]

Figure 8. Man in front of Kullu temple. Photo by author.

We sat together watching the scene, discussing tourism and changes at the temple. As if on cue, a Canadian woman and her Argentinean lover entered the shrine, and the gūr explained with a smirk that, despite being Haḍimbā's mouthpiece, he was not allowed to enter the temple because his low caste status might pollute it. One might think that a man such as this would be bitter about this strange inequity, but I was more upset about it than he was. Like other members of the temple committee, he was profiting handsomely from the temple's inclusion in the state's religious tourism circuit. But his full belly didn't tell the whole story. The ease with which he accepted the apparent inequity had more to do with the separation of Himachali religion from other spheres of life than it did with the ironies of the perpetuation of the caste system in our globalized world.

Scene two: Nine bronze masks mounted on long bamboo poles bounced against the knotted shoulders of two villagers. The deity moved back and forth across the temple grounds. On one side, the priest guided the deity's movement with a thick steel rod. On the other, a villager in a coarse wool jacket and green skullcap asked it, "Can you relieve the pain in my joints?" The deity lurched sideways, falling toward a dollop of cow dung, and the priest translated its actions. The deity would help if a series of goat sacrifices were offered. The request was extravagant, and the man walked away complaining. He offered no money or grain for the ceremony. Later in the evening, I sat with the priest in the deserted temple grounds. He was bitter. The temple was broke. The villagers no longer heeded the deity's warnings and only made tiny offerings at the most important festivals. These days, he complained, "God is a beggar."

These two scenes offer us radically different pictures of local deities in Western Himalayan financial, memorial, and political economies. In one, a temple has become a source of wealth. In the other, "god is a beggar"—destitute, forgotten, and forlorn. One temple has become so famous and is such a source of regional pride that it is commonly imagined as synonymous with Himachali religion. The other has been virtually forgotten, neglected by even the villagers who live nearby. While the fates of these two temples couldn't be more different, they have the same source. Both temples were radically transformed by midcentury land reforms, and both are now understood in relation to the concept of Himachali religion that developed in the wake of these reforms. The reforms disallowed local deities from controlling land. Their holdings were split and redistributed. They became "minors" in need of state protection. This protection entailed the delineation of a new "religious" sphere defined in opposition to the spheres of life regulated by rule of law. It is difficult to overestimate the impact these transformations had on the emergence of Himachali religion.

In 1953, socialist-leaning politicians in Himachal's newly formed legislative assembly were eager to show leaders of the Nehruvian government that they could enact the modernizing reforms laid out in Nehru's development strategy. At the heart of these strategies, in the early years of Indian independence, were progressive land reforms that sought to "return land to the tiller" and break up existing power structures that relied on large land owners (or zamindars). In 1953, the Himachal Pradesh Abolition of Big Landed Estates and Land Reforms Act was passed. In addition to proving that the legislative assembly could modernize Himachal, the act was designed to facilitate the redistribution of wealth in the region and to provide a stronger tax basis to fill state coffers. While it essentially failed on these accounts (though somewhat less dramatically than in other states), it did have unforeseen consequences that fundamentally reshaped how villagers related to their gods.

The act's second chapter contained a series of legal definitions (including the terms "adult," "minor," and "land"), which effectively divested most temples of their property within a decade, turning once-wealthy deities literally into beggars. Only a generation before, village temples were centers of economic, psychological, and governmental power; now that deities were defined as minors incapable of holding land titles and in need of state protection, they were desperate for state maintenance funds to prevent the ornate façades of their temples from crumbling. What is so telling about the effect of this legislation is not so much that the secular state defined "religious" even as it eschewed purportedly religious issues but that such a powerful formulation—transforming a god into a child (or more precisely, transforming God into an idea)—so quickly became part of the common-sense understanding of a god's place in society.

This dissolution of the deities' material power without the corresponding disappearance of the deities was intrinsically tied to the emergence of the modern concept of Himachali religion. That is, severing the ties that tethered local deities to particular spaces and lands was integral to the metonymic linking that would become so important to the collapsing of difference between the deities. The accidental religion that emerges is not simply about the restriction of local forms of power. While the material relations between deities and villagers were undercut by the reforms, the emergence of "religion" as an autonomous sphere allowed new forms of allegiance and affinity to grow. In particular, the growth of urban migration and increasing dissatisfaction with urban life, created a nostalgia for one's natal village and the village deity. So, while village deities have been cut out of most material transactions, they have simultaneously been reinscribed in a privileged place in the modern Himachali imaginary.

GODS, MEN, AND MOUNTAINS BEFORE RELIGION

The ownership, management, and cultivation of land in the Western Himalayas has long been a contentious issue.[2] In its attempt to generate and codify sources of revenue, the early colonial state sought to structure and systematize land relations throughout the subcontinent. As the Western Himalayas did not come under the control of the colonial authorities until a relatively late period (1815 for the Shimla hill states and not until the end of the First Anglo-Sikh War in 1846 for the Punjab hill states), attempts at settlement reports and agrarian assessment and codification were fitful and uneven. In fact, the pre-1857 settlement reports that were so common in Eastern India[3] did not become prevalent in the Western Himalayan region until after India gained independence.[4] For the most part, it appears that the difficulty of the terrain and its relative agricultural poverty hid these regions from the official gaze of colonial officials.

However, from the earliest of these reports and from a number of early survey missions, it becomes clear that the precolonial systems of land tenure in the Western Himalayas were significantly different from those enshrined in the North Indian plains. Large landholders were virtually nonexistent,[5] state power was weak and conflicted at best, and village structures were not built around systems of interdependent structures and reciprocal hierarchies like they were in the plains. In one of the earliest settlement reports that we have from the region, the prodigious and influential George Carnac Barnes offers the following insight.[6]

> Everybody is familiar with the economy of a township in the plains. There is the village community springing for one ancestor and possessing a joint interest in the lands of the township. For the maintenance of their rights and for the resistance of oppression they act together like one man. They regulate their own affairs, elect officers and make their own laws. There is a principle of combination and union pervading the whole body which binds them together and has preserved them unaltered from the earliest times. In the hill village, there is the common area upon which the inhabitants are collected and the village functionary who resides over them. But here the analogy ceases. They have no community of origin, but belong to different castes. There is no assemblage of houses like an ordinary village, but the dwelling of the people are scattered promiscuously over the whole surface. Each member lives upon his own holding and is quite independent of his neighbor. There is no identity of feeling, no idea of acting in concert. The headman, who is placed over them is not their own choice, but has been appointed by the Government. In short, the land enclosed by the circuit, instead of being a coparcenary estate, reclaimed, divided and enjoyed by a united brotherhood, is an aggregation of isolated freeholds quite distinct from each other, and possessing nothing in common, except that, of fiscal convenience, they have been massed together under one jurisdiction.[7]

With this lucid statement, Barnes returns us to our original assumption that the Western Himalayas were internally diverse and distinct in many ways from the plains. In this short piece, Barnes offers us some insights we will need to bear in mind as we move through this discussion. The first is that communities in the Western Himalayas should not be understood as hilly counterparts to typical Indian communities. These are neither the strong centralized towns of South India nor the interdependent communities of zamindars and their tillers. The Western Himalayas are highly variegated communities that vary from area to area, from state to state, and more importantly within the regions themselves.[8] In one "village"—although the word "village" is deceptive here insofar as it connotes a social whole—there were different languages, deities, celebrations, communities of origin, and calendars. As Barnes reminds us, and as will be clear throughout his work, the only thing that held these people together was "fiscal convenience."

Barnes made another remark that we need to examine more closely. He said that the people of these regions worked their own land. This is a point that other commentators have picked up on. In his seminal work on ecological change and peasant resistance, Ramachandra Gupta observed similar patterns in the hills to the east of Garhwal: "The hill land-tenure system inherited by the British differed no less strikingly from that in the plains. The first commissioner G. W. Traill, observed that at least three-fourths of the villagers were hissedari—i.e. wholly cultivated by the actual proprietors of the land, from whom the revenue demand was perforce restricted to their respective shares of the village assessment.... There were few large landowners. As in Kumaun [and Tehri Garhwal] division, the agrarian system was dominated by peasants cultivating their holdings with the help of family labour."[9] These communities were thus largely separate from state authorities and large organizational bodies. Land tenure was locally regulated. The majority of lands were not held by institutions, states, or influential families.

While many people agree that the systems of land ownership where villagers farmed their own land were most common, there is wide disagreement about the consequences of this. Guha himself argued: "The absence of sharp inequalities in land ownership within the body of cultivating proprietors—who formed the bulk of the population—was the basis for the sense of solidarity within the village community."[10] This is a view that is endorsed by many contemporary vernacular historians who long for the days of social equality and many villagers who spend more than a little time opining on the subject. However, Barnes was of a radically different opinion.

Turning again to Barnes, we begin to see the transition from the heterogeneous and localized version of land tenure to one regulated by the state:

> In these hills I fancy I can discern that primitive condition of landed property which at one time, perhaps prevailed throughout Hindustan.... The framework of the land system is here preserved in its original simplicity and those various and complicated tenures which have grown up with the innovations of conquest and the progress of society in our lower Provinces are in this neighborhood, almost unknown.... There are, I conceive two separate properties in the soil. The first and paramount is the right of the State to a certain share of the gross produce and the second is the hereditary right of cultivation and claim to the rest of the produce on the part of the cultivator. Such is the simple and intelligible relations between the agricultural community and the State, which, with few exceptions, exists throughout these hills.[11]

Barnes's theory relies as much on his own desires as it does on systems of local land tenure, but it does offer us some insight into the manner in which people related to their lands before settlement activities and postcolonial land reforms.[12] It is not simply that Barnes stands in as harbinger of the colonial state, but more importantly that he begins to rethink the past as a means of supporting future transformations.[13] It is clear from the account that I have quoted in full above that he understood the land tenures of the hills as simple and easily administrated. Land was locally owned and revenue was tendered to the sovereign authority. But what happened when the sovereign was ambiguous or absent? As I have asserted several times, the hills of the Western Himalayas have always been highly contested. No single ruler ever held sway over all the mountains, and those rulers that were able to expand their territories always faced threats—both internally and externally. Moreover, areas that were on the fringes of these so-called states often had no idea they were being claimed by a larger power, let alone taxed.

Colonial records from both the Punjab hill states and the Shimla hill states are filled with many examples of land disputes between two regions, both regions claiming sovereignty over particular areas. Of the records that remain, some of the most interesting document disputes over control of Hatkothi and Ravingarh and over grazing rights in Kullu, Bushahar, and Spiti.[14] The dispute over Hatkothi is particularly instructive. Located in a fertile valley in an area along the Pabbar River basin, Hatkothi is wedged between three major regional powers: Jubbal, Bushahar, and Jaunsar Bawar. The controversy chronicled in the archive involved the revision of a land settlement. The resettlement was necessitated by a legal case: Raja Sahib of Jubbal versus Mussadi, a citizen of Bushahar, filed by Major Burnett. The dispute went on for nearly ten years.[15] In a letter to the political agent in Simla, the Rana Sir Bhagat Chandra (raja of Jubbal) described the continuing escalation of tensions. In this letter, the raja complained of further problems: "On the case being filed, Jubbal sowed Kharif crop in that land on the 30th Jeth 1999-S., corresponding to 12th June, 1942. on the 10th Asarth 1999-s., corresponding to 23rd June 1942 one Jaishi Ram son of Chopnoo of village Mandhol, Bushahr state entered on the land and trespassed by destroying the Kharif crop sown by Jubbal and resowed the land for him."[16]

The case was originally filed in 1933 by Mussadi, who claimed that he was the rightful owner of a piece of land located between the larger principalities of the Hatkothi Temple, Bushahar State, and Jubbal State. The dispute that ensued clearly shows how unclear relations between these three principalities were. Most of the witnesses cited in the archives believed that Mussadi, a man who claimed allegiance to Bushahar, had been cultivating this particular piece of land for a long time.

However, when the issue of its proper ownership arose, Jubbal (a state that was very close to the British administration) made a claim to the land, disputing Bushahar's right to collect taxes on the property. Simultaneously, the temple committee, a semiautonomous body, also made a claim to the land. As the final arbiter of all interstate disputes—as dictated by the initial deeds (*sanads*)—the British government was brought in to decide the case.

I draw attention to the case to lay out how the ownership and sovereignty of particular lands was transformed under colonial management. A man and his family had been using a piece of land for generations (it should be noted that the land in dispute was particularly fertile in relation to other lands nearby) and understood themselves to have an agreement—however tenuous—with Bushahar.[17] However, with the solidification of state boundaries and land revenues, a debate ensued in which the positions of the temple committee, the raja of Jubbal, and the raja of Bushahar came into serious dispute with one another over the sovereignty of two small fields. While the records available cannot disclose the truth, extensive correspondences make it clear that the dispute was part of a larger transformation of land relations in the Western Himalayas in which states and large land owners—particularly temples—came to play a powerful role in the mediation of disputes between people and their land. Colonial courts settled disputes such as this one, solidifying boundaries between different areas of sovereignty, whether controlled by princely families or deities.

When the British moved into the Western Himalayas, they vanquished two forces. First, they pushed back the Nepali, and second, they drove out the Sikhs. One of the primary strategies they used to defeat these large powers was to employ local armies and local knowledge provided by princes and their advisors. As a reward for participation in these exploits, the princes were granted sovereignty over lands that they claimed as their ancestral property. I will not dispute whether the sovereignty that was granted to states like Bushahar and Chamba was faithful to the historical record. However, my contention is that these grants, the legal documents that they were founded upon, and the administrative apparatus that would connect them allowed for the solidification of state boundaries—geographic and otherwise—in a way that was hitherto inconceivable. As the settlement reports were drawn up, they were articulated in feudal terms. There were princes, and there were peasants. The peasants paid the princes, and the princes paid the British. There was also, just as in the dispute at Hatkoti, a third party: the temples.

Perhaps the most powerful transformation of the social and political landscape of the Western Himalayas under colonial control was the solidification of the power of independent states and the writing of their histories to buttress control and administration.[18] Most colonial writings on the Western Himalayas and the scant material published since assumed that the people of the region were to be understood in terms of states and the communities that formed around those states. This not only made possible the writing of histories from the perspective of genealogical roles and royal inscriptions[19] but also buttressed and justified a wide range of social practices, including the reorganization of land ownership and the use of slave labor for the construction of colonial hill stations. While I do not want to go so far as Edward John Thompson did in his classic work, *The Making of the Indian Princes*, I do want to assert that the British system of indirect rule and the *sanad* treaty system, which managed relations between states and supported the power of local rulers, were instrumental in creating conditions under which the princely states, as state powers, achieved more control over their subjects, defined geographic boundaries, regulated systems of revenue collection, and first systematized systems of intrastate communication and exchange.

The most powerful consequence of the solidification of princely power and the standardization of prince-peasant relations was the development and refinement of the *begār* system. This system of forced labor was used by the British to explore and map the Western Himalayas, to build roads and networks of communication throughout the region, and most spectacularly to construct the town of Shimla, which became the summer seat of British power in Asia. Indeed, *begār* satisfied a deep need for the British. In moving their summer capital, they faced formidable challenges. From the construction of roads through the steep labyrinthine mountains to the transportation of British officials and their luggage from the final train stop in Kalka, the British needed labor—enormous amounts of it. The work that went into the construction of the Kalka-Shimla Railway offers a sense of the amount of labor needed to make the hills livable for colonial officials. The railway line, which was 96.6 kilometers in length, was built almost exclusively with *begār* labor. In less than two years, 869 bridges were built, often carved by hand from nearby stone. The line ascended over two thousand meters and navigated almost one thousand curves.[20] In order to furnish the labor for this undertaking, the British took advantage of a system of relations that existed between rulers and peasantry in some areas of the Western Himalayas.[21] While the precolonial extent and parameters of this system are unknown, it is clear that the British expanded it greatly and abused their relations with princes by forcing them to provide laborers. What's more, most officials who worked within the system agreed that it was unjust and without legal or moral justification, but nearly all continued to support it, even if they did not explicitly lobby for its continuation.

The settlement reports that became the basis for relations between colonial agents and the states were organized around a set of assumptions. The first of these was that the sovereign power of an area was the prince and that this prince asserted control over all the people and land in his territory. Thus, revenues assessed for the land were to be collected through the prince, and land-revenue collection became a primary part of the relations between princes and colonial officials. As we have already seen in the Kangra settlement report, Barnes believed the precolonial land-tenure system to be a simple set of relations. Peasants lived on and worked their own land, and they paid tribute to the sovereign of the land. This basic assumption continues throughout the settlement reports. For example, in the Kullu settlement reports of 1888–1891, compiled by A. H. Diack, and the 1913 revision, officers further subdivided the state into separate sections (Rupi, Seraj, etc.). In their treatment of each of these regions, the fiscal history is understood to emanate from the raja. The question was not about who owns what land but rather about whether, in the succession from generation to generation, there had been a lapse when no direct offspring was available.[22]

There is a deep ambiguity between those that cultivate land and those who control land. While the majority of these settlement reports assume that the authority is state based, there are many others that hint at the fact that authority was much more divided, contested primarily by local deities. In many places, historians or settlement officers sought to reconcile what they understood to be a contradiction or an oversight on their part: that temple lands were independent from the raja. In some places, particularly Kullu and Chamba, there were inscriptions that intimated ties between rulers and divinities.[23] However, other than the central royal temples, temples in most areas appear to have controlled their own land. What is more, the nature of this "control" must be understood in context. For the British, controlling a plot of land meant that the people who lived on the land were obligated to render service to its owners, whereas for many who were connected to the temple, controlling land meant attending festivals, traveling with the local deity, or playing instruments at ceremonies—not forced labor in distant lands. In one of the earlier settlement records, the influential E. G. Wace criticized his predecessor, Edwards, for assuming that ownership and rent proceeded in straightforward ways in Himachal: "But what Mr. Edwards described in paragraph 97 of his report of 1859 appended as the khas or jagir lands of the families of former Rana of Kotkhai and the maáfi lands of the village temples (deotas), are of course mainly cultivated by tenants. They aggregate 415 acres. Of these 171 acres pay no rent, the tenants giving their labour (baith) in return of their tenancy"[24]

In fact, I could argue that colonial land policies sought to solidify tenuous land relations and strengthen authoritative bodies through which they could channel their revenues. While we will never know the degree to which smaller temples were autonomous from forms of state power, it is clear that the regular settlement reports conducted throughout the state solidified claims to land.[25] While the princes were the obvious winners of this process and local cultivators the losers, temples and temple committees were also winners.[26] It must be remembered that the majority of the settlements took place after the Great Revolution—after the East India Company transferred control of the Government of India to the British Crown and a greater emphasis was put on exempting religion from regulation. When she took power from the East India Company, Queen Victoria declared that she would "strictly charge and enjoin all those who may be in authority under us that they abstain from all interference with the religious belief or worship of any of our subjects on pain of our highest displeasure."[27] Thus, I believe, lands in any way associated with temples assumed the same authority as lands associated with princes. These were the conditions that led to temple committees and princes being the two largest aggregate landowners in the Western Himalayas on the eve of Indian independence in 1947.

The history of land control in the Western Himalayas is fraught with elisions and contradictions. While we have seen that the systems of land tenure in this region were different from the zamindari or taluqdari system of land organization used in the plains of Northwest India,[28] I will now explain how exactly these systems differed. While, in many plain communities, relations under the Mughal Empire were between local large landholders, Rājpūt chiefs, and emperors in Delhi,[29] the control and administration of land in the Himalayas was much more uneven, varying from region to region. It was highly dependent upon the strength of local leaders and the distance from centers of regional power such as Kullu, Chamba, and Mandi.

One of the most characteristic differences between the Himalayas and other areas in North India was the agrarian strength of temples. Our knowledge of the precolonial land holdings of these temples is compromised, being based on the need to buttress local princely control. Thus, lands that were most likely independent of princely control were classed (for administrative purposes) as part of the princely apparatus. Moreover, colonial theorists on the topic, from Charles Lyall to Jean Philippe Vogel, all seem to assume that lands owned by temples were lands granted to the temples by rajas and not lands that had been obtained by rajas through military or other exploits or lands that were outside of the administrative apparatus of the state completely.

In the early settlement reports, as officers attempted to assess tenure and revenue questions, they sought to understand the histories of these pieces of land. In so doing, they generally assumed that the British controlled all those lands that were not explicitly claimed by other parties. As they wrote their histories of these regions and tried to develop an understanding of the pasts of these lands, they relied primarily on two forms of information: royal genealogies and inscriptional evidence. While inscriptional evidence was present in some areas (such as Chamba, the explicitly royal temple of Kullu, and the temple complex at Bhīmākālī), the majority of temples and their lands fell outside the scope of these two forms of evidence. However, since these forms of evidence were supposed to be more reliable than oral testimony, they took precedence in the articulation of land rights. Despite the gross emphasis on royal genealogies and temple donations, it was still clear that, in many places, temples and their committees controlled large amounts of land. The following assessment is an example of a common conclusion for administrators in the region:

> A large area was assigned by the Rajas as endowments in perpetuity to temples and idols, and at present about one-seventh of the whole cultivated area of Kulu continues to be so held. In conferring land as an endowment, the theory appears to have been that the Raja divested himself of his lordship or proprietorship, and conferred it upon the idol or shrine. The cultivator thenceforth paid rent and did service in respect of such lands to the shrine and not the Raja. Up to present day neither the priests nor servants of the shrine, nor the cultivators of the fields make any claim to be called

proprietors of the endowment lands, though most of them claim a hereditary tenancy of office or of the cultivation. They seem in fact to consider
that to make such a claim would be an act of profanity on their art, which
might bring down upon them the wrath of the particular divinity to whose
shrine the land is dedicated.[30]

This quote illuminates the degree to which deities and their lands were
connected. It was not only through stories and periodic movement that
deities asserted their control over local lands. In many cases, they were
the sovereigns of those lands. An earlier settlement report from the same
region asserted: "Most of the tenants cultivate land the revenue of which
is assigned to temples."[31] It was thus the temples, and not necessarily the
figures of the state, that were the largest landowners. However, the push
to administer these lands through royal, rather than temple, administrators obscured the role that temples and their lands played in the history
of the Western Himalayas. It also greatly distorted what would follow
the colonial period. For example, in his otherwise excellent 1997 dissertation, Suman Chauhan assumes colonial categories:

It has already been mentioned that Rajas in pre-British times used to
endow temples with land grants. The cultivators of such lands thenceforth
paid rent and did service in respect of such lands to the shrine, and not to
the rajas who had made the grant. The temple land was cultivated by two
types of tenants. 1. Service tenants such as pujaris, kardars, wazirs, turis and
other employees of the temples. 2. The second type of tenants were those
who used to pay rent to temples. So long as they were paying this rent they
were not evicted. The rent taken from such tenants was generally fixed
amounts of grain, butter and oil. Some tenants also used to pay in cash only.
Such tenants were also liable to perform some duties in temple during the
festival and to bear the deity's palanquin during festival time. They could
also be called upon to render help for the construction of a new temple as
such a need arose, or to repair it, and also to carry loads when the idol was
taken out one a journey. Such tenants had the right to mortgage their land
but they were not allowed to sell it. In case the assignments of the temple
were resumed the tenants of such land paid the revenue to Government
and nothing was air to such temples.[32]

The mistake that Chauhan makes here is assuming that all temples were both products of land grants and in allegiance with the state, even though only some temples were clearly the beneficiaries of generous land grants from the Kullu rajas. This assumption detracts from the excellent data that Chauhan has accumulated that analyzes the relationship between land and social control.

Through a detailed analysis of published and unpublished materials, Chauhan shows that temples were large landowners in Kullu, controlling much more than one-seventh of the total area. Relying on the information in Diack's 1892 settlement report of Saraj, Chauhan writes that deities owned more than 8,788 acres of land, while Brahmins and Rājpūts combined held less than 3,800 acres.[33] This type of finding is common. In Lag Maharaj of Kullu, deities held more than one-sixth of all lands,[34] and in Wazir Rupi—where the most valuable lands are located—a quarter of all lands were owned by the deities.[35] It is important to note here that what is most significant about the relationship between deities and land owning was the relative size of the parcels. In most areas, land holdings were usually between one to five acres, but temples controlled much larger holdings. The majority of the people in the hills cultivated their own land. Settlement reports repeatedly assert that between 75 to 90 percent of all land was owned by those who cultivated it and that these holdings were very small. By contrast, the holdings of temples could be extremely large. According to Chauhan's calculations, temples were significant landowners at the end of the colonial period: in 1948, Haḍimbā held 309 bighas of land, Bijli Mahadev held 1072, Shamshi Mahadev held 3014, and Ambika held almost 5,000.[36] Apart from from the deities, the only other large land holders were the rajas of princely states, many of whom at that point had either been drafted into the new democratic project (as had the rajas of Jubbal, Chamba, Bushahar, etc.) or were being stripped of all of their power (as was the raja of Bilaspur).

To further upset some of the stability that is implicit in the settlement reports and in the historiography, we must return to the relative

instability of political allegiances in this region. The political consolidation of the Sikhs barely reached into the Himalayas, and the area was
little more than an afterthought for Mughal emperors.[37] Temples in the
Seraj, for example, such as those of Ambika and Shringa Rishi, appear
to have often been largely independent and did not maintain perma-
nent ties with either Bushahar or Kullu. Furthermore, deities like Jamlu
in Malana were never integrated into the Kullu pantheon or into the
political apparatus, of which the pantheon was such a powerful
reminder. Even within the contiguous territories of Kullu proper, deities like Bekhali mata retained significant land holdings and exercised
independence from the throne (*gaddi*) at Sultanpur. While there was an
intimate connection between deities and royal power and authority—
as in the case of Bhīmākālī and the rajas at Sarahan and Lakshmi-
Nārāyaṇa and the rajas at Chamba—it is clear that enormous tracts of
land were tilled by farmers but understood to be the property of the
deities. This is a sentiment that continues today despite radical land
reform measures, the increasing growth of horticulture, and the privatization of everything. In Himachal, one can still hear people refer to
lands titled in their names for revenue purposes as the gift of the deity,
owned and controlled by the deity.

LEGAL REFORM AND ITS "MINOR" REMAINDERS

Like in many areas of postcolonial India, land reform was one of the
first pieces of legislation pushed through the legislative assembly of
Himachal. In much of South Asia, the abolition of the zamindari system
that had sustained colonial rule was hindered by a lack of credible
and thorough land records. As the reforms moved forward, the land
revenue that had been the backbone of colonial finances and had propelled the early colonial regimes forward was radically undercut. The
absence of adequate records prohibited people from being taxed in pro-
portion to land ownership, and the connection between revenue and
reform was lost. In the heat of the historical moment, the focus was

much more on the equal distribution of land resources than on the state's coffers.

At the center of this discussion is the Himachal Pradesh Abolition of Big Landed Estates and Land Reforms Act of 1953. This act and its successive refinement set the standard for land tenure and state regulation of land holdings. More than any other piece of legislation, these reforms transformed circulation of power in the Western Himalayas, quickly erasing the power of local deities while solidifying central state authority. The act and its ramifications are extremely complex.[38] Jogishwar Singh summarized the act as follows:

> Landowners could resume land for personal cultivation up to a maximum of five acres, subject to the proviso that no tenant could be evicted from more than 1/4 of the area held by him. The term for exercise of this right was originally fixed at one year from the date of commencement of the Act, but was later extended to March 1, 1956 and then to September 1, 1956. All rights, titles and interest of landowners holding land in excess of Rs. 125 of annual land revenue and which was with tenants were vested in the state government which could transfer these in favor of cultivating tenants in lieu of payment of nominal compensation. Tenants with rights of occupancy could not be ejected from their tenancy except if they rendered land in their possession unfit for the purpose for which it was originally held or for failing to cultivate land according to local customs; or for sub-letting land without the consent of the landlord. Rights of widows, minors, armed forces personnel, students and prisoners were specially protected.[39]

In short, the act resolved the discrepancy between ownership and tenure in favor of the tenants, making it possible for anyone who inhabited the land they cultivated to assume ownership of a portion of it. The explicit goals of the act were clearly laid out. The act sought to eliminate intermediaries between the state and the farmers, whether they were princes, land barons, or deities; to make it almost impossible to eject tenants who were occupying and farming lands; and to vest all land with revenue assessment of more than 125 rupees in the hands of the state for redistribution. Moreover, as part of the dismantling of colonial and princely power, the act installed the evolving state as the arbiter of all agrarian relations, giving it the power to take and redistribute land according to the dictates of the new legislation. However, as legislative historian V. Verma noted, the act "turned out to be a sieve full of holes of which vested interest took full advantage."[40]

There is no doubt that the development of this legislation came about in direct response to a call from the central government to reform land tenure: "The future of land ownership and cultivation constitutes perhaps the most fundamental issue in national development."[41] However, the means by which the reforms were implemented were at the discretion of state and regional leaders.[42] These reforms were carried out in a number of different states throughout the region, and consideration of the different styles of these reforms figured prominently in the debates of Himachal's legislative assembly. As many scholars have reminded us, however,[43] the benefits of the reforms accrued more to the middle class[44] than to the poor farmers.

Discussions initiated by Chief Minister Parmar, the architect of the Himachali state, were directly in line with the national goals. These goals were articulated as twofold: advancing social justice and increasing economic productivity. As historian H.C.L. Merillat put it:

> Increased agricultural production was one of the major aims of India's planners from the outset. The other main object of land policy was greater social justice—a reduction in the disparities between the lots of the rich and the poor, an end to exploitation of workers on the land by landlords, a confirmation of holdings in the hands of those who actually worked the soil and the promise of more nearly equal status and opportunity for these who lived on the land. These two aims—greater output and improved social justice—were seen as mutually supporting.[45]

The question was how to bring these two goals together. Some early nationalists, such as Govind Ranade and Mahatma Gandhi, favored a moderate approach toward large landholders. Nehru, on the other hand, felt that radical agricultural reforms based on a system of peasant proprietary ownership needed to be implemented if India wanted to move forward economically.[46] Like many other facets of postcolonial

India, land reform took the track outlined by Nehru, and the central government began to encourage and articulate particular modes of land reform: "In the course of the Constituent Assembly deliberations, it will be recalled, a consensus had evolved as to how this should be done [elimination of zamindars]. Each State, subject to approval by the Central Government, would draw up its own plan and decide how much compensation should be paid to the Zamindars. The courts were not supposed to question the amount of compensation."[47]

Each state proceeded with this process somewhat differently, and the particular wording and implementation of the legislation drawn up by different states varied greatly, as did the overall success of the project. By "success," I mean the production of stated goals. As the Fourth Five Year Plan states in regard to one of the centerpieces of its land reform scheme, "the main object of ceilings which is to re-distribute land to the landless at a reasonable price on a planned basis has thus been largely defeated."[48] However, while the stated goal of the reforms was not achieved (though Himachal faired better at realizing it than some other states did), the reforms had profound consequences. I believe that this has to do mainly with the elimination not so much of intermediaries like zamindars or talqudaris but with the elimination of divine intermediaries. But before discussing this, lets look at the debates surrounding the first of several land reform bills to move through the Himachal Pradesh Vidhān Sabhā.

Many in the nascent legislative assembly had been elected because they supported the plight of local farmers, which was at the heart of the movement to overthrow princely rule and reform internal relations. The incipient political communities that became the backbone of Himachal's emerging elite were primarily those associated with Praja Mandals and with the reorganization of territorial unity, the central concern of which was the establishment of the rights of peasants as a means of furthering the development of the state.[49]

Thus, while Himachal was a Part C state, the legislative assembly of 1952–1956 passed fifty-five legislative measures, the vast majority of which were devoted to socioeconomic development.[50] Looking at the archival records from this period, it becomes readily apparent that land reform was the most important item on the legislative agenda.[51] While some politicians worked for national recognition and state reorganization and a translocal level, the majority of internal reforms were focused on land.[52]

There was broad consensus that the princes and large landowners had abused the "tillers of the soil."[53] The argument against what some legislators called the brutal tyranny of local princes had become a common theme in the midcentury political discourse. The argument also drew on a longer tradition of reform that worked specifically to overcome the abuse of indentured labor. The early legislation of land reform fits neatly into a pattern of progressive realignment of power in the Western Himalayas. There were a couple of basic ideas that guided this realignment. The first of these was the idea that whoever lived and worked on a piece of land should be regarded as its proprietor. The second guiding principal was that no single individual should be able to control too large a tract of land. Furthermore, by applying rules first developed in the 1952 Punjab Tenancy Act,[54] legislators worked to ensure that tenants could not be removed from land unless they failed to pay land revenue or utilized the land in an "improper manner." After a lengthy review process assessing the needs and potential impact of land reform, the Himachal Pradesh Abolition of Big Landed Estates and Land Reform Act of 1953 (ratified in 1954) was laid on the table. It was then complemented by a number of other acts that sought to address issues left unresolved in the Abolition Act of 1953. While this trend toward reducing the size of land holdings is clear enough, it is not evident exactly what transformation happened on the ground.

As India turned its eyes to the West and embraced visions of modernization, the earliest forms of development the country put into effect were focused on industrial development.[55] However, these new forms of production were virtually impossible to implement in the inhospitable regions of the Western Himalayas. An undereducated populace, a challenging topography, and a lack of adequate infrastructure all precluded the Western Himalayas from engaging in industrial modernization. This was a major setback for those elites who were championing modernization and pushing for state integration and reform. They sought to articulate the future of the Western Himalayas in terms that were understood at the national level, but their failure to do so greatly weakened their demands for full statehood. The natural obstacles faced by the state when it came to industrial development led politicians to turn to the other prong of national development: agrarian development. Unable to develop large cotton mills or manufacturing centers, Himachal embraced calls from Delhi to develop the agricultural sector.

In many ways, Himachal's land reforms were dictated from the central government. The federalist structure of the Indian constitution meant that land reforms were the responsibility of the states, and so their success or failure lay primarily at the state level. Through a series of planning papers and clear articulations in the Five-Year Plans, the national government laid out a plan for land reform that articulated the logic of these reforms in terms of their ability to improve social justice and economic productivity. Picking up on these goals, Himachal's planners and members of the legislative assembly followed many of the national directives, often mirroring their failures and triumphs. They began with a logic that depended on the "abolition of intermediaries" that sought to destroy those forms of indirect control that had been facilitated by British land reforms, in particular the zamindari and jagirdari systems. The broad effectiveness of these reforms was then attacked by a number of reforms that focused on the setting of land ceilings (limits on the size of land holdings). As we examine the relative successes and failures of these policies and attend to their social repercussions, it will be easy to lose sight of the broader goals of this discussion, which is understanding the centralization of power in the bureaucratic state, the elevation of a small number of elite landowners, the financial destruction of local temples and their associated bodies, and the resurrection of these temples as a visualized, almost nostalgic ideal.

As with so many of the initial reforms implemented by the nascent Himachali state, land reform was the product of intense lobbying and political pressure by Y. S. Parmar. A member of the Indian National Congress Party and a supporter of Nehru, Parmar attempted to implement the goals of the First Five-Year Plan with admirable efficiency. It was his efforts that brought land reform to the table and pushed the legislation at both the national and the local level. While particular reforms fell prey to many of the same pitfalls as reforms did in other states, Himachal was relatively successful in implementing some of the broader contours of land reform as conceived by nationalist leaders and idealistic agrarian reformists. In a speech on the floor of the legislative assembly, Parmar articulated the twin goals of land reform: "It can be expected that the future of Himachal Pradesh is its farmers. These people are working in the fields and this bill has shown them a new vision, a new way. This new way is the road towards economic and social development with this the state is proceeding further and further."[56]

Parmar believed that Himachal's future lay in rapid economic development and, given the particular geographic features of the land, that agricultural production was the state's best hope.[57] For him, it represented a great opportunity for the state to move out of its "backward" and "tribal" character into a modern, productive, and socially just society. According to Parmar and the logic that he articulated again and again on the assembly floor, the absentee landlords were spoiling the great potential of the state. Like the British before them, they were allowing good and profitable lands to go to waste. It was only through radical land reforms that Himachal could achieve the destiny that Parmar was so fond of invoking: "We only want that a policy should be accepted that we can earn more and more from the land. This is the only aim.... There will be no surplus land left with the big landlord and if they will get the fair compensation against that land then it will not be a problem for them."[58]

This type of rhetoric was characteristic of Parmar, who took the liberty to speak on behalf of "the people" every chance that he could. He was a vocal advocate of the rights of farmers and villagers and consistently set the needs of peasant before those of other members of the state. Though he came under intense criticism for favoring farmers over "those who fill the state's wallet,"[59] he continued to advocate for them and spoke unapologetically in favor of the abolition of the landed classes: "Those people who were living on the hard work of the farmer, they will have the problem. The people who were profiting will certainly be hurt, but this is only natural."[60] Parmar felt that the abolition of landlords and the redistribution of wealth was part of a broader struggle against injustice and social inequality.

Throughout his career, Parmar was concerned with elevating those who had been ignored and left outside the fold. He sought to integrate peasants and landlords and hill people with plains people and to further the progress of the nation by providing a solid economic and cultural form that was conducive to equality. In his opinion, the land reform bill was one of the biggest steps toward that goal:

> It is correct that we are attempting to bring together classes of society, to establish a classless society.... Everyone will be considered equal, whether landlord or farmer.... Both are owners.... No one will remain who lives on the hard work of others. Those who do the hard work will get the return according to their toil. According to this bill, after passing this recommendation there will be no question of lifting of a particular class. Both sides will be on their land. They will have to rise up and be equal. This is the meaning of this bill.[61]

While the land reforms of the early 1950s and those passed in 1971 and 1972 were ushered through the assembly and signed into law, they did not proceed without a fight. In fact, the reception of these reforms was quite mixed. As might be expected, the majority of the families that would be affected by the law were themselves part of the emerging political elite. This put them in direct conflict with the direction of the nation as articulated in the First Five Year Plan and the leadership of

Parmar. That any of these reforms were passed is a testament to Parmar's ardor and diplomatic skills. Their failed implementation, however, is a testament to the crafty work of other self-interested politicians. In fact, examining some of the more conspicuous objections to the bill will make some of the problems that were created clear.

The primary objection to the bill was that it would have a negative economic impact. Many people believed that the dispersal of land to peasants would undercut the growth of the middle class, which was being driven by people from the rural environments moving to urban or semi-urban centers. These people, critics argued, held the future of the state, and it was only on the basis of income from their land that they would be able to support themselves as businessmen and the creators of a new robust economy. By far the most articulate, if vociferous, spokesman for this position was the prominent MLA from Mandi, Krishanad Swami. Swami, like many of the MLAs that came after him, was a master of persuasion—of speaking out of both sides of his mouth at the same time. Reading transcripts of his speeches, one often has the sense that he and Parmar shared a lot of ground; however, they could not have been more distant from one another on most of the central land reform issues. For example, in Swami's opinion, the government had gone too far in seeking to redistribute the land of large landholders:

> I want some reform for farmers. Then their economic status will be solidified and everyone would be satisfied. But these reforms, in the case of the tenants, should not be at the cost of those people who are the main factor behind filling the treasury of the Government. They [economic leaders] will become poor or refuges. There should be some way so that they too can earn their bread. If you want to make them refugees, then I will reject this bill. Devastation is not the work of the Government and it is also not the work of the Government to favor only one class. The government has to take care of both.[62]

Swami argued that the goal of government was to look out for all levels of society and to foster economic growth through means other than agrarian reform. He believed that it was important to protect the interests of

Figure 9. Deity being moved from storage to Rāth. Photo by author.

those contributing to the development of the state's economic resources. Agricultural development was, he contended, simply about subsistence and not about what would be best for the state as a whole.

Swami thought that a land reform bill would create a widening gap between the classes of society. The redistribution of land, in his opinion, would not have the effect of leveling social difference but instead would create a deep-seated resentment between the classes that would only redouble communal differences. Swami believed that the only way to move toward social equality was to solidify minority power and allow the profits to trickle down to the masses: "To those who are saying that we are in majority and we want to eradicate existing land holdings, I say: not everything should be settled by majority. The government must care for all communities."[63] Swami was an ardent opponent of the land reform bill and attacked it from other angles as well. In sum, many of the issues that he pressed, such as protection for widows and students, ended up being incorporated into the bill. Most importantly, he planted a seed of dissent that enterprising landowners could cultivate to secure their interests, interests that were easily rested from deities that had become "minors."

SEPARATING DEITIES FROM THEIR LAND, AND THE POSSIBILITY OF RELIGION BEYOND ECONOMY OR POLITICS

The early land reforms were a legal sieve that filtered certain classes of landholders from others. To make matters worse, the reforms of 1953 were undermined by the transformation of the Vidhān Sabhā in 1954 and its dissolution in 1956.[64] In fact, the Supreme Court case of *Vinod Kumar v. State of Himachal Pradesh* (1959) was resolved in favor of Kumar because the land reforms of 1953 had been enacted by a legislative body that was no longer in existence and, as such, the reforms could not be applied to a new context.[65] The repercussions of these land reforms, like similar reforms across India, were not what might have been expected or envisioned by their creators. In an insightful analysis of the development and failures of land reforms in South Asia, Ronald Herring suggests that there was a deep divide between what officials thought they were doing and what they actually did—a gap between, to use Herring's terminology, "policy logic" and actual reforms.[66]

Far from inaugurating a peasant revolution, the reforms centralized authority in the emerging state and allowed many of the larger landowners to retain their land and consolidate their power.[67] So, if the often-repeated numbers about the abolition of 2,500 big estates and 100,000 acres of land being distributed are even remotely true, who were the landholders who were adversely affected? How did this restructuring impact those who were able to avoid the downsizing of their properties? How did these changes structure the relations between center and periphery? In particular, how did they affect relations between local deities and those associated with them? To answer these questions, I pursue three lines of thought. First, I argue that village temples were most adversely affected by the abolition act and that the redistribution of their land radically changed the material relations that were associated with the temples. Second, I argue that those who knew the law were able to manipulate emerging legal and bureaucratic structures to maintain their lands while simultaneously increasing their social status through ever more public roles (rather than less public roles, which the act was designed to encourage).[68] Third, I argue that, while undercutting the material relations between deities and villagers, the reforms created a nostalgia for the natal village and the village deity. So, although village deities have been cut out of the game of material transactions, they have been reinscribed in a privileged place in the modern Himachali imaginary. In this way, the deity becomes the heart of a new Himachali religion that is free of economic, political, and social entanglements.

In many areas, gods and goddesses were the largest landowners. Their lands were acquired through tax-free royal land grants or simply because they were outside the jurisdiction of any state (precolonial, princely, or colonial). These large land holdings include the lands of deities like Jamlu in Malana and Sringa Rishi in Banjar and even of temples like the one in Devī-Kothi.[69] While it would be impossible to examine the changes that affected all of these temples from the late colonial period until the present in this book—that would be a manuscript unto itself—we can get a good understanding of the broader changes at work in the state by looking at the example of one district, as my ethnographic and archival research suggests that the trend in this district is prevalent throughout the state.

Some of the best evidence for the relationship between temples and land ownership comes from the work of Jogishwar Singh, who was the district commissioner in the Kinnaur district at Kalka from 1980 to 1983. He went on to complete a doctorate at the South Asia Institute of the department of History at Heidelberg University. Although his work focuses on understanding the changing patterns of institutional credit, Singh examines transformations in land tenure by looking at revenue from the earliest settlement reports (1851), the first legal settlement

(1894), and extensive records of postcolonial management in Kinnaur and Bushahar, to which very few have had access. With a translation of an Urdu text by Wājib-ul-Arz of Ghodi-Kamru, Singh pushes forward one of his basic arguments: that temples were major landowners in these upper regions.[70] In a discussion of the four types of tenants and their various rights, he states: "Generally, occupancy tenants are at the service of the Mandir Devta or the Mandir Thakur, at some places also of the zamindars. Tenants of the Buddhist temple have been in cultivating possession of the temple in question."[71] More explicitly, the majority of the people in this region—those who occupy and work the land—are subject to the service of the temple that controls that land.

While "control" may not have the same legal definition as "ownership," it does indicate that the temples in this region were the locations where grain was stored, loans offered, and excess redistributed. In short, the temples controlled the agricultural production in the region. For example, in the early twentieth century, Devatā Nagjī controlled 2,443 bighas of land, Devatā Maheshwar at Sungra controlled 2,800 bighas, and Devatā Badrināth controlled 1,986 bighas.[72]

One of the primary strengths of Singh's work is his detailed elaboration of the changing credit structure in Kinnaur. The major distinction that he makes here is between the "informal sector"[73] and institutional credit structures, such as the H.P. State Cooperative Land Development Bank. Singh works hard to show the inadequacies of the early credit structure and to examine the systems that preceded the foundation of formal modern credit systems. He argues that these credit systems were deeply entrenched and finds evidence of them in the accounts of Christians associated with the Moravian mission and in colonial dispatches from the earliest revenue collectors. He demonstrates that the relationship between the largest landowners and the larger temples was an ongoing process in which the rights and legitimacy of both deity and raja continually reinforced one another through various means, not the least of which was money lending. The deities thus traditionally served as one of the core sites of authority and material exchange, although these roles were taken over by the postcolonial state. It is worth quoting Singh extensively here:

> The Rajas of Bushahr did not establish any institutional credit infrastructure to act as an economic underpinning to their rule but provided the deities, consciously or otherwise with the means of generating a surplus and functioning as money lenders. Money lending operations of the deities came to be so well organized in time that they came to constitute a kind of quasi-institutional credit network, lying somewhere between an official credit network and the network of village money lenders. They functioned for some debtors as refinancing agencies from money lenders. They gave (and give) loans regardless of purpose, unlike official agencies which give loans only for so-called productive purposes and almost refuse to admit the need of loans for consumption purposes.... The devtas' interest lay not in reducing borrowers to landless servitude but in meeting their essential credit needs so that they would have enough surplus to repay the devta with interest, thereby increasing the latter's capacity for further lending. The devtas did not impose notional, insupportably high interest rates. The total absence of mārwāri seths from Kinnaur shows that the devtas have not done a bad job as moneylenders.[74]

This passage makes it clear that the deities of Kinnaur and Bushahar[75] were involved in the lives of the villagers in very material ways. There is evidence from a number of sources that supports Singh's contention that local temples served as banks and storehouses for the villagers associated with them.[76] Moreover, I have heard it argued on several occasions that the begār system that the British exploited as a thinly-veiled system of slavery was more often understood as a form of communal participation in the activities of a deity (and many people still adhere to this system) rather than a mode of labor exploitation managed by a prince. However, with the introduction of the land reforms, the agricultural base that served as the economic backbone of many deities' support was uprooted. In many cases, even the managers of these temples (*kārdār*) we not allowed to retain more than a couple of acres of land. In fact, stories of land seizure are a common part of the everyday stories of temples in the hills.

Figure 10. A *koṭhī* in the Satluj Valley. Photo by author.

As Singh concludes, "all the affected landowners [of the Abolition Reforms] were village gods."[77] The five most adversely affected landowners were local deities in the villages of Sungra, Chagāon, Bhāba, Kāmru, and Sangla. Land taken from these five deities was redistributed to 2,284 people before February 28, 1966. This was more than one-quarter of all the land given to tenants in the entire state. In total, more than 9,000 bighas of land were taken from these five deities. Similar seizures were made all over the state, from Chamba to Spiti.

These numbers come from some of the larger villages in the region and areas where rajas had the greatest control. In areas where this is not the case, the land holdings of deities were even larger. One such case comes from a district on the other side of the state, in Chamba. Since Jean Vogel first brought Devī-Koṭhī to public notice, it has remained an area of interest. As a result, we have more information about this remote village and its temple than we have about many other villages.[78] According-ing to a report in 1956, the shrine of the goddess Chamunda held approximately 56 percent of all arable land within the revenue village and even more outside of the village: "In total, it possessed 65.2 acres out of 118 acres of cultivable land in the village, apart from the land in other far-flung areas tilled by as many as 26 tenants."[79] Like so many others, the temple at Devi-Koṭhī was relieved of its land by the 1953 reforms, and the relation it once mediated between the people of Chamba and the land disappeared.

We can get a sense of the economic and material centrality of temple and its administrative apparatus when we look at one of the major administrative structures in the Western Himalayas. Throughout the hills, areas of division are often referred to as *koṭhīs*, a term that seems to have been used extensively in the colonial period as well. *Koṭhī* has an extremely wide range of meanings. Most broadly, it refers to an administrative unit of land collected together as "grain revenue." It can also refer to the specific land on which a temple sits. However, it is more often used to name the physical building in which the collective grain was stored. These *koṭhīs* are invariably located adjacent to temples and are often described in the vast travel literature from the colonial period, such as in this passage by B. H. Baden-Powell: "In the [hill] States generally, the country is divided for similar purposes into koṭhī—that is, tracts the grain revenue of which is collected in one central koṭhī or State granary, in which also official business is daily transacted, and perhaps such justice as is required by a simple people, is dispensed."[80]

Today, however, these buildings are mostly abandoned. They are still managed by temple treasurers (*bandhārī*), but they are predominately empty. They are now used to house the ornaments and extra masks of the deity. They also sometimes house temple records. For the most part, they are closed and empty, though they dominate the visual landscape of the temple complex. They thus stand as a metaphor for the radical transformation of the role of the deity. Emptied of their material power, the temples now stand as monuments to a rich cultural history and as the objects of faith rather than serving as the center of material and spiritual life. These structures are the ones most commonly shown as a sign of Himachal's ancient religious heritage.

PART TWO

Knowledge

Making and Managing Theological Culture

CHAPTER THREE

Ordinary Miraculousness

Farmers and Pharmacists Practice
the Science of Religion

"COLLECTING HISTORY"

I was sitting with my fieldwork assistant and two local researchers in a tiny village in the upper Sutlej Valley. It was late afternoon, and the wind had whipped the clouds to the northeast into a wispy frenzy that looked like a blown-out mushroom cloud. We had just finished recording a long series of local songs that told of the time before the birth of the world, and many people were gathering around us in front of the blacksmith's shop. A young man approached us and asked my friend, a local researcher, in a familiar cajoling tone: "Uncle Jī, what are you doing? You walk from village to village scribbling in your tiny notebooks. Why are you always writing things down and asking such strange questions?" My friend and guide replied: "I am collecting history, world history. Everywhere, our history is being lost."

This chapter lays out the rationale for and content of a rapidly expanding field of practices associated with the writing of Himachal's cultural history. I suggest that the writers, filmmakers, and photographers involved in this field are providing the material for the creation of a new person, that they themselves are exemplars of this person, and that their works are fast becoming the center of a canon on Himachali religion.

Figure II. *Somasī* journal cover. Photo by author.

In Himachal Pradesh, history writing is booming. Farmers, veterinarians, and photographers are writing what they do and see. The birth of this field is directly connected to the emergence of the idea of Himachal as a bounded abstraction worthy of reflection—as well as to the creation of specific governmental departments set up to support it. The Department of Language and Culture was started in 1972, after state recognition, at which point the department and its more prolific ally, the Academy of Arts, Language and Culture, became the de facto centers of literary production, control, and intellectual patronage in Himachal. Working in combination, these two departments helped create an enormous archive of materials and a network of people and institutional structures.

In this chapter, we will see how the forms of knowledge that developed in these departments were responses to specific governmental failures and how the Department of Language and Culture was founded to help encourage regional integration.[1] We will seek to understand how the discourse on the cultural traditions of the Western Himalayas emerged out of specific problems of governance and how the people and discourses that addressed this problem straddled the boundaries of state and society. Furthermore, we will examine how ideas, discourses, and material networks first formulated under the gaze of state planning gave birth to a popular new genre in the region—ethnomedia—and how the works in the genre are becoming the center of an evolving canon.

This chapter is an argument in three movements. The first part argues that the ethnohistorians of Himachal Pradesh, whose field developed because of a need for cultural unity and was encouraged by the dictates of the new state of planning, provided an operating narrative of the state that grounded the state's authority in its local theistic practices. In so doing, they were able to simultaneously validate local deity traditions while employing them, sometimes metonymically, in the service of the emerging state. And yet, as the second part of this argument shows, vernacular ethnohistory, although it emerged in the shadow of state knowledge and logics, has not been controlled by governmental ministries that profess their own opinions and thoughts from on high to the distant masses. The hard and fast lines between state and society that were established by midcentury political science don't make much sense here.[2] Instead, the people writing vernacular ethnohistories and interacting with villagers are themselves villagers. They are farmers, astrologers, veterinarians, and photographers. They are also part of a publishing and institutional network founded and orchestrated by the Department of Language and Culture and the Academy of Arts, Language and Culture, and their work contributes to and bolsters the idea of the state. The discursive work of these figures, as explored in the third movement of this chapter's argument, is performed in a space of Himachali public culture that I call ethnomedia, which connects distant villages to publishing centers in Shimla. It also connects writers in mountaintop villages to reformers in Chandigarh and creates a space in which the content, performance, and management of Himachali religion occurs.

A now famous phrase, the Bengali writer Bankimchandra Chatterjee declared in the 1880s: "Bengalis have no history." He admonished Bengalis to wake up and begin writing the history of Bengal. He argued: "Bengal must have a history, or else there is no hope for it. Who will write it? You will write it, I will write it, all of us will write it. Every Bengali will have to write it."[3]

Within the newly formed public cultures connecting local spaces to translocal intellectual and capitalistic circuits, the new genre that is most important for the discussion of religion and the state is ethnomedia. I refer to this genre of representation as "ethnomedia," as opposed to one of a range of other terms, because it connects two things: ethnographic representations and media circulation.

The evolution of this genre is intimately connected to the work of the Department of Language and Culture and the Academy of Arts, Language and Culture.[4] Projects initiated within these departments, sponsored by them, or inspired by their work constitute the majority of productions in the genre. Early officials within these departments, such as M. R. Thakur, Banshi Ram Sharma, and Sudarshan Vashisth, defined

Figure 12. A popular pamphlet. Photo by author.

the scope and focus of the field. In many ways, the origins of the genre as a major force within public culture can be traced to the work of the state's first chief minister, Y. S. Parmar. Parmar's early works on Pahāṛī language and polyandry (see chapter 1) directly linked the projects of state modernization, ethnographic representation, and state administration. His works provided inspiration to the highest levels of Himachali society,[5] and his administrative vision provided the structural apparatus for the early formulation of ethnomedia.

In the early period surrounding the state's full recognition (1960–1980), ethnomedia took the form of several vernacular publications, the promotion and redesign of public spaces, and the reorientation of fairs and festivals. These developments worked in unison to achieve the broader goals of the Department of Language and Culture and the Academy of Arts, Language and Culture. What formed was an interconnected group of journalists, scholars, promoters, publicists, and administrators, who worked together to articulate, reproduce, and archive the traditions and practices of the state.

The works within this genre are clearly indebted more to later colonial conventions of ethnographic description than to systematic historical treatises. While they do give attention to the past and its relevance for the present, the concern is not chronological, and they do not pay close attention to time as a set of progressive moments in which people and events shape and reshape the world. In terms of models, those of John Hutchinson and Jean Philippe Vogel are almost entirely absent, whereas those that draw from Parmar's work are common. In short, the conventions of modern historiography are not in evidence. Instead, there is a close attention to the realities of daily life and a painstaking process of description and categorization of the practices.

This process is not unconnected to the logic and practices of the late colonial state.[6] As Nicholas Dirks so clearly lays out in several places in his work, the late nineteenth century saw a transformation in which the focus on the relationship between land, revenue, and the colonial state was replaced—following 1857—by what he terms "the ethnographic state."[7] While Dirks's concern in much of his work is to show how caste became "the primary object of social classification and understanding,"[8] many of his conclusions ring true in the context of Himachal. Dirks believed that the project of categorization and control became tied not to the identification of land that could provide revenues but to the correct identification of the character and pasts of the colonized so that the diverse masses could be more effectively and more smoothly known, understood, and thereby ruled.[9]

The process of land regulation and identity formation in Himachal Pradesh is very similar, although the connection with the logic of rule is somewhat more diffused. Whereas, in the colonial period, the development of an ethnographic state and its associated forms of knowledge emerged from the threat of rebellion, ethnomedia in Himachal emerged more out of a need for national recognition at the political and cultural levels and a need for geographic integration. Thus, in the period immediately preceding 1971, ethnomedia played a central role in integrating disparate populations and then representing those populations in public forums, and this role continued to grow in the following years.

The genre that formed created a readily accessible archive of the various traditions of the state. It cataloged the songs and dances of geographically isolated people. It systematized information about fairs and festivals. It rethought practices as part of historical progressions, as symbols of cultural patterns, and as signs of uniqueness. It helped people who once understood themselves as isolated and different to feel like they were part of a community and then represented that community to the public. These last two functions were arguably the most important development of early forms of ethnomedia.

STUMBLING TOWARD A SCIENCE OF RELIGION

In 1961, as India was pushing its way into the promised land of modernity, the administrators of the national census operations and the registrar general, Ashok Mitra, decided to supplement their normal task of collecting, collating, and publishing statistical information in primarily numerical form. The demands of the postcolonial state were changing as India's Planning Commission took aim at the village level.[10] In his introduction to the 1961 volumes, Mitra stated: "After the independence of India in 1947, the orientation of census data underwent considerable change to meet the new requirements of social planning and development. The shift from the administrative needs of a colonial government to that of a national government for economic reconstruction and welfare measures brought in its wake changes in data requirement."[11] While the collection and distribution of census information had become a vital component of the proper functioning of the state, it had also become clear that there was a growing disparity between the facts as they were represented in numerical and mathematical models and the mess of human life.

Ashok Mitra and his cadre of Indian Administrative Service officers embarked on an ambitious project to address this gap. As Mitra put it, in order to "try to invest the dry bones of village statistics with flesh-and-blood accounts of social structure and social change, it was accordingly decided to select a few villages in every state for special study, where personal observations would be brought to bear on the interpretation of statistics to find out how much of a village was static and yet changing and how fast the winds of change were blowing and from where."[12] Each state was to conduct at least thirty-five studies focusing on three types of villages. The first were small one-community villages of between three hundred and seven hundred people. The second type were villages having significant "scheduled tribe" (ST) populations. The third type was large, well-established, socially complex villages. These studies would be used to produce a single volume focusing specifically on each state's fairs and festivals.

This work was undertaken in Himachal Pradesh by the energetic and intelligent Ram Chandra Pal Singh, who was then superintendent of census operations. Under his able control, thirty-five volumes[13] were published, surveying villages from the high peaks of Kinnaur to the warm valleys of Mandi. These village surveys were developed in the period that also saw the heated struggle for Himachal's statehood. Consonant with the concurrent independence movement, the volumes give consistent attention to the prowess of Himachali development. As one examines these volumes, it is essential to remember that, when they were created, the States Reorganization Committee had just rendered its decision to assume direct control of the region and that, by the time the last volume was published, Himachal had grown extensively in area, population, and political stature. Thus, these studies are inflected by the struggle for statehood, and they laud the progress of Himachali development and the growth of regional identity on almost every page. They sing the song of modernity.

Great care was put into producing these volumes, which contributed to their consistency in both form and content. Although the questions asked differed from survey to survey, the manner in which the information was managed and the styles of analysis were highly consistent. Most of the studies are divided into four main parts: the village, the people and their material equipment, the economy, and the social and cultural life. While some studies subdivide these sections, every study addresses these four primary concerns. For the detailed examination of these studies that I will carry out here, the sections on social and cultural life are most important. I will use these sections as a way of understanding the formation of the relationship between religion and state in Himachal.

Before moving forward, a note on the works themselves is in order. These studies are excellent resources for the study of Himachali society and history. There is really nothing else like them when it comes to the detail, precision, quality, or diversity of the information they provide. They are excellent records of what various regional administrators thought of the relationship between religion and state in the period from the late 1950s through the late 1960s. Moreover, in contrast to other types of census records, these studies specifically sought to understand how Himachal was changing and to document and explain those changes. I have chosen these studies as a point of inquiry because I believe they are the precursors to the genre I am calling vernacular ethnomedia. These studies, in combination with the volume on fairs and festivals,[14] introduced many new scholars to the world of publications and validated the important role of the village historian. The volume on fairs and festivals is a foundational work of the genre. The pool of talented researchers and writers who prepared these texts became the first ethnohistorians and the foremost among a generation of new experts.

In his fabulous essay "The Character of Calculability,"[15] Timothy Mitchell examines how, in the formation of colonial administration in Egypt, administrators sought to draw a perfectly accurate map of the Nile River basin. This would make it possible to accurately measure and register land owning in the region and to map and administer water usage, crop rotation, planting, and harvest. "Begun in 1898, the survey was based upon a novel technique of figuring the relationship between people and land embodied in the law of property: The large-scale map.... In less than a decade the countryside had been transformed from a place in which maps played no role in administrative practice, legal argument, or financial calculation, to one of the most closely mapped terrains in the world. The making of these maps introduced new forms of measurement, representation and calculation."[16]

What is so important about Mitchell's essay, however, is not that he shows how the British created new forms of knowledge to better rule and extract resources from Egypt but that he describes how these forms of calculability, planning, and abstraction inevitably brought about their own undoing. With the production of the map, administrators no longer had to travel to the places that were mapped. They could use the knowledge and measurements on the map to make administrative decisions. However, due to Egypt's hot and humid climate, the map shrank as it absorbed moisture and then dried out again, distorting calculations, and the boundaries of the river and the placement of rocks and other landmarks shifted over time. Moreover, it was better to set the

price of crops (e.g., cotton) in direct collaboration with the farmers har-
vesting their crops rather than setting prices by consulting maps and
measuring the price against the potential of the fields to produce cotton. As a result of these issues, Mitchell argues that the map and other
forms of knowledge like it "opened up a distance, a gap that came to be
seen as an absolute divide. The movement from the field to the survey
office was not to be experienced as a chain of social practices, but as the
distance between reality and its representations, between the material
and the abstract, between the real world and the map."[17]

The village monographs in Himachal were conceived of because of
a similar perceived gap. Increasingly, administrators were aware of the
"inaccuracy" of census data, a perception that continues to pervade the
census office in Shimla. These monographs developed because of this
growing gap and the need for state managers to retain control of the
areas they were administering. Moreover, by explicitly focusing on
questions of change and social transformation, these surveys examined
sites of analysis easily overlooked in charts and graphs. As one surveyor
perceptively observed:

> The census is essentially a statistical survey, and as such it partakes of the
> limitations of such surveys because of its dealing with such aspects of
> human life as are capable of being expressed numerically or quantitatively.
> A census report deals with the total population, rate of its growth, its dis-
> tribution over land and according to age, sex, marital status, literature, lan-
> guage, religion, occupation and other allied subjects. But the census report
> does not satisfy completely the reader desirous o f knowing little informa-
> tion on social structure and material culture of the population—the types
> of houses they live in, the clothes they wear, the food they eat, their house-
> hold equipment, their livestock, their hours of work and recreation, their
> beliefs and customs and their traditions and aspirations.[18]

Thus, as the administrative apparatus of the state emerged in
Himachal, administrators were well aware of the growing gap between
official knowledge and lived worlds. While the need to develop a body
of information about the state was ever present, there was an attempt to

keep this knowledge locally relevant. While these studies were dictated from the national level and organized from Shimla, they are nevertheless local village studies conducted by surveyors living in or near these villages, and they are tied to locality. What is ironic, however, is that the space that they open—that of the vernacular ethnohistorian and indeed of the possibility for state history altogether—made possible the radical abstraction of place and the creation of translocal forms of identity and community that were so fundamental for Himachal's formation. Examining how these studies treat the relationship between religion and culture will show how this happened.

As noted earlier, each of the monographs contains a section on "social and cultural life," which is understood as different from the economy,[19] the village (its geography, flora, fauna, buildings, etc.), and the people (their castes, ages, education, food, dress, etc.). In the sections on social and cultural life, authors make a connection that is fundamental to the premise of this book: the unification of religion and culture. The word "religion" receives little attention in these monographs. When it is used, it serves as a shorthand for "Hindu," indicating a unity of religion. By contrast, however, the most important part of these sections is invariably the role of village deities and temples within everyday life. Listing the topics covered in the social and cultural life sections of a couple monographs will give a better sense of the way that themes are grouped in these monographs. The survey of Shakroti includes "village temples, fairs and festivals, Satya Narayanki katha, Navrattas, beliefs in spirits and unseen powers, social taboos, [and] superstitions."[20] The survey of Gijari includes "religious institutions in the village, fairs and festivals, recreation and games, dances, common habits and important customs, [and] superstitions and general folklore."[21] While the components of these sections vary, they always include information pertaining to the local deities, the temples, and their fairs and "superstitions." In making the connection between culture, deities, and temples, the authors of these studies opened a connection that became central for vernacular ethnohistorians and for everyday identity constructions in Himachal: they associate culture and deities. Himachali conceptions of religion are not limited to the dharmic associations of nationalist reformers. Rather, it is more common to link culture, religion, and regional identity in the familiar phrase, *hamārā devīdevatā saṃskṛti* ("our theological culture").

It is worth noting some of the central components of *devīdevatā saṃskṛti*, as it appears in these volumes. In general, there is a consistent attempt to place the local deity and the temple at the center of social and cultural practices. The following is an excerpt from a village survey of the village of Chirgaon, above Rohru in the Pabbar River valley: "People have deep rooted faith in various beliefs and superstitions. The Supreme God is Jabal-ke-devta. All rituals and customs connected with their birth, marriage, death, house construction, and others are directed by the wish of the devta [deity] through its oracle [gūr]. Even the out-break of any epidemic and big disputes are referred to the devta."[22] That the village god is the supreme authority (although Jabal is actually located in an adjacent village) and that all social life revolves around it are consistent themes in the literature on deities and villages. Many of these monographs begin their section on social and cultural life with sentences like this: "The villagers believe that their lives are governed by the dictates of various gods."[23] This not only indicates that the category of religion does not correspond to the same semantic field as it does in many Western contexts but also implies a form of translation that plays on the synergistic relationship of religion and culture. These census reports, like all forms of knowledge, are invested with political consequences. Like the work of the ethnohistorians that followed them, the surveys offered a translation of religion and culture that helped create a new entity (*devīdevatā saṃskṛti*). The semantic shadings of this concept vary wildly, but its emergence is inextricably tied to the modern category of religion.

This form of translation creatively reconfigures the conceptual fields of both religion and culture. The authors of these surveys understand culture as everything that is somehow associated with the people and deities of a place, and as something that can be or has been inherited. It is first and foremost not a part of economy or of the state. Perhaps more importantly, the concept of culture is not quite enough to convey the authority at work here. For this, the authors of these monographs use the word "religion" and refer to the deities of the villages. However, because of the development of secularist discourse and the work of religious reformers in the colonial period, there is also a certain perception that "religion" proper has negative dimensions and that certain parts of it are on the decline. Most authors of these studies worked with the concept of superstition, separating superstition from religion and culture from ignorance.[24] Therefore, one of the primary analytic tasks of the social and cultural life segments of these monographs was to unify religion and culture, employing the apolitical and supersocial dimensions of both while at the same time attempting to free the concepts of their negative connotations.

One of the most common reflections these studies offer is the idea that the youth are being transformed by the processes of modernization. In Himachal, according to these authors and other modernist reformers, change was predominately the result of exposure to new horizons. They claimed that the construction of roads and communication networks, which was just beginning in the early 1960s, radically transformed the region's youth, and nowhere was this clearer than with respect to religious beliefs. The coauthors of a survey of Brahmaur, one of the more "disconnected" villages, reported: "The younger generation does not feel so much drawn towards religion, but this is a common feature everywhere and the people of Brahmaur cannot escape this all-pervading influence of march of time."[25] This statement reveals the deep residue of midcentury modernization theory. Although these words were written in a multiethnic, pluralistic society in which "religion" as such was just coming onto the horizon as a category of social organization, the survey's authors were already pronouncing religion's future elimination. No one can stop the march of time. Just as Parmar argued, they believed that modernization would bring about the gradual development of the people of Himachal and that this would lead to the progressive dissolution of religion.[26] Indeed, it is common for the authors of these studies to simultaneously lament and celebrate observations such as: "A trend noticed among young men is that they do not respect the old beliefs so much now."[27] These statements, pronounced forty years ago, have not stood the test of time. They do, however, herald the introduction of an important concept into the everyday matrix of life: historical dynamism.

As Y. S. Parmar and colonial administrators had, the writers of the village monographs subscribed to an understanding of the past as a space of static tradition where lives were cast in dark and repetitive forms. They believed that religion, beliefs, and superstitions had all made their way, intact, from the earliest migrations to the present. But now, the people of this region had entered a new stage.[28] They were moving from stasis to dynamism, from poverty to wealth.

Shathla, located in the old state of Kotgarh, is one of the few villages in Himachal Pradesh that has undergone many changes during the past decades. The area of Kotgarh was merged with Himachal Pradesh after India gained independence. Shathla was once the typical hill village, where life remained static for centuries and there was not enough agriculture for even subsistence living. No one could ever imagine that this land would produce rich crops that would change the very face of the village life. Some of the more significant changes that have taken place are the increase in economic standard, the construction of better houses, a higher level of social awareness, improved education, the introduction of urban-influenced village administration through panchayats, and the diversification of employment opportunities.[29] Thus, the light that people like Parmar brought to Himachal—through the expansion of roads, education, and systems of planning—has enabled the state to move from the stale waters of its own repetition to an expansive future of possibility.

I have dwelt at length on these village surveys because they are foundational for the formation of ethnomedia. These texts and the world they inaugurated contributed in two powerful ways to the creation of ethnomedia as a genre and a profession. First, they offered a few select people their first possibility of making a career representing Himachali culture, a career they would embrace for decades. It is worth noting the importance of three people in particular: Mian Goverdhan Singh, V. C. Ohri, and O. C. Handa. At the time the surveys were being published, Singh was the young and energetic librarian at the Secretariat Building in Shimla, and he provided the bibliographic backbone for the project. His references and leadership allowed field researchers with little knowledge of Himachal Pradesh to complete their surveys and write up their works. Singh went on to write numerous articles and books that have informed and inspired the current generation. Ohri was the curator at the Bhuri Singh Museum in Chamba, and his insights into Himachali culture can be read all over the pages of the surveys, not only in those sections that cover Chamba, where he was an active contributor. His ideas made their way into the general vision of R. C. Singh, the superintendent of the census operations. Finally, the work of O. C. Handa cannot be overestimated. While the majority of his contributions to these monographs were photographs or paintings, Handa later became one of the most prolific authors on Himachali culture, and his career begin with his work on the surveys.

Second, these studies provided an archival basis for further training and served as an aspirational target for the following generation of writers. The studies themselves also created their own ripples. While the monographs were used primarily in administrative offices and rarely circulated outside of bureaucratic circles,[30] the enormous survey of fairs and festivals is widely available.[31] It has been reprinted and can be found in a tattered form in most district headquarters. The text helped produce an enormously influential and growing body of literature on the fairs and festival of the region, and it continues to ground an important distinction between fairs and festivals for contemporary Himachalis: fairs are "secular," while festivals are "religious."

VERNACULAR HISTORIANS AND THE POWER OF
NAMING

The earliest vernacular publication explicitly addressing the cultural resources of the Western Himalayas was *Himaprastha*, a monthly journal published by the government press. *Himaprastha*, which put out its first issue in April 1955, is typical of a broad range of vernacular publications that emerged following India's independence. The journal collects a wide range of materials. There are historical and ethnographic essays, short stories, reports on development, and poetry. The issues range widely in their content and the quality of their articles. What holds them together is an abiding concern for the state of Himachal and a focus on describing life in the Western Himalayas. There is very little attention paid to national issues and virtually no attention given to international issues or news. Instead, *Himaprastha* assumed the roles of cultural expansion, mediation, and publication.

In its early days, the primary concerns of *Himaprastha* were twofold. It sought first to publish materials about the cultural practices of the Western Himalayas. Many of the early essays were dedicated to articulating practices from regions not connected to Shimla or other major population centers. These essays generally dealt with fairs and festivals or particular ritual practices. The most important contribution of the journal, however, was its literary content. For the first fifteen years of its history, the journal was an integral part of the formulation of Himachal as a land of cultured and sensitive people who were neither barbarians nor illiterate. Even today, in many national Hindi literary circles, the writers of Himachal are regarded with great esteem. And it is the unification of their particularity and their control of Hindi that reviewers point to as their special contribution. In a 2001 review, Satyapal Sehgal summarized the contribution of Himachali fiction:

Therein is the socio-cultural landscape of this hill-state which may be of immense value to people who treat literature as a source material to construct social histories, people who are interested in knowing the anxieties and aspirations and the self-image of this fast changing society, especially in villages. In this regard, the fiction writers of Himachal have done their work with a simplicity, both at the level of sense and sensibility, and also at the level of expression, which is refreshing.... Hindi fiction of Himachal has its own rhythm, its failures apart, if any. And that comes out in the backdrop of deodars, chinars, heights, seasons, songs, dances and customs of Himachal![32]

Seghal's review discusses Sudarshan Vashisth and Keshab Nārāyaṇa, two of the most important figures not only in Hindi fiction from Himachal but also in the development of ethnomedia more broadly. Vashisth has occupied various positions in the Department of Language and Culture since its inception, and Nārāyaṇa has been the primary editor of *Himaprastha* and the journal *Girirāj* for more than two decades. Thus, in trying to understand the development of ethnomedia, it is important to understand the way that genres blend into one another, writers cross platforms, and the missions of the media are intertwined with one another.

While *Himaprastha* was important in supplementing the census studies in the early years of the formation of the Himachali state, no serial has been more important for representing the cultural diversity of the Western Himalayas than *Somasī*. Published by the Academy of Art, Language and Culture, *Somasī* is the primary publication outlet for vernacular ethnohistorians in the state. The flagship journal of the academy, *Somasī* was started in 1975 as part of a flush of activities in the newly formed academy. Although the circulation numbers of the journal are relatively small (five hundred to a thousand), its influence has been enormous. Its power comes not from a wide circulation or even directly reaching a popular audience. Rather, the real power of the journal is its prestige. It is the most prestigious place to publish serious work on the history and ethnography of Himachal Pradesh, and is thus a staging ground for elite narratives about the state. As the state's most highly regarded journal, the pieces it publishes are circulated widely. They are reprinted in popular newspapers and become the basis for advertisements. They are integrated into tourism pamphlets and read on radio broadcasts. The power of the journal is its ability to define the discourse and the terms of public debates. It is in the pages of *Somasī* that narratives of Himachali ethnohistory are codified.

The academy and its publication outlet provide an institutional and publication space in which knowledge can be created, represented, and then preserved. It is not simply the circulation of the journal as a piece of material culture that is important. Equally important is the circulation of the people who create this knowledge at the local level.[33] The authors of the works that appear in Himachal's literary journals are not exclusively well-educated urban elites. While some people who write for *Somasī* are intellectuals living in Shimla, the majority are local doctors, teachers, and farmers who are interested in the preservation and reproduction of local culture. Not only do these people participate in the disembodied forms of linguistic production, they also live in communities and influence the daily workings of rites and temples through their actions. Just as media connects people across time and spaces, these people serve as mediums in the production and consumption of knowledge in specific places. They mediate the local and the translocal.

While the articles themselves vary greatly with respect to content and style, the overall thrust of *Somasī* has not changed significantly in the past twenty-five years. Early in the journal's history, editors M.R. Thakur and H.S. Parashar defined it as a space in which the cultural diversity of the Western Himalayas could be researched and published. The early issues opened an almost clinical approach to cultural research. The driving desire behind the articles was the collection and presentation of things that were unknown, from areas that have been cut off or from people who were outside of the regional centers. In terms of content, the focus was on topics that would have come under the colonial heading of "custom."[34] Close attention was paid to marriage practices and dances, local songs, and storytelling traditions. There are several essays and one entire issue dedicated to local sayings and proverbs, a favorite source of vernacular historians for the reconstruction of history.[35] In fact, in the stories published in these early issues, much more so than in the later texts, there is a careful attention to language and the problems of linguistic definition. Many authors, for example, worked hard to counter the Grierson hypothesis, which argued that Kangri was actually a Punjabi and not a Pahāṛī language.[36] Others struggled to maintain a space for Pahāṛī within the pages of the journal, and all struggled with their own prose. Writing style, word choice, and syntax all varied greatly from author to author. Some authors, such as the journal's first editor, H. S. Parashar, wrote in a heavily Sanskritized style that is largely unintelligible to most people in Himachal these days. In fact, a vast number of the words he uses are not to be found in any Hindi dictionary. Other authors, such as Y. S. Parmar, used language heavily influenced by Urdu and Persian, while still others used words and grammar derived from local vernaculars. What united the authors, however, was an almost obsessive desire to represent and archive what they knew or had heard. Like Japanese tourists at the Taj Mahal, they sought to document everything they saw.

A NORMATIVE TRADITION CRYSTALIZES

Vernacular ethnohistorians have created an enormously rich public space in which their representations of Himachal's culture and history circulate. Their narratives have become the ones that most people, from Shimla to Chirgaon, tell themselves about their pasts and their practices. They have helped to forge pieces of authorized and authorizing narratives. As such, they become sources for the normalization of Himachali religion as well as a standing reserve to buttress the authority of the secular state. By describing some of the most common elements of these narratives, I will show how they are inextricably coupled to the ascendancy of the secular, developmental state. That is, the narratives of Himachal's past, its distinctive culture, its divine sanction, and its singular character are not simply connected to the formation of a community but serve as the legitimating narrative on which the enduring authority of the state rests.

Figure 13. Himachal Tourism office in Manali. Photo by author.

I seek to establish here how the authority of the state is located in the fractured circulation of narratives of Himachal's connection to divinity and to its distinct cultural traditions. The state relies on religion for its authority. As the publisher of authoritative texts, the state manages fairs and festivals, a practice that is as much about the state's own employment of the mimetic power of Himachal's religious traditions as it is about preservation or economics. In almost all of its public forms, the state draws on the mimetic power of Himachali religion to authorize itself. For example, the front of Himachal Pradesh Road and Transport Corporation buses are painted with *Himachal Dev Bhoomi* (Himachal, God Country). While the state provides its citizens with transport to regions that were once disconnected, it draws its sanction from the image of Himachal as a divinely blessed land.

Furthermore, emerging out of a matrix of state-society relations—in the figure of the vernacular ethnohistorian—the state is itself constituted in this relationship. So "the state" is not an atemporal entity persisting through time and undergoing a few minor alterations in the passage to modernity. Though it is experienced as singular and impenetrable, the state is constituted in the everyday relations of people, such as the interactions between a language officer and a deity's medium or a vernacular ethnohistorian and a festival attendant.

In these negotiations, the "leaders"[37] who speak for the state employ the mimetic magic of representation. Throughout his compelling body of work, Michael Taussig has tracked the logics of mimesis—the power of representing, mimicking, and working at a distance. In his thoughtful (if not always coherent) work, *The Magic of the State*,[38] Taussig gives us many examples of the state's invocation of "death-spirits"—the powerful possession of the state by the dead—the most common being Simon Bolivar.[39] In this case, the state became possessed by this dead man and the powerful narratives that were condensed in him (liberation, decolonialization, continental unity, strength, equestrian prowess, etc.). The uncanny connection between the state and the spirit world is energized through the power of mimesis, and mimesis is best understood as the connective tissues of the world, those filaments that connect representations to one another. Taussig, following Walter Benjamin, calls the capacity to see these resemblances "the mimetic faculty."

The connections the two men write about are not stripped of time. They have their own histories, trajectories, and disciplines. Benjamin says it best in his essay "On the Mimetic Faculty":

> Nature creates similarities. One need only think of mimicry. The highest power for producing similarities is man's. His gift of seeing resemblances is nothing other than a rudiment of the powerful compulsion in former times to become and behave like something else. Perhaps there is none of his higher functions in which his mimetic faculty does not play a decisive role. This faculty has a history, however, in both the phylogenetic and ontogenetic sense.[40]

The history that Benjamin refers to here is how "the gift of the production of similarities" and "the gift of recognizing them" are transformed over the centuries. It is possible to see the entirety of *Becoming Religious* as an attempt at writing a particular history of the mimetic faculty. That is, I trace the transformations in the structure of authority—in the ways that deities, kings, ministers, and populations rely on transformed systems of similarities. What this chapter argues is that the state, in all of its Indian enchantment,[41] relies upon being possessed by the narratives of vernacular ethnohistorians and the forms of recognition they entail.

In his introductory notes to Mian Goverdhan Singh's classic work, *Festivals, Fairs and Customs of Himachal Pradesh,* O.C. Handa—a prolific author in his own right—writes:

> In the traditional societies where the monstrous tentacles of the hybrid modernism have not yet affected the life-style of people, their fairs and festivals are the frank and unabashed index of their socio-cultural inheritance and the collective psychological response to the challenges of the world around them. Himachal Pradesh, situated in the northwest corner of the sub-continent in Himalayan seclusion has been the abode of such people.... Since the very dawn of civilization in the Indian sub-continent down to the middle of the present century, people of diverse cultural strains, religious affiliations and racial characteristics have been drawn to this region to seek peaceful and secure living. That continuous and profound process has inspired a socio-cultural metamorphosis to form a distinct Pahāṛī culture of Himachal Pradesh.[42]

In these few lines, Handa offers us his vision of Himachal, a vision that condenses many of the most common themes of Himachali writers. When writing about Himachal Pradesh, most scholars begin with a pair of assumptions: Himachal is an autonomous cultural region distinct from other regions in South Asia, and it has remained impervious to the radical social changes around it. Moreover, throughout tumultuous periods, Himachal has stood as a peaceful region untouched by the "monstrous tentacles of the hybrid modernism." What Handa does not clearly articulate in this passage, but which pervades all of his writing—as it does that of all other vernacular historians of Himachal—is the idea that Himachal is the land of gods (*dev bhūmi*) and that, as the land of gods, it has a privileged relation to God. As Goverdhan Singh writes in the first sentence of his book: "Himachal Pradesh [is] popularly known as the 'valley of gods.'"[43]

In the section that follows, I will focus on five primary narratives: that Himachal is the land of the gods; that it has an uncannily peaceful past and present; that its theistic traditions are tied to the natural landscape; that its religious practices and myths are radically different from those of the plains peoples; that these practices and myths are unchanged from aboriginal time; and that the unique character of hill people allows them to simultaneously embrace the past and the future, thereby making them superior not only to the inhabitants of other regions in India but also to those in "modern" societies in general. I will track these themes through the work of two prominent ethnohistorians currently working in Himachal, Molu Ram Thakur and Deepak Sharma. I will examine how, in their work, they create an idealized narrative of the past in order to understand the present and project a future. While there is certainly nothing novel about such projects, their pedestrian character does not discount their centrality in the construction of daily life. Moreover, this chapter is not simply about the creation of these idealized pasts but also about the ways these creations circulate in public culture and are reinscribed as authorizing narratives for the state.

I also suggest that the work of these historians is part of an ongoing process of defining the canon of Himachali religion. That is, these writers and the public spaces they invigorate are engaged in a process of collection, arrangement, and redaction that is foundational for current and ongoing forms of interpretation, by both younger historians and outsiders and people in villages performing rites and carrying deities. I believe "canon" is a useful term for explaining what these people are doing because it helps us to see how community, authority, and orthodoxy are being produced. It will also help us to see the vernacular ethnohistorians as "leaders" not simply in a political sense but also in a theological sense. These leaders are situated within their communities much as theologians are situated within theirs, and we might usefully examine their works as we would those of theologians.

Figure 14. Yashwant Singh Parmar, Himachal's first vernacular historian. Photo by author.

What is a canon? How is it formed? What does it do? In order to answer some of these questions, it will help to begin with a quote from Heinrich von Stietencron:

> In the context of religion, a canon is the result of a deliberative attempt to collect, arrange and preserve the original message of a religious community, and to protect it against all corruption, It transforms haphazard individual recollection into authoritative tradition or sacred scripture. As such, it itself becomes endowed with an aura of sacredness which derives both from the original seers, ṛṣis, prophets or teachers who formulated the message, and from the eternal truth which is thought to be encapsulated in the text of canonical scripture. Such a canon is one of the strongest possible forms of defining and securing a specific religious identity.[44]

This statement offers us a relatively strong place to begin our examination. A canon is the result of a conscious act to formulate important narratives that define a specific religion's religious identity and the identity of the religion. This is, I argue, an accurate description of the project of vernacular ethnohistorians in Himachal. These ethnohistorians consciously collect, arrange, and interpret elements of Himachali cultural life and offer those elements to the public, where they are preserved, repeated, and debated. These narratives then become authoritative sources for the analysis of daily life.

The core component for the production of a canon is repetition and exegesis. In his thoughtful and influential reflections on canons, J. Z. Smith writes that the production of a canon might usefully be understood as analogous to the development of cuisines from foodstuffs. That is, from the immense array of possible foodstuffs available, groups of people choose a limited number of ingredients, from which an almost unlimited variety of combinations (cuisines) are created. Similarly, a canon is a human process of selection and interpretation. As Smith states: "I have argued that canon is best seen as one form of a basic cultural process of limitation and of overcoming that limitation through ingenuity."[45]

For Smith, one of the most important components of a canon is the perception that the canon is closed. Its elements, whether they are texts or divinatory technologies, must be limited and require the interpretation of an exegetical community. These concepts are helpful in understanding how the narratives of Himachali history inform Himachali identity, statehood, and daily ritual practice. One of the most important elements of these discussions is the manner in which elements, narratives, locations, and locutions are repeated from author to author and medium to medium. So, we will see the way that the five main themes mentioned above are repeated by different vernacular ethnohistorians and in other public forms. These are the narratives that define the boundaries of the canon; they are the core components used for the interpretation of new information.

One of the things Smith is so good at is showing that the notion of a canon does not rely simply on the idea of revelation (an idea he wants to "bracket"). He argues that a canon relies on notions of human ingenuity and creative exegesis. It relies on the creation of a limited set of material from which an unlimited number of interpretations can be created. As someone who believes that theologians should be historians of religion's "prime object of study,"[46] Smith considers the process of canon formation and its exegesis to be central to the task of historians of religion. For our task here, what is important is how Himachali scholars have assembled materials from disparate regions, times, and languages and, through creative exegesis, brought their materials into line with the five core narratives of Himachali religious history.

As I noted earlier, that Himachali scholars have engaged in this process is not necessarily interesting. This is a process repeated in innumerable other places and times. What is interesting, however, is how and why they have done it—questions that get at some of the other important elements of canons. In order to understand these questions, it might be helpful if I drew out a connection that I have been alluding to in the last couple of pages. It is useful to understand vernacular ethnohistorians not simply as historians or "not-quite-historians" but as theologians. This indicates that they are people whose primary concern is illuminating a canon of materials, offering this illumination to the public for the public's self-edification, and using the works of that canon to define what is and is not part of a tradition. This may also help us better understand the new forms of authority that are enabled by evolving relations between religion and state.

As will become clear in our discussion of these figures, the reasons for writing about and researching Himachali cultural traditions are varied. Himachali scholars are, however, united by a felt duty to remember and preserve practices that are being lost. Much of their discussion and work takes place in the shadow of decline or threat. The perceived threat is twofold, coming from forms of forgetting and competing religious visions. The threat is perceived differently by each writer, and the perception of the threat structures his or her response to it, but the following example offers a good general survey.

There is a spring festival (*biśu*) performed in the upper Shimla hills that culminates in the annual reestablishment of a tree in front of the village temple. Before the tree is raised at the end of the ceremony, it is brought before the temple. As the crowd swells, women and men hurl sexual insults and provocative invitations at one another. The senior ritual officiate, in this case the deity's gūr, is joined by a young virgin (*kumārī*) from the community. They walk the length of the tree, which has been stripped of its branches. As they walk, the people continue to hurl insults and make propositions, and the gūr paints the tree's trunk with streaks of red. The sexual overtones of this festival are not subtle. Having attended the rite and been crudely propositioned simultaneously by grandmothers and their daughters, there is little room for misunderstanding. As a result, this part of the rite has faced strong criticism in the press and in some government ministries. Critics have argued that the rite is a debased form of spring ritual that is badly in need of reform and claim that it does not accord with Hindu practice and values. However, several local ethnohistorians, most pointedly Deepak Sharma, have undertaken a campaign to retain this part of the rite. He has written extensively of the rite's heritage and cited other vernacular ethnohistorians in support of his point. He has formed small local coalitions to combat government pressure and influence the local community. He has even petitioned local governmental officials, including the district commissioner and the MLA, to preserve the rite as it is performed. Here, then, we see how these scholars are working to define and structure local communities in conformity with the broader trends of Himachali practice. The effort to preserve this rite has been successful, and its preservation must be understood in relation to the growing body of authoritative works on Himachali culture and practice and the writers/theologians who marshal it.

ETHNOHISTORIANS IN THE FIELD

Our detailed consideration of the work of vernacular ethnohistorians begins with M. R. Thakur, a man who has arguably done more than anyone to define the shape of this discourse. Before retiring, Thakur was the longstanding editor of *Somasī*, secretary of the Department of Language and Culture, and a prolific author. He has written the only systematic grammars of the Pahāṛī, been a kind and generous mentor to scholars interested in the religious history of Himachal (including me), and shaped the research agenda of the state for more than three decades. There are few people either inside or outside of Himachal who know as much about the religious history of the state as he does. Indeed, his writings inform much of what is being written today. His work has been published in various journals, newspapers, and short manuscripts over the past thirty years. This chapter uses Thakur as a guide, just as aspiring scholars have used him as a guide. Examining a range of materials, including English and Hindi texts and many interviews I have conducted, I will outline his reading of the religious history of Himachal Pradesh. This reading, I believe, has been the base weave on top of which new narratives have been written.

Thakur's work is easily distinguishable from much of the writing emerging from Himachal, which simply collects stories or assorted evidence without any regard for structure, narrative, or argument. Thakur, on the other hand, has a clearly delineated project: he articulates, initiates, and sanctions a unified narrative of the religious history of the area. All the elements of this narrative are present in the first pages of his widely read *Myths, Rituals and Beliefs in Himachal Pradesh:*

> For the English speaking people "if there is any way to heaven it is through hell", but for the Indians the path to heaven ascends from the Himalayas. And the Himalayas with preponderant mountain chains are inhabited by very interesting people with splendid religious history, mythology, folklore and traditions. They hug their primitiveness as much as they embrace the pinnacles of civilization. They present a rare blend of the old and the new. Their myths and rituals speak of their hoary past.... The social and religious life on the hills is very much different from the plains. The hill people are neither exclusively Shaiva nor Vaishnava.... The hill people rather worship a large number of village gods and goddesses.... The western Himalaya is the home of gods and goddesses and of god-fearing people who have respect for all the religions. Their old conventions have never

stood in the way of progress in this science dominated world. Their gods never fought for religion. Their fight was always aimed at promoting peace and harmony and feelings of mutual trust among the people.[47]

This long quote outlines the work that lies ahead. He offers us guide-posts for the articulation of primary narratives of Himachali ethnohistory. All five of the above-mentioned major themes are here.

Let us begin with the first and most influential of these themes: Himachal is the land of gods. Thakur begins his work with a strangely anachronistic assertion and a reversal. Rejecting English-speaking approaches, he analogizes Himachal with heaven and thereby validates Indian paths to heaven. In doing this, he locates Himachal at the center of nationalist soteriology. This equation of Himachal with the land of gods, spiritual insight, or the gate of heaven is a common trope. As Thakur explores the religious and cultural history of Himachal, he continually reminds us of Himachal's divine sanction. He explains the predominance of divinities in Himachal on these grounds. He begins another of his works emphatically: "Himachal is the land of gods. Every village here has its own deity, every deity its own temple and every temple its own radiance."[48] This is a theme that will reoccur more forcefully when we return to the manner in which Himachal is marketed as a religious space, but it should be continually held in mind that this perspective is assumed in everything being written about Himachal. It frames the way readers of these texts understand them and how authors and readers integrate them into their personal experience of local ritual spaces and the operation of religious authority in villages.

As Thakur emphasizes in this quote and throughout his published work, Himachal is a land of natural powers. Vernacular ethnohistorians across the state also emphasize this aspect of Himachal, and no one who has spent more than a few days in the Himalayas would argue that these mountains are not sublime. These scholars argue that the radical natural features of these mountainscapes and the intricate ways they have shaped social and political life speak to the larger religious history of the state. That is, the religious history of Himachal is indelibly marked by its natural context. In fact, the majority of Himachali scholars writing today subscribe to a narrative that begins with powerful natural forces that people could not understand and proceeds through a series of transformations that end up in the present as a baroque embrace of natural spirits and scientific rationalism.

One of the primary elements of this narrative is the migration and settlement of different ethnic groups. The diverse histories of Khaśas, Khanets, and Rajputs are inevitably read by Thakur in a way that supports the animistic origins of Himachali religion. In his narrative— which exists in countless different forms in village origin stories— these tribes encountered a wide range of demons when they migrated to Himachal. These demons are undoubtedly the most common theme in the mythopoetic histories told in villages and towns. They serve as evil counterpoints to the benevolent founders of villages and families. When migrants came to Himachal—from Kashmir, Rajasthan, Nepal, and Central Asia—they needed to be protected from the malevolent demons of the hills. In order to combat these forces, they began to communicate with the benevolent powers of the region, powers that constitute the essence of Himachal.

The reason that there are such a high number of deities in the hills is apparent. It is believable that the every group of settlers occupying the small and hitherto desolate and deserted areas among the thick forests and shrubs that they believed had been the abodes of dangerous and devastating demons, devils, and spirits felt the need for divine protection.

Immediately after becoming aware of the region's divine patterns, these migrants tamed the local demons and began to live in harmony with both demons and gods. They searched for the natural forces of good and established shrines dedicated to them, seeing them as guardians. The subsequent religious history is a progressive systematization of the original impulse and orientation. As the traditions progressed, they became ever more attuned to the natural order. As Thakur described it: "The galaxy of gods in this part of India is infinite. They are worshipped in towns and cities, in villages and localities, in temples and shrines. They dwell in rivers and ravines, in springs and streams, in brooks and lakes, in valleys and dales, in stones and rocks in trees and plants, in fields and high peaks, over mountains and hills, in woods and forests."[49]

This particular religious history, rooted in a symbiotic relationship between humans, nature, and divinities, is often cited as the reason why the region is "peaceful." Himachal's past, like its present, was peaceful. That is, even though most vernacular historians are quick to admit that it was only in the past thirty years that unity in the Western Himalayas was achieved, they nevertheless assert that the history of the region is one of peaceful coexistence. Contemporary rhetoric, from sources as diverse as wall hoardings and school textbooks, addresses and constitutes Himachal as a land of peaceful harmony, as a place and space essentially of harmony. Any evidence to the contrary is read as a historical aberration. There are indications that there have been wars, tyranny, human pain, and suffering, but the vernacular ethnohistorians of Himachal have effectively dealt with this in a number of ways. Violence is interpreted as the work of power-hungry tyrants, neighboring warmongers, colonial hegemony, or postcolonial corruption, as it is seen as running against the essence of Himachali religious history. In Himachal, in contrast to the rest of India, Hindus and Muslims worship together: "In practice, however, they [a group of Hero deities] are venerated by both the communities with equal faith and even after partition there are many mazars and dargahs which attract large crowds of devotees. At the mazar of Pir Baba Dumey Shah at Nagrota the caretaker of the tomb is a Brahman and the devotees are almost all Hindu."[50] Thus, Himachal looks past the simple communal violence that has characterized post-partition India.

To summarize, Himachal sees itself as a land specially touched by divine forces, in which its people are in harmony with their deities and therefore are able to maintain a peaceful society. These three factors, and

Figure 15. Anointing a fresh-cut cedar for Biśu. Photo by author.

several others, buttress the common assertion that Himachal is special. It is peaceful, whereas other areas are plagued with violence; it has gods everywhere, whereas other places have only deities like Śiva or Viṣṇu; and, importantly, the people of Himachal live in harmony with the land, whereas the land in other regions is ruthlessly exploited. The people of the hills have an intimate bond with their deities, a bond that guides them and sets them apart from the rest of the country: "Since time immemorial, there has been a steady and perceptible process of humanization of gods and now, they are almost human beings. They eat, drink, walk, live and dance with their worshipers. The deity talks with them face to face."[51] These connections ground all of life, and in contrast to other modern societies, the people of Himachal follow their deities' lead.

Thakur summarizes his view:

> The village devtas in Himachal Pradesh are not simply objects of worship. They, rather, constitute an institution which governs all social, cultural, moral, economic, religious and political life of the village folk. In the faith

of the people of which these devtas are held and the manner in which this faith is expressed, they have large number of traditions and conventions governing their day-to-day life. These traditions, superstitions and conventions which, at present, prevail in this area go a long way to show that the area might have been, once infested with supernatural forces and what people could not understand they began to worship.[52]

While many would argue that a quote such as this betrays a commitment to divine agency that invalidates a modern scientific and rational outlook, Himachali historians go to great lengths to bring the worlds they are living in and describing in line with "modernity," "science," and "development." As quoted earlier, Thakur argued that Himachali religion was superior to that of "the English speaking people" because of its unique ability to embrace both the past and the present: "They [Himachalis] hug their primitiveness as much as they embrace the pinnacles of civilization."[53] Indeed, this is a theme most vernacular ethnohistorians emphasize. Some focus on the "scientific" basis of ritual practice, others point to the understanding of the natural processes that guide the rhythms of life in the hills, and still others indicate that there is a rational basis for "superstitious" beliefs. Thakur believed that the embrace of both tradition and modernity was embodied in people like himself, people who continue to practice their faith according to local traditions (he is from a village above Kullu) while simultaneously embracing many of the claims and conveniences of Indian modernity. This ambiguity is clearly summarized in the following quote:

> The myth and ritual behavior function as a conceptual apparatus in the life of a family, a tribe or a community. A large number of rites are performed with a view to achieve some goal or end. The end may be physical like good health, beauty, longevity, etc. social like fame, wealth, power, status and so on; and naturally like rainfall, floods, droughts, plentiful crops etc. These goals are achieved by combination of meritorious actions and ritual performances. Thus, the myths and rituals of ancient people that have come down to us are of scientific value because their analysis throws light on the peculiarity of primitive thoughts. They speak of the mental perception of their environmental phenomena.[54]

This quote, however, is far from transparent. For Thakur, myths are not simply textual tools employed by scholars to get at the logic of ritual and practice, as is intimated at the end of the quote. In his personal communications and in the majority of his published work, it is clear that he believes that myths and rituals are themselves scientific and rational—not simply that they can represent something coherent but that they are in themselves coherent and complete. However, the conflict felt by those who engage in the "scientific" study of the history of religions in Himachal while practicing these same religions fills pages and pages of texts. It is often this tension that animates a text. Indeed, the question of how to approach the history of religions in Himachal Pradesh—the question of method—is present in many of the emerging texts.

The next scholar we will examine is Deepak Sharma, a man of boundless energy and creativity. Born in the village of Nirmand in the district of Kullu, Sharma is a veterinary pharmacist intensely committed to the history and future of Pahārī culture. Sharma, an immensely generous and prolific contributor to the Himachal public sphere, helped introduce me to the valleys surrounding his village and unraveled innumerable mysteries for me. My debt to him is incalculable. His writings have appeared in books, newspapers, journals, and numerous other publications. His editorial guidance has shaped several local video productions and public performances. In short, he is one of the most powerful public voices in the region and its adjoining districts. His writings range from short opinion pieces on other local writers to lengthy treatises on local deities. Amid all this writing and sociopolitical activity, there is a central animating force to his work: his reading of history and its role in the present. This understanding of history runs throughout the narratives of vernacular ethnohistorians.

Aside from his complex diction and resounding passion, the first thing one notices about Sharma is the frequency and importance of his discussions about history. For him, history is foundational. It provides a point of movement and orientation. However, his understanding of history does not resemble that which has been constructed by modern Western historiography. How exactly does he understand history then? In short, Deepak Sharma sees history as the accumulation of the works of deities in the world and the marks they have left on the directionality of the present. He does not consider history to be an ordered set of events temporally distinct from and culminating in the present or a record of the forgotten moments in relation to other objects. Rather, history is a medium; it is a mode of disclosure: "There are facts [*tathyoṃ*] hidden [*chupe haiṃ*] behind this [the world we see]. Today especially history is being twisted [*toṛ-toṛ*]. This makes me very sad. Many times through the medium of newspapers I have raised my voice about this issue. History is not made [by people], it has already been made."[55] It is the job of the historian to uncover this history, to let it speak again in the public sphere. Sharma believes that history provides the key to a better a future, one that is not misguided and dissolute. How can history provide that? Through the work of deities.

For Sharma, history is the space where deities have left their mark (*nišān*) on the present. Once, he concluded a long monologue explaining how a set of deities had come to the places where they are now worshipped with the following rhetorical flourish, which he often closed his longer narratives with: "They [the objects of worship he was discussing] gave direction to society. This is history, literature. This isn't some blind-faith, not some fraud. There are facts hidden behind this."[56] This theme pervaded his thought. In the past, various deities had guided works in the past, just as they had guided the development of local communities and kept things in balance.

Sharma is fond of allegories. On one occasion, in response to a question I asked him about the role of history in the present, he told me the following story to ponder:

> Today every house has a [water] tap, every house has facilities, but today's man, he is dealing with difficulties, he is troubled. What is the reason behind this? The cause? We are not moving with history, we are not moving with the teachings of history. We are forgetting everything. A tap is

installed in the house. What is happening at the local pond [*bāveri*]? People are throwing garbage in the bāveri. I am an independent thinker. Let me tell you [the village of] Nirmand's situation. There is a bāveri up there with a deity Banaba, an incarnation of Mahādev. He is believed to be Śankar. There is a Ganeṣa image there and now the bāveri is lying dry. People have thrown polyurethane bags into it. Close by, there are two or three more bāveris they have also dried up ... Down below [the village] there is a bāveri there are also bushes on it, which means that people's attention isn't going there. If ever there is a drought, famine, then these bāveris will be useful. Ponds and springs will all dry up. This will save us, this is our history.[57]

In memorial traditions throughout Himachal Pradesh, the primary way the dead are commemorated is with the creation of a well or tap, a space that can become a communal *bāveri*.[58] The dead and water taps are fundamentally related, and this connection is continually emphasized by older villagers. In his quote, Sharma is mourning the connection sullied by trash and forgetfulness. He wants to resurrect the intimate connection between the present and supernatural agency. The wells created by people and the taps that supply houses, including Sharma's own tap, will all dry up in a drought. Only the *bāveris* can provide sustenance through drought and famine. This is not because the *bāveris* go deeper. It is because they are the embodiment of divinity in the world. They are now dry, but this is precisely because they have been forgotten. The connection with the past and with the direction they provided is now lost. That is why remembering is so imperative for Sharma—for him, history is first and foremost an ethical project. Only by remembering the past will Himachal be able to preserve itself; only remembrance will allow the nourishing waters of the past to flow.

In other discussions, Sharma is fond of telling different versions of the following story:

The difficulties in society today, with which society is grappling, today man is standing on the crossroads, he cannot figure out which direction to go. On the crossroads, there is a soldier posted, cars come from this side, cars come from that side, if the soldier doesn't signal there will be an accident. This has become man's condition today. This is my heart's sorrow. I am very sad and upset these days.... That is all my objective. The medium? Through the pen, divine powers, through divine power this is all happening. And this is my purpose.[59]

Implicit in this statement, as in the one preceding, is a critique of state authority and of the conditions of modernity. While the earlier critique questioned the panacea of the modern state apparatus (power, water, roads, etc.), this statement goes further in its criticism, although both point in the same direction. Here, Sharma questions the ability of the state—in the guise of a soldier—to guide the actions of the community. In his opinion, it is precisely the loss of connection to the divinely directed past that has left individuals without purpose or direction. He does not believe that the modern state can offer guidance. It can provide lots of important things, but without the overarching guidance provided by local deities, people would be lost. However, he does not reject modernity outright. He lives in a house with electricity and water, and he uses the roads that now crisscross his valley as much as anyone else. What he rejects is the idea that the things brought by modernity are enough. He rejects the enchantment of the state. For Deepak, everything in life, from the gathering of water to the writing of history, must proceed from and with the blessing of local deities. The gathering forces of the state cannot usurp that function.

This belief continually comes up in conversation when he is distinguishing his type of history from that of others. He is often upset about the writings of others, and he fills the editorial pages of local newspapers with his tirades against historians who do not share his views. He argues that their "distortion" of facts, by which he means the secular parsing of history into distinct moments unconnected to a divinely ordered narrative, is one of the primary reasons why people are so confused. Sharma feels that historians must attend to the problems of local communities; they must read history against issues of local concern rather than against an abstracted index of "truth." For him, history writing is, again, a moral obligation. He asks:

When will we publicize and propagate history, when will we expand it to people? And in practical ways, not just that you write, yes, I have written a book, I have done a PhD in history, we have written fifty books, they are rotting in libraries, it is infested with bookworms, you don't call that history. History needs to be spread to the public consciousness [*jan mānas tak*] to every person in the form of a people's movement [*jan āṇdolan*] we will have to propagate history. Only then … I remain centered on Nirmand, so as far as Nirmand is concerned, we will have to save Nirmand's history, compile it, beautify it, and bring it consciousness to all the people. Today, if you ask a child from Nirmand, "What is this?" she will say, "I don't know." "What is this?" "It is some stone." Who is at fault [*doṣī*] here? Is that girl at fault? Our elders say, "Today the children know nothing." Who is at fault? I believe we're at fault.[60]

For Sharma, history has both revelatory and ethical dimensions. It is revelatory insofar as it describes the hidden workings of supernatural actors over temporally or spatially distinct areas. The majority of his work is devoted to this revelation. The hundreds upon hundreds of pages he has written describe how deities have founded villages, performed miracles, sanctioned rulers, and healed communities. In this regard, he is working to support three of the five tenets of the narrative described above: Himachal is a land of gods, Himachal is a peaceful and blessed land, and Himachal is different from the plains. Interestingly, the second dimension of his work is ethical. In this regard, his work is devoted to history writing as a space of social reform. This reform presents an interesting conundrum. While Sharma is somewhat involved with the broader national trends represented by the Sangh Parivar (there are posters of Keshav Baliram Hedgewar in his main sitting room), he does not agree with the communalism these organizations facilitate. I have seen him sit and eat with tailors, Muslims, and Sikhs. What he is seeking is not a simple return to the Vedic golden age, though he does understand the past as a more perfect time than the present. Rather, his work attempts to walk a middle ground between the advances of modernity and the guiding authority of local divinities. Sharma feels that they are both necessary, and bringing one to bear on the other is a fundamentally ethical act. He believes that modern historians must understand, unearth, and propagate the relationship between material and divine history. His view of the state is much the same as his understanding of the role of the historian. He believes that the state can provide fundamental guidance and educate, feed, and provide for the people of Himachal Pradesh, but he maintains that all this must be carried out in accordance with the "natural" and "historical" patterns of the regions, meaning it must be in line with the demands and desires of local deities. In other words, the policeman cannot tell the oncoming cars which way to go. Only local gods can see the past and the future, though it is government ministries that must provide the roads and the electricity to houses.

CHAPTER FOUR

Managing Religion

Government, Gūrs, and Gods

RELIGION IN THE SECRETARIAT

When Himachal's current chief minister, Virbhadra Singh, was elected to office while I was carrying out my fieldwork, I wanted to interview him about a number of things. He was the descendent of the royal family of the Bushahar kingdom and was rumored to possess many of its historical documents. Moreover, much of the information I had gathered about him and his family was contradictory, and I wanted to try to get my stories straight. His office is located in the Secretariat building, a fortress guarded at all points of entry by several heavily armed guards, metal detectors, and a retinue of assorted officials. I was well versed in the baroque logic of access that governed this building, as it also houses the main library, which was run for years by the inimitable Mian Goverdhan Singh and is now ably managed by Jaideep Negi.

Detached from the primary building is a smaller circular building. When I arrived, I thought that this was a small canteen for tea and paratha. I parked my motorcycle next to it and started to walk into the Secretariat building. A policeman screamed at me, shaking his fists in rage. Though all the areas nearby were unmarked, I had, it seems, parked in an area reserved for police vehicles and the most important of

Figure 16. Gūrs performing diagnostic rites. Photo by author.

ministers. This was a good lesson in the unwritten logics of Himachali governance. Luckily, a quick retort to his abusive Hindi, spoken loudly for the benefit of those waiting nearby, brought the blood to his cheeks and bought me enough time to move my bike to the proper location, which was also unmarked.

Finally, after trying unsuccessfully to get into the building from another point, I made my way to an entry room filled with people waiting to see various ministers and officials. The spatial design was an apt metaphor for my situation. The room itself was a circle, with only a few chairs around the edges. The space was crowded with people of all kinds, though most were men and many were angry. The room was cold, and the floor was threadbare and worn through in places. The walls were empty except for a fading poster, torn near the bottom, showing a pretty woman on a ski boat speeding across Revalsar Lake. "Himachal" was written across the top. While the typography and the woman's fashion spoke to me of 1972, for many of those in the room with me, it spoke of a dream of pleasure and plenitude that they imagined was just beyond the secretary.

There was a small adjoining room enclosed in cedar plywood and Plexiglas. Only a tiny slit big enough for papers and thin books was open to the crowd. Men pressed their faces into the hole, speaking over one another to request security passes and private meetings. Inside, there were three indifferent, almost unconscious people sipping tea and guarding their prized possessions: a black phone with direct access to any office in the Secretariat and a book of security passes. I had been through similar experiences many times before and was careful to observe the strictest of etiquette concerning the initial interaction. The first few words would determine whether I would ever get past the machine gun–toting guards—most of the people in the waiting room would not. I edged my way in, having spied the man who seemed in control—the one who held the phone. I waited until he looked free— or more dazed, really. In my best Hindi, I dropped the names of three ministers inside, said they were my friends, offered my academic credentials, and asked to be allowed entry to the secretary of the chief minister. I said "Sir" four times. He eyed me wearily but with a tiny sliver of recognition. He picked up the phone and dialed. The call was short. "Ji Sir.... Ha Sir.... Thank you Sir." He set the phone down and stared absently as I held my breath in anticipation.

Then he picked up the phone again and appeared to call his wife, his mistress, or an old friend. They were talking about nothing in particular. Finally, exasperated, I interrupted him. "Sir?" "Fine," he responded. He looked to the pass guard and nodded, and then he looked back at me and asked, in Hindi, "You were in the paper, no?" Yes, I had been. Too many times, but on this occasion, I was thankful for the recognition it provided. I had passed the first test.

I entered the Secretariat with a backpack full of recording equipment and cameras that failed to set off the metal detectors, although the guard scrutinized my pass with the acumen of a *New Yorker* copy editor. I was finally escorted into a small room crowded with freshly shaven men all wearing their finest clothes. They were a bit shocked to see me and seemed threatened in a way I did not immediately understand. Even the guard in this room seemed somewhat hostile to me. He sat silently as I showed my pass and asked to enter the office of the chief minister's secretary. No such luck. I waited, sitting on the thin felt carpet that covered a concrete floor that seemed to be directly conducting the cold of an underground glacier. Finally, the secretary came out to call another man into the office and spied me on the floor. He gave the guard a scowl and asked me who and what I needed. I handed him a business card[1] and briefly explained why I was there. He apologized profusely for the treatment and moved a well-dressed man from the chair next to his desk, urging me to sit. I was immediately served tea spiced with clove and cardamom, different from most tea served in Himachal. He was curious about me and asked some questions about my research. What did I think of Shimla? Of Himachal? Where had I been? He too had seen me in the paper and asked about the documentary I was shooting. Once he was satisfied, he got up and walked into a room partitioned off by velvet curtains. There were about ten people sitting in the office. One was the chai boy, and another was assigned to answer the phones. The rest—all men—were newspaper editors, major contractors, and two of the state's most important ministers. The secretary came back, and I was led into the warm, spacious, and well-lit office of the chief minister.

This somewhat self-indulgent story highlights an experience common to many villagers of Himachal Pradesh, with two important divergences: the speed and depth of my access. An average villager could never expect to be allowed a personal visit with the chief minister. Although I was quickly granted a private meeting for a number of interesting reasons that space does not permit me to explore here, for Himachalis, frustration and the number of barriers to access are an important part of daily life. The personal secretary has become synonymous with access, as he or she can either deny or provide access to valuable information and opportunities. Gūrs liken their role—serving as a medium between villagers and their deities—to that of a secretary. Indeed, this metaphor was repeated by many gūrs and reiterated by countless people trying to explain the importance of the gūr to me. This was not an explanation that was given to me simply because I was a foreigner. Rather, the discourses on religion and the state reinforce one another in Himachal. They are metaphoric and symbolic systems used to understand one another.

Describing the gūr as the personal secretary of the village god offers a vivid metaphor to visualize his role. However, it does not go far enough to clearly outline the gūr's status and function in contemporary Himachali villages. He is understood as the medium of connection between villagers and their deities and is the person who facilitates a host of transactions or prohibits them. Yet, as it was explained to me many times, like the personal secretary of a government official, he can interject his own agenda into the transaction. He can interfere with, shape, or transform relations between the villagers and their deities. This is a common complaint among villagers who dislike, for one reason or another, the gūr of their deity. However, like the majority of secretaries in the Secretariat, most gūrs claim to be unable to control what they say when they are in trance. They simply communicate messages. They are mediums facilitating the flow of information from gods to people, just as personal secretaries mediate the flow of information between government officials and citizens. Ironically, this grounds their authority; they are both guided by a power that exceeds them. In the case of the gūr, it is the deity, and in the case of the personal secretary, it is the state.

In this chapter, I investigate an anxiety that emerges as the state government asserts itself in ever more areas—such as regulating festivals, limiting the authority of temple officers to decide local disputes, and publishing works that purport to explain "authentic Himachal." Many villagers are uneasy with the blurring boundaries between state power and the power of deities. Who gets to speak for a deity, and in which contexts? In Himachal, each deity has its own gūr, a person who is specially trained, adheres to certain behavioral standards, and knows how to invite the deity to enter his body. These gūrs are the lifeblood of the community, communicating the desires and displeasures of the deity, predicting rain, and warning of calamities. Even as scientific rationalism has become prominent in the region, very few people question the legitimacy of these individuals to speak on behalf of deities. But it is increasingly true that the scope of their statements is circumscribed, in effect if not always in locution. The content of this chapter comes primarily from extended interviews I did with these mediums as well as with members of their communities. These conversations show how anxiety over the extent of the gūr's ability to speak clarifies the boundaries between the deity's sphere and that of the state as well as a growing nostalgia for a time when society was governed by gods and not the secular state.

RELIGION RELATES TO ITS "OTHERS"

One of the most important questions in debates on secularism is the location of the secular. Where is the secular? Where are its boundaries, and how are they maintained? In India in the 1960s and '70s, many of these debates were folded into the question of whether the country could be considered secular at all. Some argued that the concepts of "the secular" and "secularism" were alien to the native soils of India and that they would be impossible to implement there.[2] But they also contended that the postcolonial state had been obliged to intervene in so many spheres of public life (particularly the regulation of temples and ritual practices) that it could not be considered secular.[3] Others, such as Donald E. Smith, took the opposing position, enthusiastically endorsing Indian secularism. Through a detailed historical examination of the development of the secular postcolonial state, Smith argued that, despite facing major challenges, India was a secular state.

Much of the discussion was not centered on calls for a Hindu state, for religious institutions to direct legislative processes, or for compulsory religious education but rather on the way that the state defined religion through actions such as the Prevention of Dedication (Madras Devadasis) Act of 1947, the Madras Temple Entry Act, and the solidification of the Hindu Code.[4] An important question that emerged was about the location of religion. Could religion be included within the state, or should it be kept separate? How could the state regulate religious spaces to ensure fiscal responsibility, individual liberty, and proper management practices while leaving religion a space of its own? I suggest that this particular question demanded by the logic of the secular is somewhat misguided in the Indian case. While the "wall of separation" may be an apt metaphor to describe American secularism, it is not appropriate here. As the following chapters will make clear, strict separations between religion and state and between public and private are impossible to maintain in India. What I propose is a reorientation of the discussion of secularism. Indeed, I agree with Partha Chatterjee, who asks why all relations between religion and state are named with the term "secularism."[5] Let us turn away from the question of whether or not religion is located inside or outside the state. I assume throughout this work that, in Himachal Pradesh, religion and state are interpenetrating systems.

In this chapter, I will ask whether early developments in Himachal Pradesh are consistent with an abstract notion of the secular and how the lines between religion and state are drawn within the space of contemporary social life. Specifically, I will examine how the conundrum of Himachali religion—that modernization in Himachal demands the simultaneous elevation and marginalization of religion—developed and provided the context in which state-religion relations took shape.

THE MANAGEMENT AND MAINTENANCE OF RELIGION

The forms of knowledge we are examining here have roots that reach deep into the past of the subcontinent. The first of these forms is colonial, and the second is postcolonial. In the 1800s, as the British Empire developed and the British felt a greater need for control and command, they developed sophisticated forms of knowledge to manage and control the Indian population. Nick Dirks argues that there was a massive shift in the organization of the state after 1857, going from being organized around land and the revenues produced by that land to being organized around the management of populations. The latter type of management required the production of sophisticated forms of ethnographic knowledge that went beyond the historiography and surveys that had been developed previously.[6] This, in turn, helped to produce the literature that emerged as district and state gazetteers, district reports, censuses, and so on. The ethnohistorians of Himachal Pradesh are inheritors of this tradition, as were the writers and organizers of the village monographs discussed in chapter 3.

The ethnohistorians of Himachal, having inherited many forms of literary presentation and knowledge formulation, including the model of the gazetteer, combine many forms of representation in their work. In his classic work on colonialism and its forms of knowledge, Bernard Cohn argues that the British employed different investigative modalities "to classify, categorize and bound the vast social world that was India so that it could be controlled."[7] According to Cohn, most investigative modalities "were constructed in relation to institutions and administrative sites with fixed routines."[8] I will examine how Himachal's ethnohistorians emerged out of the Department of Language and Culture and its administrative dictates. I will also show how the knowledge gathered there was used not simply to heal cultural schisms in the region but also to formulate a cultural ideology that legitimated the state while simultaneously drawing on local resources.

My account of this process, however, will differ from those of Dirks and Cohn. While their work has powerfully uncovered the interdependent relations of knowledge and power and has helped us to realize that the project of knowledge creation was not the work of innocent, if curious, colonial officials, I believe they both have a tendency to impute a greater degree of personal and institutional agency to the processes than is warranted. Colonial administrators and authors were not always the conscious architects of policies of oppression and control.[9] Furthermore, I do not believe that the guiding logic behind this process of knowledge creation was the grounding of command and control enterprises of the colonial state. My argument is that, while there is an indissoluble relationship between knowledge and power, knowledge production in Himachal, as in the colonial contexts Dirks and Cohn examined, came about in relation to the specific demands of governance, the systems produced, and the processes set in motion exceed the boundaries of the state. They bleed out into everyday life and transform all they touch. In turn, the sites they touch reflect back in ways that no amount of calculation, systematization, or control can fix or prefigure.[10] I have already discussed how the system of land reform designed by Himachal's early legislative body failed to achieve its intended result and proceeded instead to abolish the land control of local deities while reformulating the control of new landowners. I have also shown how the production of numerical census information broke down in the process of state planning, giving rise to the need for more-detailed nonstatistical data. Throughout the remaining chapters, I will be attentive to places where the logics initiated through the ethnohistorical project of the Department of Language and Culture are exceeded by the messiness of daily living and to how the accidents of history conspire to undermine the logics of state planners.

When Parmar ascended his self-made throne, the need to fully flesh out his bureaucratic apparatus weighed on him. While many of the basic programs and departments—such as those dealing with roads, power, and education—were already in place, others—such as the Department of Language and Culture and the Department of Tourism—took shape in the months following the granting of full statehood in early 1971. The new departments, like all government departments, emerged out of perceived needs. Parmar and Lal Chand Prathi,[11] the two major players in the formation of these departments,[12] were responding to three acute needs: the need to define the state's relationship to language, the need to catalog the region's cultural traditions, and the need to unite the state's diverse regions.

The first of these, formulating the state's relationship to language, required a delicate balance. Language was a contentious issue, dividing sections of Himachal along regional lines. The various languages of Himachal were not mutually intelligible, so trying to use them all as the basis of administrative or even everyday commerce was impossible. Thus, Hindi was set as the state language, and one of the primary goals of the Department of Language and Culture was the creation and distribution of administrative vocabularies. This continues to be one of the main functions of the department; it translates forms and creates new words for novel situations. When Hindi became the official language of administration, an allied set of forces within the department was devoted to the preservation and promotion of Pahāṛī dialects. In the early 1970s, the department arranged a number of literary workshops and publication venues for Pahāṛī, and they sponsored the compilation of a Pahāṛī-Hindi dictionary, the expansion of which continues today.[13] Furthermore, through the publication wing of the Academy of Arts, Culture, and Language, essays in vernacular journals such as *Himprastha* and several independent manuscripts were published.

The second was an acute need to integrate the diverse regions of Himachal. Just as India was being torn apart by factions in the 1970s (in Punjab, Arunachal Pradesh, Kashmir, Ladakh, etc.), so too was Himachal threatened by regional disintegration. Parmar's most pressing need was to build roads to connect communities that were isolated from other regions. With the incredible increase in roads, the diversity of Himachal's cultural traditions was brought into clear view, and the need to bring these regions into the Himachali fold became acute. In fact, many at the department still consider this to be its primary goal. Prem Sharma, the department's current director, once told me: "This is our main purpose, our goal: to join the regions of Himachal."[14] Since its inception, the department has pursued an active agenda of integrating the state on a number of different levels. For example, when the 1961 census survey on fairs and festivals was released, officials realized that these events were capable of uniting not only the communities in which they were held but also the state more broadly. So, thereafter, the construction, promotion, and management of select fairs and festivals became a way for the department to project the message of integration by bringing together local villagers, deities, interregional travelers, and state officials in annual ceremonies. Festivals like the Lavi fair at Rampur, Śivarātri in Mandi, the Daśaharā festival in Kullu, and Manimahesh in Chamba have become powerful signs of state integration. They are also symbols (*pratīk*) of cultural integration. The state has actively promoted these fairs by paying deities to travel to them, by using the state marketing apparatus, and by managing the content of these fairs, for example, by making sure that practices such as animal sacrifice are sidelined.

The management of state image and regional unity is not a part-time job. For the daily administration of linguistic and cultural affairs, the department has set up offices in each of Himachal's districts. Staffed by three to five people, each of these offices is headed by a senior language officer, who attends to the management of local fairs and festivals, temples, and publications and administers small funds to various people and institutions that fulfill the needs of the department. These employees are local-level figures of the state, managing its desires and demands.[15] While conducting my fieldwork, I spent time with a number of these individuals, and it seems to me that this is where the lines between religion and the state are being negotiated on a daily basis. Villagers are constructing their image of the state by interacting with these officers and others from the department, while the department, through its portrayal of the villagers and its forms of promotion, seminars, and management practices, is shaping what religion means.

In one of the more prominent districts of the state, I spent a great deal of time with the senior language officer, who, in the process of one day's interview, summed up the conundrum of the state with unusual clarity.[16] I asked her what the primary role of the department was in the district and what they did. "We have so many schemes," she told me. "All these go through this department and I am the head in this district. We do seminars, we do all the cultural programs, and we coordinate the fairs and festival. Here we have so many fairs and festivals just like the Daśaharā—Daśaharā is an international festival. Then there is a state festival, winter festival in Manali, ... so we cooperate the local bodies and organize these festivals."[17] I then asked her what she thought of some of the things that happen at these festivals, giving the example of animal sacrifice. "We can't interfere in religion," she replied. "India is a secular country [*Dharma Nirpeksha desh*]. It is written in our constitution. We cannot interfere in the religion of any person, so it's not easy, because it is related to their religion. So the government can't interfere in religion and culture. Religion, which is culture, culture, which is related to religion. So we can't pass any law against any religion or culture. So it's very difficult."[18] As a Brahmin fiercely opposed to animal sacrifice, she is speaking here of walking the line between constitutional separation and the management of the religion and culture in her district. For this woman, it comes down to the difference between law and custom. While the legislature is unable to write any law against the free exercise of religion, she has the task of managing religious practices and communities on a daily basis, which, in her district, has led to the widespread eradication of animal sacrifice.

Finally, in connection with its role as the manager of cultural traditions, the Department of Language and Culture, and particularly the Academy of Art, Culture and Language, has been given the third task of creating an archive of the cultural traditions of the state. This task has been taken up by a wide range of people. The woman discussed above, for example, has written two books and more than ten articles on the traditions of her district. The importance of the creation of this archive is difficult to overestimate. It began with the village monographs discussed in chapter 3 and has been continued through scores of small manuscripts, innumerable newspaper and radio productions, and several different academic and semi-academic publications. The creation of this archive was instrumental in helping state administrators govern in isolated regions. The work of language officers and regional researchers in remote places like Pangi, Kalpa, and Poo gave central administrators a glimpse into the cultural lives of those they sought to manage, control, and develop, and it allowed them to better pursue the ends of the development state. The information was folded into tourism plans, road routes, school construction, and even government service selection.

The formation of an archive of Himachali culture and history must not be seen simply as an administrative move servicing the ends of the postcolonial state—a sort of key text for the deconstruction of power interests and political strategies. While it definitely fit into this sordid matrix of desires, it has been more influential in shaping Himachali public culture. It is this information that has allowed for the creation of Himachali history—for the production and reproduction of the belief that Himachal is an entity that is the subject of history and able to realize itself as a state within the Indian union. The archive has helped forge the opening to every book on Himachal that invokes one or another Puranic text and equates Himachal with the Himalayas.[19] Through the authority of this archive, signed both by the state and by history, Himachal has emerged as an entity and an idea, and it may someday even emerge as a nation.[20]

During the past several decades, a large body of scholarship has developed exploring the transformation of religious practice in colonial and postcolonial India. These theories are generally composed of three interrelated parts. The first emphasizes the hierarchical character of South Asian society and explains religious modernization as a function of Brahmanical reforms: Sankritization, the standardization of ritual activities, and the canonization of divinities, sites, and saints.[21] This argument generally portrays Brahmins as "cultural brokers" for the reform of South Asian Hinduism. There has also been a parallel track of theorizing that has centered on caste as the key to understanding religious modernization. This group of studies, which is still tied to the idea of Indian hierarchy, argues that religious modernization has been propelled by reformers who have been able to dispel the "traditional" caste boundaries that have defined religious communities of practice.[22]

The second part of these theories asserts that the very idea of religion in South Asia is, itself, a product of colonial rule.[23] The contention is that colonial categories developed in the census in combination with regulatory force and Western education condensed the diverse practice and beliefs of the subcontinent into a singular "world religion." The "religion" that emerged looked a lot like other religions across the globe, assuming an interdependent, if distinct, relation with the colonial state. Many of these studies pursue their line of attack into the late colonial period, adding the third important dimension of these theories: the idea that the primary force driving religious reform is Indian nationalism. Following the decline of the Congress Party and the rise of religious violence across the subcontinent, this literature has grown tremendously.

While these approaches highlight some of the important dimensions of religious modernization, they cannot account for the changes seen in the Western Himalayas. First, Brahmins are not a predominate caste in the Western Himalayas, so their role in defining and organizing practice in the Western Himalayas is highly attenuated.[24] Second, colonialism in the Western Himalayas was a highly variegated affair. There were princely states, British-administered territories, and other areas that were almost totally ignored. These multiple pasts preclude us from seeing colonialism as the most significant binding string in shaping the present. Third, nationalist narratives have not affected daily life in the Western Himalayas in the way they have in Allahabad or Madurai. We must look somewhere else for the arbiter of religious modernization in the Western Himalayas.

I will examine four instances in which the character of religious authority is being redefined. Each suggests that older figures of religious authority—such as particular divinities, gūr, and raja—are slowly being superseded. While two of the examples come from festivals and two from ritual sites, they all suggest that the state is replacing these older forms of religious authority.

I argue that, at least in the Western Himalayas, the mechanism of religious change has not been Brahmins, colonialism, or nationalists. In fact, I do not believe that it has been a response to any single agent personal or corporate. Instead, religious change has come about in relation to those forces of calculation, planning, control, and organization that mark modern forms of power. It is these forces, multiple and conflicting, that have produced the very fields of religion and state.

Religious change in Himachal Pradesh is an unauthored process. However, this does not mean that it hasn't followed a particular logic. It means that neither government actors, nor subalterns, nor puritanical Brahmins, nor colonial forms of knowledge are its architects. Rather, I argue that all of these entities, like "religion" and "state," are caught up in larger processes that seem to move by themselves: calculation, organization, and specialization. In making this claim, I am not arguing for the inexorable teleological development of modernization. To say that these forces are at work and that they have formed the warp and woof of life in Himachal is not to say they have a direction. I am arguing, for example, that the idea of projects has reshaped these worlds, not that the forces that this idea is a part of are themselves a project. The difference is subtle but massive. In the following pages, I will be attentive to sites where these forces have conjoined to restructure religious practices and give flesh to the state.

MEETINGS, METAPHORS, AND MODERN SOCIAL ORGANIZATION

As noted earlier in this chapter, fairs and festivals are some of the most commonly discussed concerns of vernacular ethnohistorians. From the early explanations of Pandit Tika Ram Joshi[25] to the classical works of Mian Goverdhan Singh[26] and others, fairs have figured centrally in the development of the evolving archive of Himachali culture. This

Figure 17. Deities entering a village during Mandi
Śivarātri. Photo by author.

interest is predicated on the assumption that these fairs and festivals
condense historical and cultural meanings. Journalists often describe
these events at meetings (*milan* or *samāgam*), and just as these fairs and
festivals collect Himachal's deities, so too do they collect narratives
about the region's cultural history: "Himachal Pradesh, popularly
known as the 'valley of the gods', lies in the heart of the Western Himalayas. It is a land of thousands of fairs and festival. And its centuries old
culture rightly commands deep interest and respect."[27]

First, I will look at the logic of one rite, *indralok yātrā*, in which the
structures of modern governance used to organize the logics of state
ministries are translated into theological frameworks. I contrast two
different readings of this rite to elucidate differing approaches to theological efficacy and the unseen power of deities. They speak of differing
logics of authority and of the reframing of religion in the age of the
modern state.

Next, I will examine the recent history of one particular festival,
Mandi Śivarātri, and the ramifications of the state's practices on it,
arguing that the repositioning of the festival precipitates a renewed
relationship between the state and its people. The rite thus serves as a
means of mediating the relationship of state and villagers through a

local festival. What happens in the process is ambiguous and conflicted. Broadly, however, there is a semanticization[28] of the practice, a translocalization, and an inclusion of the rite within state-managed development projects. The relationship between state and religion as mediated through fairs and festival is not simply the after-image of managerial control and touristic promotion.

The deities of the Western Himalayas are mobile. They travel from village to village, solving problems, dispersing blessings, and gathering income. Some even move between villages on an annual basis.[29] They travel during prearranged cycles throughout the year, going to homes where they are called to do work. In many regions of southeastern Kullu, northeastern Mandi, and northern Shimla districts, there is a tradition commonly called *indralok yātrā*, a rite that commemorates the annual journey of the gods to the world of Indra.

In the middle of winter, after the festival of Lori (generally celebrated in mid-January), the village deities disappear. They remain absent anywhere from a month (the most common pattern) to only a few days. This begins the prolonged festival of *indralok yātrā*, which opens with a ceremony of closure. On the first day of the festival, the village deity is brought from the temple into the village square, where it is undressed. Its ornaments and mountings are all unhinged, and it is placed in a box that is then sealed and placed in the temple.[30] The period that follows is inauspicious. Many people spend their days at home, avoiding social contact. During this time, no rituals can be performed in the home or village. The deity is completely absent. The rite is considered by many to be the end of the year.

When the deity returns, there is a large festival that celebrates the commencement of the new year. The deity arrives through the medium of the gūr. The gūr becomes possessed by the deity's spirit and relates its entire history, including how it originally arrived in the village and the difficulties that it had to undergo to get there. Once the stories of the deity's origins have been told, the gūr moves on to business. The speech that follows is not unlike the chief minister's annual budget speech and has even been compared to these on several occasions.[31] The gūr begins by relating how all of the deities interacted in heaven. How did Banar get along with Mahasu? Was there a quarrel between any of the deities? How did the deities address human grievances between communities? This is then followed by a long piece of oratory that details the coming year. It answers the questions on everyone's mind: When should crops be planted? Will the rains be good? Will there be a flood? Who will die? Who will marry? Who will have a child? Is the village in danger?

Great variability surrounds the explanation and interpretation of the rite. People in the same village interpret the rite differently and attribute radically different meaning to it. The interpretations range widely in both content and sophistication.[32] I believe that *indralok yātrā* presents us with an excellent example of a space that is discursively unsettled. The obscurity associated with *indralok yātrā* is due to the lack of a common interpretive history or institutional body that regulates the explanation of its performance. It is also due to what happens in the period between the opening and closing of the rites. The rite is itself built around invisibility, beyond final, objective proof and evidence. This discursive ellipsis, this space that cannot be brought under the control of the authority of the archive or the witness,[33] has become a space where people are able to work out their own understandings of the relationships between deities and themselves.

Because of the sheer paucity of historical information, it is impossible to say when, how, or why the rite began. However, the fact that the deity disappears during the winter and that it travels points to the previous migratory patterns of many groups that are now settled in the hills and others that continue to live nomadically. The tradition of closing temples and sealing deities in boxes for extended periods of time may relate to the annual practice of people moving from high regions (where this practice is most common) to places at lower elevations, where their sheep and goats could spend the winter. It might also relate to the environmental necessity of remaining indoors during the harsh winters of the past, which are remembered with nostalgia in these areas.[34] There are also several different mythological accounts of the origin of this rite, ranging from Brahmanical interpretations that argue for the need to perform austerities in the winter in order to gain the graces of Śiva to explanations predicated on logics of leisure, which argue that the rite began because the deities, like people, get tired. Just as the British used to come to the Shimla hills for a break, so too do local deities need a break from their difficult job of ruling and organizing the populace.

I will explore two different interpretations of this rite to show how it is used to render intelligible things that are themselves opaque—in this case, the past and the operations of state power. Furthermore, these two strategies show how villages and state level discourse on theology are interdependent. Local deities are just as dependent on the logic of the state as the logic of the state is on practices in the villages.

One of the common ways *indralok yātrā* is explained is in terms of a popular myth of the Western Himalayas: the aboriginal and continual war between demons and deities. Many of the deities of the Western Himalayas are believed to have originally been demons but were domesticated and placated by the offerings of villagers. The deities of Haḍimbā and Sikru are good examples of this. The process of domestication is remembered nostalgically as a civilizing process and is often folded into accounts of modernization.

This next explanation of *indralok yātrā* combines these historical narratives about the war between demons and deities with an account of how the deities came to have only heads rather than full bodies. In the valleys east of the Satluj, *indralok yātrā* is also known as *patya poaino*, which points to the importance of keeping the masks of the deity in a wooden box.[35] According to a local singer I spoke to, who came from a family of poets, the deities begin their travel to heaven (*svarg*)[36] as soon as their jewelry has been removed and their masks placed in the wooden box. After arriving in heaven, they begin their annual war with the demons of the region. This is the same war that was fought at the foundation of the world, the war that established the Himalayas and the lands on which the people telling these stories live. It is the yearly fight for control, in which the deities must defend their lands and the people they protect. The singer explained to me that the outcome of the war directly affects the lives of the villagers. The successes and failures of the deities dictate the events of the coming year. They determine whether the villagers' children will be sick or the crops will prosper. When the deities return and the gūr narrates the deity's origin story, he also narrates the war and how the deity fought demons to protect the villagers, after which he gives a narration of the events of the coming year.

This rite is not an exercise in theological palavering. It involves the entire community and is enacted by them in the form of a game called *gindu*. In this game, the villagers mimic the actions of their deities. The population is divided into two teams, and a large ball of rags is formed, which the teams will fight for. The game begins when the ball is thrown in the air, and the competing teams fight to gain control, which is the primary goal of the game. As my friend Deepak Sharma told me, "this game reveals the war between the gods and the demons."[37]

Both the game and the recitation of the gūr reveal the hidden machinations of the divine and point to the manner in which people use alternate frames of reference to interpret their worlds. In this case, these rituals simultaneously reveal a nostalgic past and a hopeful future through playful gestures—both the playing of the game (*khel*) and the playing (*khelnā*)[38] of the gūr. The rite harnesses the narrative tension between gods and demons and analogizes it with the civilizing power of settlement and modernization in the region. This metaphoric coupling relies on two popular myths about historical change in the region. The first of these is the settler myth. This widely circulated myth tells of the arrival of deities and lineage founders to the region. They face enormous difficulties, natural and supernatural trials, famine, and disease. Finally, they triumph over this enormous adversity and found a village.

The second of these is the modernization process associated with colonial rule and its postcolonial fallout. In the everyday speech of these villagers, there is a common distinction drawn between the superstitious and the modern and between the simpleminded, or backward, and progress. For the most part, this is not read as another pernicious form of cultural imperialism but rather as a hopeful promise. Many people use the analogy of this ongoing war between gods and demons to characterize the struggle to overcome superstition and what they have internalized, and often speak of, as their own backwardness. *Indralok yātrā* harnesses this power and uses it to simultaneously reinscribe the promise of modernity and the logic of a local ritual practice. Thus, embedded within the logic of this festival is the logic that undergirds the modernization process itself: just as the deities always win the war against the demons, so too will modernization triumph over superstition and backwardness.

Indralok yātrā is also implicated in a dialectical relationship with the logics of state bureaucracy. Some of the most interesting accounts of why the deities go on this annual journey come from gūrs who communicate with the deities during their absence. For them, this is a period in which their services are not available. At this time, people cannot have any of their problems or hopes mediated; however, when the deities return, things are different. The gūrs set the tone for the year.

In discussions I had with several of these mediums, they all emphasized similar points. The world of Indra is not a heaven where the deities relax and recharge their batteries, nor is it a place where the battle that founds the world is replayed. Rather, it is more like the modern Secretariat building in Shimla, where the daily tasks of the state government are performed. Throughout the year, the deities keep track of everything happening in the village and the surrounding area. They carefully measure and record everything. As one gūr put it, the deity goes to Indralok "to have meetings, like the government [*sarkār*], and to plan what will happen."[39] These large meetings, in which each deity brings a large ledger of everything that happened in their village

during the year, can be compared to the yearly meeting of the legislative assembly (Vidhān Sabhā). The deities exchange these ledgers and
assess the previous year. What happened? What went wrong? How can
we improve? After this, they begin to plan for and argue about the
future. One of the gūrs reminded me that each deity has to negotiate
with the others to attain what it wants for its particular area, just as the
members of the legislative assembly have to negotiate with other members for the benefits and attention of state ministries. This is a difficult
process that entails balancing and counterbalancing the past with the
future.[40] Once a policy for the new year has been decided, the deities
can return to their villages and give the people news of what has happened and what will happen to them in the future.

  In both of these explanations of *indralok yātrā,* there is a logic that
relies on the intercourse between local deities' practices and state ide-
ologies and structures. In the first explanation, the departure of the
divinity is understood in a broadly construed rhetoric of struggle and
progress. In the second, the structures of the modern state are used to
understand cosmological orders. The structures of the modern state
are not only used to understand the machinations of vacationing deities. They are also used to understand the very logic of the interaction
between humans and deities. I do not take this to mean that the state
has somehow imposed itself on local religious spaces or that this is part
of a greater strategy to control the unruly "backward" masses. Instead,
I believe that it points to the pervasiveness of a transformative logic
that is as important for the formation of the state as it is for religious
spaces. The point, to put it in Ranajit Guha's terms, is that we do see a
move from forms of control predicated on dominance to those predicated on hegemony.[41]

  Śivarātri is a festival celebrated throughout the Indian subcontinent.[42] It has been observed since at least the eighth century and most
likely much earlier (the fifth or sixth centuries).[43] Some of the earliest
textual records describing the festival come from the Śāntiparvan of
the *Mahābhārata* and the Garuḍa Purāṇa. These textual sources, how-

ever, give us little insight into contemporary performances of these festivals. The way the festival is performed in Mandi offers a particularly
anomalous example.

In Mandi, Śivarātri has become the most celebrated festival of the
year. The government accords it "international" status. However, while
there is agreement that the festival is popular, there is no agreement on
its origin, meaning, or structure. Rather, the festival shows us the layer-
ing of the past and the changes brought on by the ascendancy of the
state. I will explore competing narratives about the history and meaning of the festival and competing ritual performances in order to better
understand how local religious practices are being transformed by state
organization and promotion.

While this festival is ostensibly devoted to the honoring of Śiva,
commentators agree that Śiva is only one of many important deities it
celebrates. Most narratives of the origin of the festival begin with the
establishment of Mandi.[44] It is said that, in 1527, Ajbar Sen set up his
kingdom on the banks of the Beas River. He also built a Śiva temple,
Bhutnāth, around which the town first revolved.[45] In popular accounts
of the settlement of the left bank of the Beas and the founding of New
Mandi, people emphasize a common origin story: the mysterious offering of milk.

It is said that, in the time before Mandi, the left bank was a dense
jungle that no one visited. Once, a milkman noticed that one of his cows
was traveling to the left bank every day and disappearing. When she
returned, she had no milk. Suspicious of thieves, the milkman decided
to follow the cow to see who was stealing his milk. He followed her and
saw that, as she rested in the shade of a tree, her milk poured forth onto
a stone. Having heard stories like this, the milkman told his friends,
and they tried to remove the stone. When it became clear that it couldn't
be moved, a temple was established on the site.[46] This common origin
trope provides a powerful form of legitimacy for the city and its past.
The story is commonly recited, and residents and nearby villagers use
it to justify their divine sanction.

In 1648, the character of Śivarātri and of the Mandi kingdom changed radically. Suraj Sen was an ambitious king, who built many forts, annexed large tracts of territory, and defeated the rulers of his rival state, Suket. While Suraj Sen was not always successful in battle, his biggest problem was the continuation of his lineage. The king had eighteen sons, but all of them died in his lifetime, leaving him with no heir. In 1648, during the later years of his rule, he commissioned the creation of a silver icon of Mādhorāy, and he dedicated his kingdom to the trust of the deity. The inscription on the icon reads: "Surya Sen, lord of the earth and destroyer of his rivals, has this blameless image of the Blessed Discus-Bearer, and master of all the gods, illustrious Madho-Rai, made by Bhima the goldsmith in Vik. 1705, on Thursday, the fifteenth Phagan."[47] The dedication corresponds to the date of the celebration of Śivarātri, and it is clear that Surya Sen took advantage of this festival both to glorify Mādhorāy and to integrate the kingdom. Mādhorāy continues to be at the center of ritual activity.

These stories of the festival's origin compete with at least three other narratives of its origin and meaning. While they are not mutually exclusive, the usage of one usually implies the exclusion of the others. A very few people associate the origins and meaning of the festival with its earliest textual renderings, which extol the virtues of worshipping Śiva and emphasize simple acts of fasting and offering on the festival day. They revolve around a story of Purāṇic fame: that of Śiva and the hunter. Though the details (name, kingdom, the reason the hunter was in the forest, etc.) vary, these narratives tell a story very similar to the following version, which is one that is told currently in Himachal.[48]

Once, a hunter traveled deep into the forest to gather meat for his wife and family. He wandered all day, but did not meet with success. As evening fell, he was ashamed, and he kept searching until it was dark and the jungle became very dangerous. To protect himself, he climbed a bilva tree to wait out the night. He couldn't sleep in the tree, and in order to stay awake, he passed the night plucking the leaves of the tree and letting them fall to the ground. Beneath the tree, hidden in the ground, was a Śiva *liṅga* (a phallic symbol of Śiva). As he sat there, he thought of his wife and children and began to cry. The tears, like the leaves, fell onto the *liṅga*. Inadvertently, this hunter had spent the night worshipping Śiva, who was so pleased that, when the hunter died, Śiva brought him and his family to his abode, where they resided. So, it is said that, on the night of Śiva, people who remain awake all night, fast, and make offerings of bilva leaves and water will be released from the cycle of rebirth upon death.

Another tradition maintains that Śivarātri is the night that commemorates the wedding of Śiva and Pārvati. This narrative focuses on some of the ritual elements of the festival. One month before the festival begins, the city is decorated as a bride. The *liṅga* at Bhūtanāth is worshipped with an offering of *ghī* (ghee) on a clear night on which stars can be seen. After this, Śiva is not worshipped again until Śivarātri begins and the *ghī* is brought out of the *liṅga*. For those who emphasize the nuptial elements of Śivarātri, this rite is the center of the festival.

However, the marriage narrative is not exceptionally popular. While it moves us in the direction of contemporary practice, from which people draw their explanations, it does not explain what most people do when they come to the festival.

In seeking to understand Mandi Śivarātri as practice, it is best to approach it from the position of different observers. As is evidenced throughout *Becoming Religious,* I refuse to take a position on the ontological status of categories, practices, texts, and so forth. I believe that the being of any thing is relative to the world and people within which it is situated. Therefore, I will not say that Śivarātri is one thing or another. Rather, I find it more useful to describe it from the position of those who celebrate it. This is not to say that I endorse an impotent form of subjectivism. I do not. As will be suggested in the following examples, I use a many-angled approach to suggest direction and trend.

As mentioned above, one of the primary historical narratives of the festival centers on the arrival of Mādhorāy and the transfer of the Mandi kingdom to the deity's control. Despite the festival's ostensibly

Śaivite character, manuscript and inscriptional evidence suggests that, from at least the time of the transfer of the kingdom to Mādhorāy, Śivarātri has been an important festival for the kingdom and its Vaiṣṇava rulers. Like the festival of Daśaharā in Kullu, Śivarātri serves as a powerful means of integrating local deities into large royal relations. This is the only time during the year that all the deities of the various regions of the kingdom are brought to the same place. As each deity arrives at the temple of Mādhorāy, carried on the backs of its worshippers, it bows to Mādhorāy. This moment of deference signifies the renewal of a relationship that is as much financial and militaristic as it is cultural. Despite Mandi's inclusion in Himachal Pradesh since its earliest formulation, the rite of royal obeisance continues to be performed. In fact, many feel it is the most important part of the festival.[49]

For others, the most important performative component of the festival is a rite separated from the main events. This rite points to a common practice at smaller festivals in the hills. I will quote a description of the festival in order to give the reader an impression of how rites like these are described:

> On the last evening of Śivarātri a primary rite (pramukh prathā) called "Jag" is performed. On a day before the festival is over, the primary officials of the temple, the gūr and the kārdār of the deities, are collected at a specified location. The rite is announced by the playing of instruments. Between all the assembled people, a platform about 2 square feet and 5–6 inches above the ground is constructed and some sacred symbols (pavitra aṅkan) are drawn on it. After that, a fire is lit on the stage and the instruments continue playing their music, increasing the excitement. Then the gūr, having been pierced by divine power (daivī śakti se āveśit) twirls a piece of burning wood in the four directions. It seems like he is calling some unseen power (adṛśya śakti). He then takes the burning wood, walks around the crowd, and finally sits with the royal family and other important people assembled there. The gūr then makes predictions (bhaviṣyavāṇī) for the coming year.[50]

This type of rite is very similar to those at the center of smaller festivals in the surrounding hills. On the final day of these festivals, two or three deities are gathered with their gūrs and other officials, and the deity is invoked. Once the gūr is playing (*khelnā*), the people ask about their problems and petition the deity for help. These rites are primarily pragmatic, and they are crucial for the management of everyday problems. They are an integral part of the festival.

Without a doubt, the component of the festival that is most commented upon in state ads and newspapers and other forms of publication is its unitary function. The deities come to the festival to meet one another, dance, and celebrate their peaceful coexistence. The festival is a meeting. While the ritual of appearing before Mādhorāy intimates the importance of the deities meeting, it emphasizes a singular relationship between Mādhorāy and each deity. It recalls a system of sovereignty, patronage, and persuasion that is no longer present in the Western Himalayas. What most commentators discuss these days is that there is a new association connected to new forms of patronage. This is the gathering of all the deities on the grounds of the Mandi government high school.

Each day of the festival, after leaving the places where they stay for the night, the deities travel to the field at the high school, where they spend the day. They are preceded by trumpets, drums, and flutes. The musicians (*bajaṇtrī log*) blow their horns and pound on their drums as the bearers of the deities enter the grounds in a long line. The deities then greet one another. If they are of relatively equal stature, they dance around, bobbing and weaving and tipping their chariots toward each other. If they are of unequal status, the lesser deity defers to the more powerful deity. These greetings can be short, lasting only a few seconds, or can go on for a very long time, up to twenty minutes. When those carrying the deities speak of this dancing, they assert that they are not in control. They say the deity does what it wants. If it wants to dance, it dances. If it wants to stand still, it does not move. If it wants to offer obeisance, it does. In fact, this is one of the most common ways of justifying the strength of the deity. The movement of the deity is considered miraculous (*pratyaksa*), and it is confirmation of its power.

Once they have greeted one another, the deities line up in rows. One deity, Mahasu, stands at the head of the line and is said by many to be the most powerful deity on the grounds. Once assembled, the deities and their administrators sit all day being viewed and receiving offerings from the community. This aspect of the festival (its unitary function) has been used to stand in as a metonym for Himachali religion more broadly. The anonymous author of the pamphlet "Mandi Śivarātri: Meeting of the Gods," explains: "Himachal is known as the land of the gods (devbhūmi). Here, the gods are always celebrating fairs and festivals. One of these is Śivarātri.... On the day of the festival, the town resonates with the sound of the drum, and the people of the town are filled with happiness. The dancing together of the deities is the most important part of the festival. After they dance, the town reverberates with the sound."[51] In fact, for many writers, this joining of the deities has come to be a symbol of Himachali religion more broadly. In one article, Sudarshan Vashisht relates the meeting of deities at Śivarātri to the very structure of Himachali religion: "Festivals, Fairs and celebrations are related to the life of culture and society. Local traditions are associated with the development of society. Almost every tradition in Himachal is related to religious beliefs. Mandi Śivarātri is also a symbol of the union of tradition and religion."[52]

The conception that the festival unites the region is not an accident. It is the result of a broader set of forces linking the Department of Language and Culture, the Department of Tourism, district offices, and local temple committees. In spaces like Mandi Śivarātri, the Department of Language and Culture's goal of joining the regions of Himachal, mentioned above, has been brought to fruition. It is a union orchestrated by a convergence of departments and local bodies. The Department of Tourism and the Department of Public Relations promote the festival in print and visual media, and the Department of Language and Culture, in collaboration with district officials and local committees, organizes participants and festivities.

There is a small committee organized by the district commissioner's office that is in charge of the administration of Mandi Śivarātri. They decide which deities to invite, how much money to give each deity, where they will stay, and how they will participate. This committee began its work in 1983, and the ascendancy of the festival is directly related to this committee's work and its promotion of the festival. Before that, the festival had begun to fade. Fewer deities were attending, and only people from Mandi proper visited the fair. The district commissioner clarified in an interview: "Now the organization of the festival lies with [district] administration. Formerly, it was done by the rulers of Mandi state. So, the administration invites all those deities that were invited by the king, and, of course, some new deities have been added. Some of these deities are rejoining this *melā* [festival] after twenty five years, others after forty, and still others after forty-six years."[53] The committee is therefore responsible for the resuscitation of the festival and for giving the festival its current shape.

In this example, we see clearly a transformation in the shape, style, and meaning of the festival. Where, previously, the festival was predicated on the sovereignty of Mādhorāy and was used as a means to bolster the revenue and status of the deity and its state—not unlike mercantilist economic systems—now the festival is part of a broader system in which it has become a symbol of cultural unity, joining cultural practices with state practices. In the process, certain forms of practice (e.g., *jag*) have been discouraged because they do not fit into the broader emphasis on meeting and unity, and certain deities (e.g., Mahasu) have been favored over others (e.g., Kamru Nāg), which have been excluded. The festival, therefore, condenses new forms of governance and cultural celebration in a peaceful meeting that conforms to the main narratives articulated by ethnohistorians. What this example helps us to see is the way that the state has helped to remake religion in public performances and how, reflexively, the state is constructed in these spaces as the organizer, promoter, and arbiter of these festivities.

VOICES OF POWER: SEPARATING RELIGIOUS AND
SECULAR POWER

In a small village in the Pabbar River valley, I met Rajan, the gūr of a deity often equated with Bhīmākālī. He was originally from the Baspa Valley in Kinnaur and, by his early teens, regularly suffered from fits during which he would shake uncontrollably and lose consciousness. He had heard of a deity, Banar, that was famous for controlling these kinds of fits, so he traveled to the home of Banar, and the gūr told him that his fits would cease for five years. For that period, Rajan was totally free of any fits or seizures. After five years, though, the fits returned, and he was forced to retire from his government job.

Finally, when he was at a festival, the meaning of his fits became clear to him. The gūr of Kimcho, a local deity from Kinnaur, had begun to become possessed by the deity so that he could answer the questions of local villagers, and Rajan immediately lost consciousness and began to play (*khelnā*). As he was relating this story to me, he spoke of this moment in the third person and with the reverence and pride of a chosen man. When he began to play, he spoke in a local dialect of Pahāṛī, which was very different from his own Kanwari, a sign to many of the authenticity of his connection to the deity. That was the beginning of Rajan's career as a healer. For many people in surrounding villages, Rajan became their mode of communicating with the deity. He is a particularly interesting case because the deity that possessed him was not from his natal village and he does not feel limited to speak for only one deity. The deity who speaks to him is a violent incarnation of Kāli. The times he becomes possessed are invariably dramatic and violent. The first time I saw him, he was seated in a small temple devoted to Bhīmākālī overgrown with dry brush. He was screaming. His arms moved erratically as he answered the questions of a small group of male visitors.

Rajan traveled throughout the valley addressing problems through his mediumship and the agency of Kāli. While the interpretation of fits and seizures as a special blessing of power resembles patterns seen in many places across the subcontinent, it is important to note that Rajan and his style were highly unusual. He and his traveling companion were even viewed by many people I talked to as charlatans preying on the villagers.

A family of apple farmers who lived in a house near the Bhīmākālī temple believed strongly that Rajan's stories of sickness were lies and that his violent performances were simply for the benefit of superstitious villagers. They considered his dramatic performances to be signs not of authenticity but of the cheap veneer of his marketing strategy. The invocation of this powerful word—"superstitious"—appeared to me to be an important proclamation of these farmers' desire to speak on behalf of the village's history and its traditions. This word, despite the contemporary discomfort with it, plays a vital role in the everyday Hindi vernacular of Himachal Pradesh. In this case, the farmers, who were educated up to the eighth standard class, used it, as do others, to indicate a particular weakness on the part of some villagers. It is important to note that the people who use this term are not strict rationalists who attended English schools in Chandigarh or Shimla. They too are villagers who offer praise and obeisance to photographs of their ancestors, consult local gūrs for answers to important questions, and host the local deity when it visits their village. The word is thus an important marker used to position oneself relatively. It is used most effectively as a marker of difference that often serves to reify village boundaries. This is the same strategy that has been used against the state as a whole and which was an important factor in the slow process of state recognition. The difference is that the word is increasingly being utilized as a marker from the inside to distinguish Himachal from the plains. In those cases, "superstitious" villagers are lauded as special, singular, and important sites of reverence and preservation.

But in this case, the men of this village used the term to distinguish themselves from what they saw as the inauthentic practices of an illegitimate gūr. They did not believe that Rajan could be an authentic medium because he was not connected to the deity of his own village. It was immediately impossible to them that Rajan could be possessed by the deity they had lived with all their lives. In this complex interaction, one can see the deployment of a set of allied discourses that have emerged in and through the representation of the local traditions of the Western Himalayas and which have become visible through the machinations of the state and its representational apparatus. The first of these is the use of "superstitious" as an index of cultural authenticity. In this case, "superstitious"—which emerged most powerfully in the public speeches of officials such as Parmar but had been present from the time of the earliest colonial reforms—serves as a powerful marker of difference that allows people to position themselves vis-à-vis a set of practices. This is, itself, tied to the production of locality as authenticity. As I discussed earlier, postcolonial land reforms helped create the conditions in which natal villages and local deities became spaces of nostalgia and authority. With this came a sense of authenticity that tied deities and their traditions to the spaces in which they were situated. Thus, the translocal religion of Dev Bhūmi was an abstraction that had cultural currency only within strictly circumscribed spaces. It was a means of uniting people and a means of claiming cultural singularity. It was produced, however, in and through the lauding of local practices and, more specifically, of locality as the site of authenticity. Here, one can see a blurring between the state discourse on locality and authenticity, in daily interactions at more than three thousand meters above sea level, nine kilometers from the nearest dirt road. The boundaries between representation and reality and between the ideal forms of knowledge and the material conditions of everyday life blur into one another. The local and the translocal cannibalize one another. What is most important here is the very emergence of the possibility of "authentic" and "inauthentic" religion, which the gūr is able to condense because of his proximity to the deity.

Once a man attains the status of gūr and learns to access the power of the deity and translate that power into words, answers, blessings, and

Figure 18. Various powerful substances used in Tantric rites. Photo by author.

solutions to problems, he becomes a foundation of social relations. When asked to explain the role of the gūr within the village and the broader community, people generally use a number of phrases and metaphors that reference his role as a medium (*madhyam*). The gūr, in short, is the connective tissue of the deity's public. Many villagers simply said that the gūr was the medium of transaction between themselves and the deity. Many others compared the gūr's position to the most powerful metaphoric system available in Himachal Pradesh: the bureaucratic structures and organizational schemata of the state government.

In the previous chapters, I have shown how various aspects of the state bureaucracy have sought to represent discipline and to remember the local cultural traditions of the region. The ministries that I examined are only one part of a much larger bureaucratic apparatus that increasingly defines the lives of people in the Western Himalayas. From the surveying of land holdings by the revenue office to the management of Panchayat resources to the offering of animal injections and the stabilization of agricultural prices, new systems of discipline, organization, and representation create the frame within which daily life takes place.

It is commonly assumed in secular states that the state agrees to carve out a sociological space in which religion can exist unencumbered by the dictates of politicians and ideologues. In India, freedom of religion is one of the fundamental rights the constitution sought to protect:

> The Fundamental Rights of the Constitution are, in general, those rights of citizens or those negative obligations of the State not to encroach on individual liberty, that have become well-known since the late eighteenth century and since the drafting of the Bill of Rights of the American Constitution.... These rights in the Indian Constitution are divided into seven parts: the Right of Equality, the Right of Freedom, the Rights Against Exploitation, the Right to Freedom of Religion, Cultural and Educational Rights, the Right to Property, and the Right to Constitutional Remedies.[54]

The framers of the constitution and many of the nation's early leaders believed that freedom of religion was one of the primary rights that would allow for the production of a modern, multicultural, pluralistic society. However, the dream of the unification of secularism and modernity has largely been shown to be a dream of the early twentieth century. Everywhere, religion is poking its head into public spaces, from which it was supposed to have vanished. I will examine a system that transgresses the simple divisions between religion and state and between state and society, but in a way that is different from many current discussions.

The majority of contemporary discussions of the so-called failures of secularism center on the all-too-common arguments from the religious right: these are failures constituted by the rupture of the religious into the political. The ascendancy of groups like the BJP and its cultural wing, the RSS, are good examples of this type of failure. Other examples abound. The central development here is the gradual movement of religious values and religious modes of being into the public spotlight and the shifting of authority from the state to religion. While studies of this type of transformation are central to understanding the dynamic between religion and state, they generally overlook a more fundamental shift in the relationship between religion and the state that is instituted by the very powers that make the modern state and religion as it is today possible. I am interested in the ways that the logics of the state, in their forms of knowledge, structures, and organization, have created the conditions for understanding and practicing Himachali religion.

In the upper reaches of a remote valley in the Outer Seraj, in the village of Sarāhan, there is a man with more than three meters of matted locks, who is continually surrounded by children and petitioned by their parents. In his midfifties, he has earned the respect of the people in his village and many in the lands surrounding it. While his long dreadlocks and perpetual chillum smoking are typical of the many renunciates in South Asia, he is far from being a reclusive wanderer in search of personal dissolution. He lives in the center of his native village with his daughter and grandchildren. His house is adjacent to that of his brother, the village president (*pradhān*). His humble home is comfortable; its thick walls of stone and cedar protect him from the harsh winter storms that swirl through these valleys.

A shelf in the receiving room[55] is filled with photographs from his early life. There are pictures of him in an army uniform. In some, he is confident and handsome; in others, he is gloomy and despondent. His early life was difficult. He joined the army when he was young, taking a respected and lucrative appointment in the hopes of earning a better life, but he realized almost immediately he had made a bad decision. He longed for the landscape of his childhood. For generations, his family had been the custodians of the village deity. Although he knew that going back would be difficult and that the shame of having quit the military would weigh heavily on him, he chose to return. On his homecoming, he remained distant and introspective. He spent weeks in the forests with a man who lived alone, surviving on the sparse products of the pine forest. During this time, he learned many skills, both technical and spiritual, that allowed him access to the local deities.[56]

When he talks about this period, he emphasizes the importance of three lessons. The first of these was the importance of clarity. He asserts that no deity is attracted to a person with a dirty soul. A person who is confused or conflicted cannot attract a deity. But it is about more than simply being clean or dirty. He explains that being clean enabled him to make space in his heart for the deity to enter him. While he rarely speaks ill of anyone, he is clear that those gūrs who are without power and influence are predominately in this state because they force the deity to communicate with them. These gūrs are not clear; they sully the message of the deity, misunderstanding or mistranslating it.

The next things he learned in the course of his informal training were the stories of local deities and their proper recitation. These stories (*devbāni* or *bhārathā*) are the key to communicating with the deities. Normally, they are lists of places that outline the history of the deity and its travels before establishment at its current home. In order to contact and thus communicate with a local deity, a gūr must be able to tell its story in either expanded or condensed form. In particular, they must know how to recite the order of locations such that the deity can recognize who is speaking and show itself. Gūrs throughout the Western Himalayas emphasize this technology as foundational to their work. In addition to having a familial tie to the deity and a predisposition for possession, the gūr must be able to recite the *devbāni*.

The gūr from Sarāhan, trained in local systems of tantra-mantra and located a full day away from the nearest dirt road, provides a clear example of the extent to which state logics have penetrated the everyday ontology of villagers in Himachal. It is important to note that this man was remarkable not because of his connection to the state or his knowledge of its operation but rather because of his distance from it— his rejection (in his early life) of the disciplinary apparatus of the army and of the spoils of modernity. His account is therefore exemplary not because he is located within the state, explaining local practices from the state's perspective, but because he is located at the very fringes of the state's power networks yet remains fully implicated in them.

Having spent several days with this man, I finally asked him to explain to me what a gūr was and what he thought a gūr did. He offered the following explanation: "Our knowledge of Tantra is connected to the deity. The gūr is just like the personal secretary who analyses all that is given by the deity. [The deity] reveals [*pratyakṣa*][57] to us every ghost and affliction. Whatever work we must do, the deity will show us the miracle [*pratyakṣa*]. For example, if there is a particularly violent ghost, we will be given the necessary revelation/sight [*pratyakṣa*] before we will be able to heal. Whatever we are shown cannot be told to the people. We can see the planets and the constellations of people, but we cannot tell people about these because the deity will become very angry."[58]

The term that he used to explain the gūr's position, "personal secretary" (he used the English term), refers to a government official who acts as a medium between politicians or government ministers and the public. These secretaries are powerful figures within the state bureaucracy. As such, they are the objects of hatred and jokes, as well as the recipients of lavish praise and other transactions. For individuals who have any association with the broader governmental body, these secretaries are the first—and often final—line of contact with the state. They control interactions between state power and the public and are able to see on both sides of the perceived partition with unequalled clarity. What is so interesting about this connection between the gūr and the personal secretary is that this gūr, like many others, used the metaphor of the secretary to explain himself, to understand his position as a medium between the villagers and the deity. The metaphor was one that I heard many times. It highlights the perceived gap between the people and the state and the parallel between the relative distance of state officials and deities. But what does it mean that the gūr understands himself as a personal secretary?

For many, the suggestion that the gūr is like a secretary is reminiscent of common associations across South Asia that analogize deities with various official positions. For example, the deity Kala Bhairava is understood to be the chief policeman of the sacred city of Varanasi, and innumerable other gods are thought of as village protectors.[59] However, the self-identification of the gūr as the personal secretary of the deity points to a radical transformation, one that gets to the heart of my argument. The doorkeepers and village protectors are operating according to the logic of territorial sovereignty. They protect the boundaries of a distinct entity, between forest and village and between temple and village. By contrast, the gūr, as described by this man, is not concerned with protection, of the strict separation of inside and outside. He is concerned with maintaining order and organizing personal and social worlds—of transforming the social. The logic in this difference is not unlike the logical difference between the forms of sovereignty marked by early British colonialism and late colonialism, more precisely in the movement from the logic of sovereignty to that of governmentality.[60]

PART THREE

Ethics

Becoming Religious and the Mysteries of Being

CHAPTER FIVE

Negotiating Religion

Normalization, Abjection, and Enrichment

ART AND THE POSSIBILITY OF RELIGIOUS EXPERIENCE

M.C. Saxena's most famous sculpture, *Woman with Pot,* stands in a small Shimla garden, lodged between the colonial façade of the Gaiety Theater and an enormous public square teeming with children on ponies, Bengali tourists being photographed in "authentic tribal clothing," and Kashmiri migrants selling hashish to young backpackers. The sculpture, as if mimicking its surroundings, plays with the boundaries separating art and icon, ancient and modern, East and West. It grafts Himachali symbols onto a pan-Indian villager and combines European realism with normative traditions of South Asian iconography. The woman's scarf is from Kinnaur; her pot is from Kangra; and her jewelry is from Spiti. Her hips and posture resemble Ravi Varma's traditional village women, and the color evokes Nehru-era nationalist memorials. At the same time, she is adorned with multicolored lights and rigged with a motion sensor that, when it isn't broken, sprays water onto the statue as visitors approach. She is painted gold, as are many other state-sponsored sculptures, but the surrounding space is marked with the signs of ritual exchange.

For Saxena, the sculpture's power emanates from its harmonious arrangement of these oppositional forces, which generate a supersensory

Figure 19. Grandmother and child in Bushahar. Photo by author.

experience that transcends the limits of body, space, and language. After I had worked with him for a few months, we shared several July afternoons in the garden discussing the sculpture's power with both locals and tourists. These visitors rarely mentioned the sculpture's representation of a Himachali woman, its unique style, or—much to Saxena's disappointment—the technical skill involved in making it. Whether speaking in English or Hindi, they usually discussed the statue's uncanny "spiritual" power. Their stories, like accounts of local deities (*devbāni* or *bhāratha*), revolved around the sculpture's miracle work. However, these were more than fables fabricated to satisfy the theories of a curious visitor or the ego of a praise-hungry artist. They were tales of personal transformation and self-orientation. One woman told us that she visits the sculpture every week and that its miraculous power allows her to speak with her husband, who works in the Persian Gulf. Another man, who owns a local hotel, recounted how the sculpture's power helped him realize that his financial preoccupations were inhibiting his "true spiritual work."

Saxena often returns to these stories about the image's mysterious power. Trained as a psychologist in Lucknow, Saxena argues that true religion is hidden, immaterial, and produced by what he calls "self-work." This conception of religion, a perennialist recension of Protestantism, is increasingly common among Himachal's urban elites. Perhaps more importantly, this conception fits naturally with the consumer-inflected ecumenical aesthetics of Himachal's media worlds and has become one of the foundational components of these worlds. These mystical experiences are fundamental for Saxena because they reveal the world as it is. They reveal truth (*satya*). External rituals (*rīti rivāj*), devotion (*bhakti*), faith (*śraddhā*), and even seeing his beloved statues (*darśan*) can only point us toward what is actually real. They are means, not ends. Only mystical experience can transcend distinctions between religions, nationalities, or races. Only mystical experience can return us to our true selves.

To some, Saxena's theories may appear stale, nostalgic, or even nihilistic. They are interesting in the context of this book not because they reveal the ineradicability of the sacred, Saxena's artistic originality, or even the multivalence of images but rather because they exemplify the impossibility of separating the city, religion, media, and subjectivity in Himachal Pradesh. This book does not refute, support, or even assume a normative conception of "religion" that is tied to tradition, belief, or experience. Nor is it interested in winnowing genuine religion from its ideological husk. Instead, it traces the construction and incalculable effects of the emergence of a new conception of religion in Western Himalayan cities and villages. The question here is not how the city changes religion, how the urban embodies the cosmological, or why religion persists within the modern city. I am interested in the following questions: how does the development of "religion" and "the city" as problems affect what Himachalis value as true, and how do individuals style themselves according to these truths? This chapter examines how these developments simultaneously create and perform a particular art of living. It attempts to understand "religion" and "the city" as aesthetic rather than epistemological or ontological problems. Turning from epistemological or ontological problems (the existence of God, true versus false religion, absolute versus relative values, religion's place in a secular state, etc.) to aesthetic ones allows us to pull back from the imperialist assumptions of Enlightenment reason and instead center analysis on lived bodies and their variegated histories.[1] This appeal to aesthetics is not a clever dissimulation vainly substituting one object for another—the body for the mind or experience for the intellect. It marks a transformation in the style of analysis—its texture, its scope, its method, and its goal.

APPROACHING A CIRCLE

This chapter argues in circles. It traces a media circuit, starting in the remote villages of the upper Himalayas, traveling through a small regional city and into the state capital, only to return to where it started. This circle is a hermeneutic, as much spatial as historical, that uncovers how religion and the city become problems in need of definition, defense, or reform. As this circuit feeds back on itself, centripetal forces draw in energy and inspiration from colonial reformulations of Hinduism, new forms of governmental and spatial organization, and an ascendant cosmopolitan subjectivity. We will see how individuals and institutions embody and exploit "secular" post-Enlightenment critiques of religion even as they attempt to preserve and celebrate the region's religious heritage. These media reflect a normalized recension of Himachali religion authored by urbanized elites and authorized by a constellation of interdependent forces (the modern state, neoliberal economics, and global visual norms) that reproduce themselves in the subtlest desires and imaginations of the people they represent, producing new styles of relating to oneself and to others. Local ritual practices are indexed as signs of authenticity; evacuated of specificity and materiality, they are transformed into symbols in new regimes of meaning. Knowledge, rather than practice, becomes the guarantor of truth. The individual becomes the privileged site of religious experience, the state becomes the primary locus of communal identification, and villages become estranged from the details of their pasts as they turn into "ancient Himachali villages" that model themselves on museological simulacra.

Focusing on a circuit that travels from rural to urban illuminates how new relations between cities and their peripheries are implicated in reshaping religion and secularity. Until recently, the textual bias of religious studies in combination with the presumed inevitability of secularization has dramatically inhibited critical analysis of religion and modern cities as dynamic and interdependent problems. The extensive body of research on religion and place has myopically examined cosmological and spatial mimesis. Studies examining religion in modern urban spaces often understand religion as a substance to be mourned, resurrected, or excised like the diseases of poverty or unemployment. Ironically, even more historically oriented research, guided by the hobbled hope of recuperating the rich pasts lost in secularization's heady embrace, continue to abuse the feeble categorical caricatures we recognize as "world religions."

While guided by radically divergent methods, all these studies make several problematic assumptions. First, they assume that religion is a natural category. It may take many different forms, go unrecognized, or be miscategorized, but its essence is the same across time and space. It is as natural and common as carbon or nitrogen. This assumption is clearly evidenced in the unreflective usage of "religion," "the sacred," and "spirituality" as synonyms. Similar to current discussions of liberals, neocons, or pornography, debates about religion and the secular intensify as the slippage between these terms feeds back into the discourse as ignorance, insensitivity, or imperialism. While such escalation between rival sects is common (if not constitutive), it is shocking when it occurs in the reflective and critical utopia of the modern academy.

Second, they assume that religion and the secular are mutually exclusive categories that provide definitional foundations for other domains. Furthermore, as the preeminent space of secular modernity, the city does not, or will not, have religion. The individual conscience—the location of "natural religion"—remains unscathed even when cloaked by the secular. Setting aside the problematic understanding of religion as a substance to be cleansed or accumulated—like disease or wealth—these assumptions confuse the constant negotiation between religion and its others across spaces of difference. I am not interested in proving that religion is a discovery or a creation, that true religion is free from politics or that religion is a political technology for the reinscription of the power-hungry elites. Instead, this chapter tracks the effects of an increasingly important discourse on religion that understands itself as nonmaterial and apolitical, which proves effective in urban spaces and delocalized media worlds.

RELIGIOUS EXPERIENCE AND
THE PROMISCUITY OF "RELIGION"

Examining how "religion" circulates from margin to center and back reveals a puzzle: even as religion becomes more concrete in visual and verbal media, the object it references becomes more abstract. I will show how the definition and delineation of religion as a distinct sphere of life comparable with politics or economics defines the term's scope. This redaction culminates in the ineffable experiences of an individual. While many would argue that such a transformation is a necessary and epiphenomenal effect of media (or Protestantism), this development is not inevitable. The widespread disclosure of political violence and dictatorial dissimulations suggests a more rational and deliberative future. However, despite the good intentions of judicial inquiries and multilateral institutions, neither constant surveillance nor international treaties can ameliorate the bloody belligerence of war. Televising "surgical strikes" and passing resolutions against "terror" do not make the acts any less violent. The violence of war afflicts bodies as much as it does imaginations, and, despite the core assumptions of the BBC, Fox News, and UNICEF, revealing injustice is not the same as removing it.

The dynamic inflecting the mediation of religion in Himachal is different. Increasingly, religion is recognized as the secret sinew stitching Himachalis together. It is the subject of endless cultural production, and it plays a starring role in history museums and hotel advertisements alike. Across the mediascape, religion is given an awesome power even as its materiality dissolves, its spaces of practice are systematized and resignified, its gods are transformed into abstractions, and its activities are replaced with intentions. The delineation of Himachali religion hides as much as it unveils. It enables translocal identification between individuals separated by time and space, yet it does so by sacrificing existing differentials (of space, gender, ethnicity, etc.). While this narrative might seem familiar, this is a story of revelation and concealment, of possibilities and transformations without agents or ends, not further evidence of the homogenizing power of global capital. Here lies the heart of *Becoming Religious in a Secular Age.*

This story takes some if its cues from what Richard King and Jeremy Carrette call "neoliberal spirituality" while resisting the seductions that draw King and Carrette to the nostalgic chimera of religion before liberal capitalism. According to King and Carrette, recent decades have seen a "silent takeover" of religion by capitalism. Evidence of this transformation is abundant—from the ubiquity of yoga studios to Deepak Chopra's assault on borders and boardrooms. For King and Carrette, the growth of "spirituality" is ineluctably tied to a double privatization: the internalization of religion formulated by Enlightenment philosophes and the recent transformations of global capitalism that many call neoliberalism. King and Carrette argue that neoliberalism consolidates financial and social power in the hands of a few elites. While they have a tendency to conflate neoliberalism with capital consolidation and to equate capitalism with corporate monopolies (thereby distorting neoliberal theory beyond all recognition), connecting spirituality to

contemporary economic paradigms reveals an important transformation in the history of religion. It shows how an internalized, self-
oriented concept of religion dovetails with a powerful new conception
of the subject-as-consumer.[2]

On this account, the internalization of religion is more than an
important component of secularization. It also inaugurates a constellation of differentiated spheres (politics, ethics, governance, etc.), which
can be variously configured. As "self-work" becomes the starting point
for understanding religion, the city, media, and the community, the old
problems (the decline of religion, the ascent of the city, the distortion of
media, the loss of authenticity, etc.) are entirely recast, inaugurating
new styles of being and new aesthetics, supplementing and supplanting
these problems with a new set of concerns and assumptions. Here, the
history of religions becomes a mail-order catalog to augment the self, a
form of personal enhancement akin to private education or a Kate
Spade handbag. The city becomes a space for indulging personal fantasies of consumption, and media become spaces to project self-identity
and voyeuristically enjoy spectacles of self-performance.

These hyperboles capture the spirit of King and Carrette's analysis,
but we must look beyond their reactionary approach to the assumptions
guaranteeing neoliberalism's success. Critiques of neoliberalism often
fail to interrogate why so many people excitedly embrace it or to ask
why so many people excitedly embrace their own demise. The success
of neoliberal capitalism cannot be explained away by invoking the history of postwar multilateralism, corporate greed, or Reagan's cowboy
charisma. Instead, we should look at two basic assumptions underwrit-
ing this seduction (and its critique): faith in individual sovereignty and
the (self-regulating) managerial prowess of the market. Establishing the
individual as the arbiter of all value sets a horizon of intelligibility
within which it is impossible to think otherwise. Coupled with a self-
regulating market, state governance becomes redundant.

To put it simply, the logic of neoliberalism is irrefutable. Locating
authority in personal desires mobilizes an internalized space of atten-

tion to each and every individual in a manner that appears self-chosen. True freedom is natural, unaffected by market machinations or other social forces. Because it is natural, it is beyond sober scrutiny, much like the "noble savage" that has haunted Europe for centuries. From this position, then, resistance to neoliberalism is logically impossible. How could one resist what is natural? All grounds for opposition are absorbed as permissible opinions freely chosen by the individual. Crucially, I am not arguing that neoliberalism is never resistible. Of course, many people continue to resist its intrepid spirit, but once neoliberal paradigms have been established, it becomes difficult to resist them by appealing to nature, freedom, or humanity. For example, in the late 1990s, during the Seattle World Trade Organization protests, rioters performed the paradox of their own positions, expressing their personal freedoms while condemning neoliberalism. To be anything other than a parody, such protestors would have to institute radically different paradigms. To understand how neoliberal paradigms have established themselves in Himachal, I turn now to some of the ubiquitous video CDs (VCDs) filling Himachal's bazaars and village shops.

VILLAGE VIDEOS AND THE THEOLOGICAL WORK OF POSTPRODUCTION

Every Himachali village with even the smallest of bazaars has a photo studio. If there is a chai stall and a bus stop, there is also a photo studio. As well as taking photographs, many of these studios also offer video services. While most of the commercial value of these services revolves around wedding videos, many of the videographers would rather spend their days recording local rituals. At nearly every festival I attended over the past several years, there was at least one local videographer recording the event, and at some of the better-known events, there were as many as four.

These popular videos range in length from ten minutes to several hours and circulate mainly within the village itself, passed from house

Figure 20. *Bhunda* (human
sacrifice) rite performed in 2007.
Photo by author.

to house as VHS tapes or VCDs. The content is remarkably consistent, and postproduction work is almost nonexistent. They focus primarily on the main ritual transactions of the festival (ritual preparations including rope sliding, ecstatic "playing" [*khelnā*], sacrifices, and various types of transgressive acts). There is almost no concern with interpreting individual sections of the rite symbolically or to having the rite stand in metonymically for the village, region, or state as a whole.

A good example of these videos is a four-hour VCD of a Kahika festival that is enormously popular with locals.[3] This video, filmed over five days, includes all the major ritual events of the festival without any commentary, interviews, or explanations by participants. This elaborate and expensive festival, which is performed every five or seven years, revolves around the transfer of sins (*pap*) by the temple officials and the village deity onto a man from the Nar caste (a subgroup of the Kolis caste). The festival climaxes when the Nar, reciting Pahāṛī mantras and throwing leaves of barley and bhekhal, takes the sins of those present upon himself, a sacrifice that will kill metaphorically him. He is then enclosed in a circle and begins verbally assaulting the deities and the temple officials. After this, the deity's gūrs become violently possessed. The music is frenzied, some of the spectators also become possessed, and several of the men (spectators and mediums alike) even pierce their cheeks or tongues. At this time, the Nar is lying under a special cloth, and the primary gūr shoots an arrow over him. This marks the final death of the Nar. According to many people I inter-viewed, shooting the arrow over the Nar, as opposed to directly into him, is a recent modification, as is the final rite. In this rite, the Nar, who is unconscious, is loaded onto a funeral bier and carried around the temple seven times. Meanwhile, others from the Nar caste hurl insults at the temple officials. Again, the deity's mediums become pos-sessed and attempt to revive the Nar. In this particular VCD, he is revived, but many villagers tell stories of other festivals when the Nar died from the weight of the sins he had assumed.

How can we account for the popularity of videos depicting rites that most Hindu nationalists would find abhorrent and many others would denounce as primitive or superstitious? I believe their popularity high-lights the absence of religion as a problem for these filmmakers and their audiences, who have yet to be disturbed by the problem of defin-ing themselves in relation to religion. This is not to say that these vil-lagers do not "have religion" in the normative sense articulated by early European travelers, missionaries, or colonial administrators. Rather, my argument is that the separation of religion as an autonomous sphere of life—distinct from governance, economics, or politics and composed of specific beliefs and practices—has no palpable reality in these vid-eos. Accordingly, there is little need to defend or define it. This lack of conscious defense or definition is reflected in the response I was repeat-edly given when soliciting an explanation of the rite and its various ele-ments from spectators. Whether I was asking why the Nar is carried around the temple seven times or why participants needed bhekhal thorns and leaves instead of cedar branches, the answer was always the same: "Because this is our *devīdevatā saṇskṛti*" (literally "our god-goddess culture").[4] As I discussed in the introduction, this phrase pro-vides its own explanation; it does not need further clarification.

In postulating the absence of religion as a problem, I do not mean to suggest that that the villagers producing and watching these videos cannot recognize the difference between government and temple authorities or that they are unaware of categories like Hindu, Buddhist,

and Muslim. They are as acutely aware of governmental property regulations and the neglected schools and roads of their villages as they
are of disputes between Hindus and Muslims across the subcontinent. I
only wish to indicate that the rites appearing in these videos are not
understood as markers of communal difference, as somehow distinct
from political economy, as foundations of personal identity, or as signs
of superstition or authenticity. Yet, as these videos, and the people
making and watching them, move toward urban centers, they are reim-
agined in precisely these ways.

As they circulate, the videos are increasingly subjected to delocaliz-
ing pressures. In the villages where they were initially produced, they
were never sold. They were passed from house to house and occasionally shown to small groups. Yet, as they move outside these villages,
they are subjected to market forces and the particularities of Himachali
urban sensibilities. New aesthetics, new public demands, and new audiences redefine what can be shown and what will sell. Accordingly, videos of festivals and temples that are aimed at gaining wider distribution
must undergo extensive postproduction work. This is demonstrated by
the lumbering arrival of a talented young filmmaker to the state's capital in Shimla.

Raj Kumar is an ambitious young artist from a small village near
Kotkai in the Shimla district. Buoyed by the success of his festival films
in Kotkai and surrounding villages, he moved to Shimla to sell them to
local cable networks and national distributors. Yet he quickly discovered that the aesthetic in Shimla was not like that in his natal village.
His films were well shot, well lit, and well framed. From a strictly technical perspective, they were much better than most videos airing on
local television or for sale in Shimla. However, producers and distributors have been hesitant to broadcast or distribute them. Kumar has not
been to film school and had spent little time outside the valley of his
birth before moving to Shimla. The style and content of his films developed from intimate engagement with the ritual practices he has known
since childhood. Like the videos of Kahika, they revolve around ritual

transactions, pragmatically picturing ritual preparations, sacrifice, possession, and ritual piercing.

Recognizing the need to adapt his videos for new audiences, Kumar and a small group of editors laboriously reedited his videos. They removed all images of ritual slaughter, added calendar art[5] of pan-Indian goddesses to translate local deities into transregional mythospheres, and shot new scenes of snowcapped mountains and local dances to fill the holes where the controversial rituals has once been. However, none of these adjustments boosted the commercial success of the videos. So Kumar is attempting a new approach that reflects the cinematic norms of documentaries produced in Shimla and the short clips that pepper local news broadcasts, clips the producers refer to as "soft stories." He is adding voiceover commentary by several local experts on Himachali traditions, who are able not only to make structural comparisons between the rites or stories of one region with another but also to translate onscreen bodies into marketable idioms.

Kumar's final attempt to render his films marketable highlights the agency of a new class of experts who are integral to the production of Himachal as a site of identification. Over the past three decades, local historians, scholars, and thoughtful villagers, who collectively call themselves *sāhityakār,* or "writers," have developed a large body of information about the diverse traditions of the Western Himalayas. These writers acquire the authority to speak for Himachali culture by mastering this body of literature and thus become the gatekeepers of authentic Himachali religion. The addition of expert voiceover by these writers should be the final addition Kumar's films need to break into the market in Shimla. While expert voiceover has always been a common element of documentary film, the addition of it here is much more than a response to new media methods. It reveals the introduction of religion as a problem that must be addressed by anyone representing Himachal.

The introduction of this problem is further evidenced by the changing meaning of *devīdevatā saṃskṛti* ("god-goddess culture"), a phrase that Kumar's commentators employ to name Himachali religion. In most rural areas, the term denotes the practices represented in Kumar's unedited videos. It names the diverse forms of performance and thought accompanying Himachal's local deities. It can refer to traditions of pro- pitiating deities in towns, villages, springs, mountains, fields, and else- where. It also includes the practices associated with these gods, includ- ing fairs (*melā*) and festivals (*utsav*), ritual prognostication (*pūchnā/ panā*), temple management (*adhikārī*), and even songs (*gāthā*) and stories (*kathā*). However, when it is used in these village settings, it is a descrip- tive rather than a normative term. In those milieus, the term is used to name what people do, not what they should do.

However, when it is used in urban centers and elite media, the term asserts normative force, becoming virtually synonymous with the Eng- lish word "religion." In fact, the terms are often used interchangeably. The semantic condensation implied in this shift is similar to that which has occurred to the Hindi word *dharm,* which is also equated with the word "religion" in much of Northern India. In that compression, as Simon Weightman and S.M. Pandey have argued, the English word "religion" becomes the "determinate factor in Hindi usage."[6] The trans- formation of *dharm* into "religion" evidences an amazing feat of linguis- tic compression and homogenization. The term is common in early Vedic sources and texts of the classical period, yet its range of usage was enormous, including everything from ritual action, law, and duty to universal order and customary practice. Moreover, before the nine- teenth century, it was almost never used to signify anything like a vol- untary system of beliefs. The term closest to this conception was *darśana* (literally, "viewpoint"), which is generally translated as "phi- losophy" or "school thought."

Yet, as impressive as this compression is, the fact that *dharm* was increasingly understood as "religion" starting in the early nineteenth century did not mean that the people using it in this way all had the same conception of religion. Weightman and Pandey, like most scholars who fail to appreciate the nuanced conceptual and practical histories of religion, assume that what they call "the English concept of religion" was unified. The semantic slippage here between English as a language and the English as a colonial power is instructive. The shift Weightman and Pandey identify was first formulated under colonial rule and was facilitated by missionary activity, colonial forms of knowledge, new state organization, and the increased use of English as an administrative and educational language. Yet the conceptions of religion mapped onto *dharma* were anything but singular. For early Christian missionaries in Bengal and their interlocutors, *dharma* signified a system opposed to their true religion, which they termed *satyadharma*. For radical reformers like Dayānanda Saraswatī, founder of the influential reform movement Ārya Samāj, *dharma* sounded a lot like the natural religion of Enlightenment philosophes: "I believe in a religion based on universal and all-embracing principles which have always been accepted as true by mankind.... Hence it is that the religion in question is called the primeval eternal religion [*sanātana dharm*], which means that it is above the hostility of all human creeds whatsoever."[7] Tweaking Saraswatī's formulations almost two decades later, the *sanātana dharma* textbooks, written with the help of theosophist Annie Besant, understood *dharma* as an inclusive ecumenical framework in which all traditions could be situated within Hinduism. And finally, for V.D. Savarkar, the patron saint of Hindu nationalism and the whipping boy of Indian secularism, neither *dharma* nor "religion" could encompass what he meant by *Hindutva*.

So if *devīdevatā saṇskṛti* is increasingly understood in Himachal as a translation of "religion," what kind of religion does it signify? How does this definition separate religion from the secular? Where are the boundaries between tolerance and tolerability? One illuminating response to these questions is Mandi's famous photo gallery, Himachal Darshan.

HIMACHAL DARSHAN

Mandi is a small regional capital experiencing rapid urban growth. The city sits at the confluence of two rivers and is a crossroad between the upper Himalayas and the North Indian plains. On the outskirts of the city, on the bank of the Beas River, there is a small concrete building with a brick and cedar façade and a name that unites regional identity with pan-Indian temple practices, Himachal Darshan. This space is the brainchild of Birbal Sharma, Himachal's most famous photographer. Displaying more than one hundred of his photographs, the gallery combines the aesthetics of a museum, a temple, and a rest stop. The physical space is similar to many provincial Indian museums: the lighting is poor, the guard is disinterested, and the dry smell of unwashed floors hangs in the air.

While innumerable writers have attempted to represent Himachali culture in textual form, Birbal's photo gallery is the first to represent it in images. He chose the images that hang on the walls from an archive of more than thirty thousand, many of which were used in magazine brochures, tourist ads, and newspapers of the 1980s and '90s. As the visual condensation of three decades of visual memory work, the collection reveals some of the most characteristic assumptions about Himachal, particularly what is shown as Himachali religion. Yet Birbal's intervention is more than a translation from one medium to another. Taken as a whole, the museum advances two positions that may strike some as antithetical. It presents Himachal as simultaneously modern and spiritually authentic, and in so doing, I argue, it both pictures and promotes a new aesthetic, a new manner in which "Himachal" pierces the flesh.

Two themes dominate Birbal's photos: the modern and the timeless. Old temple spires are pictured against snowcapped peaks, and cedar carvings are set in verdant gardens. Next to these images are panoramas of the state's major cities and its industrial landmarks. This strategic juxtaposition of the ancient and the urban must not be read as a sign of incomplete modernization. It illustrates the style of Himachali modernity. The state's authenticity is grounded simultaneously by its antiquity and its progressiveness, a unique combination that, for present-day Himachalis, testifies to the state's divine election. Birbal's

Figure 21. Himachal Darshan photo gallery. Photo by author.

museum hypostatizes this style by announcing Himachal as *dev bhūmi*, "the land of gods"—a popular slogan that is commonly seen in buses, hotels, and filling stations. Invoking divinity to justify claims of cultural singularity is hardly novel, but Birbal's museum is more than a simple reflection of the region's changing character. It is an integral part of the creative matrix from which this character is created, generating the very practices it represents.

To understand this matrix, we must probe beyond the gorgeous scenery and boastful slogans to find that which is excluded from the frame. The gallery contains no pictures of animal sacrifice, ritual possession, or even the dancing of the deities in the chariots (*rāth*). These practices are the most common rites performed in and around village temples, and they are foundational to the ritual logics linking villagers and their deities. Birbal's omission of these rites is as conscious as it is understandable. He has excluded these rites from the normative understanding of Himachali religion because he considers them to be signs of "superstition" and "backwardness" that should be removed from *devīdevatā saṇskṛti.* This exclusion refocuses the shape and scope of Himachali religion. But if the most common ritual interactions between villagers and their deities are not permissible in these contexts, what replaces them?

In a 2000 interview with the *Tribune,* Birbal offered some clues to answering this question. He said that he is most interested in picturing "the innocent people [of Himachal], their dances and songs, their faith in the village gods." But the urge to present these images is more than an artistic impulse: "It is a matter of regret that today we are leading an ostentatious life and are oblivious of our rich cultural heritage.... With my camera I am trying to preserve this heritage. The camera freezes particular events which become valuable for our future."[8] This quote illuminates the normative dimensions of Birbal's project; he seeks to capture specific events that can be valuable for the future of Himachal. The key to understanding which particular events will become valuable lies in the gallery's name itself, which is a conscious play on the pan-Indian temple practice of *darśan.* Understood in this light, the gallery is simultaneously a place where one sees the natural and cultural diversity of the state and a space to participate in the ritual of *darśan,* which is a visual exchange between the eyes of a deity and a petitioner. While *darśan* has been an important part of temple practices at sites across South Asia for centuries, only in the late colonial and postcolonial periods has it functioned as glue binding the domestic rites of urban dwellers in Mumbai with the village practices of Madhya Pradesh in what Diana Eck calls "the central act of Hindu worship."[9] In both the style of engagement it elicits and the content of its images, the gallery constructs Himachali ritual practice as a personal visual exchange. This construction allows Himachalis as well as tourists to have Himachal *darśan.* Moreover, it defines, as it simultaneously performs, the essence of Himachali religion. As one visitor aptly put it in the gallery's comment book, "Birbal Sharma has revealed the true inner form of Himachal." This revelation also transforms Himachal, much as India itself was transformed during colonial rule, into a deity capable of participating in *darśan*.

While many would consider the combination of a photo gallery and a temple a transgression of the secular, it is deft negotiations such as Birbal's that define the boundaries and relations between religion and the secular. Birbal's selection of specific images, exclusion of others, and framing of the experience in terms of *darśan* reveals the region's true form and defines the boundaries of what is and is not legitimately religious. All of those things that are excluded are subjected to different logics—of politics, of economics, or of social reform. In spaces like this, we would do well to pay close attention to how these boundaries are established rather than condemning or celebrating these spaces as a challenge to notions of religion and the secular. They are part of a broader ongoing negotiation to define Himachal and its god-goddess culture, a process facilitated by the circulation of these new conceptions to and from cities.

To completely understand this process, a thorough reception study of these media and the development activities of different state ministries would be necessary, but here I can only offer a short example that is symptomatic of these interactions. In addition to creating and distributing different types of media, the Department of Language and Culture and the Department of Tourism employ officials to mediate the state's relations with its villages. These officials are supposed to promote local literature, write about village practices, preserve rituals in danger of disappearance, help manage local temples, and prepare village temples for pilgrim traffic.

Radha Sharma, a language officer working in Kullu district, is typical of these officials. She is well educated, articulate, and compassionate. She attends planning meetings in Shimla, designs policies for the development of her district, allocates governmental resources, and attends nearly every festival in Kullu district. As one of the primary links between remote villages and Shimla, her influence can hardly be overestimated, as the following story illustrates.

Figure 22. Goat sacrifice. Photo by author.

After returning from a distant village festival one afternoon, she boasted proudly of her work that week. The festival was an annual celebration attended by other deities in the region that are bound together by mythic family relations. The festival was accompanied by dancing, prognostication rites, and the reestablishment of a sacred tree outside the village temple. Traditionally, it culminated in the sacrifice of several hundred goats, the meat of which was shared by all those in attendance. But Sharma, a vegetarian and advocate of nonviolence (*ahiṃsā*), was offended by this. She has been deeply influenced by the new conception of religion that identifies ritual slaughter (*bali*) as a superstitious vestige of the past. She told me she was ashamed of such practices and appalled they were still happening. She was offended by the sight of blood and disturbed by the rapacity with which the villagers consumed the meat.

So, rather than helping coordinate the festival, as she normally would, she offered its organizers a choice. She told them that she would eliminate the modest monetary support provided for the festival by the government unless they eliminated the sacrifices. Already hamstrung by migrating populations, decreasing crop yields, and the seizure of temple lands in the 1960s and 1970s, the temple administrators were in no position to argue. I asked her how she could restrict religious practices in the name of the government. Doesn't the Indian constitution prohibit this? "Yes," she said. "Of course we have a secular constitution. We cannot interfere in religion, but animal sacrifice is not religion. It is a barbaric and violent practice."[10] Like Shimla's video editors, Birbal, and the Department of Tourism, Sharma performed a separation defining the boundaries of religion. For her, as for the others, "true religion" is contemplative, devotional, and peaceful. It cannot be divisive or violent. Religion is what binds Himachalis to one another and encourages what Ashok Thakur, director of both the Department of Tourism and the Department of Language and Culture, calls Himachal's "culture of peace."

URBAN ORBITS: COMPLETING THE CIRCUIT

The previous section traversed Himachal, from its remote villages to its state capital and back again. This journey began with rough videos of sacrificial rituals, largely unedited footage that was circulated within small villages and valleys. As these videos moved toward urban centers, they were edited. Voiceovers and images of pan-Indian deities were added, and potentially offensive rites were eliminated. Even with these adjustments, the circulation of the videos was limited to the homes of curious elites. They had to be further digested, further stripped of their practices and contexts, to serve as cultural masala to the daily news. This section orbits the perimeter of several interrelated issues. But what are they exactly? If this is not a pallid academic imitation of the region's popular pilgrimage circuits, what is the gravitational force attracting video editing practices, exhibition aesthetics, and religion in contemporary Himachal Pradesh? And more importantly, why does this matter?

The force binding these different themes can be summarized by turning the subtitle of Himachali writer Pankaj Mishra's eloquent novel

Temptations of the West: How to Be Modern in India, Pakistan, Tibet and Beyond (2006) into a question: what does it mean to be modern in Himachal Pradesh? This question pervades the issues discussed here, but not as an imperial assessment—"how natives really think"—that contradicts what Himachalis *say* they think or do. While the question's history is too complicated to be adequately discussed here, it must be recognized that it is coextensive with the question of Himachali identity. It is a question that Himachalis themselves feel compelled to ask. Since Y. S. Parmar first sketched the faintest lines of Himachali identity in his fight for Himachal's statehood, these two questions (how to be modern and how to be Himachali) have been inextricable.

Establishing this question as the gravitational force aligning the disparate sections of this chapter, it is now possible to understand why "religion," "the city," and "media" must be examined as dynamic and mutually constitutive. In contemporary Himachal, it is not possible to separate these concepts or to describe them with terms like "modern," "secular," or "liberal," which place them in historicist narratives. Religion in contemporary Himachal doesn't persist in spite of urbanization or mediation. Rather, as Bob Orsi has argued, the city and its technologies are "the very materials for such expressions and experiences."[11] Urban spaces and mediascapes are more than locations where religion happens. They inflect the conditions in which modern religion is allowed to appear and are reflexively altered by these appearances, producing nothing less than a new aesthetics, a new way of being in the world.

This chapter has attempted to enact the gravitational force described above rather than belaboring its implications or tediously cataloging the inadequacies of other scholars. However, to avoid misinterpretation, allow me to lay a few cards on the table. From the perspective of this book's orbit, many questions driving present-day work on religion—whether in religious studies, urban studies, or media studies—are ill conceived. "Problems" like religion's resurgence in so-called modern secular states, the media distorting Islam's "peaceful" character, or Christian charlatanry are problems only in relation to erroneous assumptions. Modern is not equal to agnostic; world religions are not natural, timeless categories; secularism is not equivalent to religious equality; and cities are not only spaces with public sanitation and high population densities but also sites of creative possibility. To make these assumptions is to perpetuate the politics of truth many of these studies criticize.

By contrast, this book employs a radically historicized concept of religion in its limited attempt to make sense of what religion means, how it is inhabited, and how it is represented in an increasingly urban, globalized, and highly mediated region of the Western Himalayas. I have attempted to resist the sticky-sweet seductions of reducing religion to religious experience, assuming that modernity equals secularism, and using "sacred," "spiritual," and "religious" as synonyms. I have also resisted interpreting globalization, urbanization, and mediation as limitations on human creativity or salves against global poverty and inequality.[12] Resisting these tendencies creates an analytic space in which religion, the city, and media emerge as products of human agency and creativity while being implicated in the very production of this agency, a space in which knowledge is embodied and desires are produced rather than discovered. Arguing that thought and desire are positioned is not to invoke a simple "culturalist" stance that validates the often arbitrary boundaries dividing contemporary geopolitical arrangements but rather to turn toward the messy vitality of human life with its inconsistencies and assumptions, its blind spots and illuminations. Most importantly, this approach avoids unproductive debates over origins, authenticity, and teleology (whether historical or theological), which reveal little more than personal agendas and the limitation of imagination.

My goal is not to lament the loss of local specificities or to celebrate cosmopolitanism. I am interested in how Himachal's conceptual, practical, and aesthetic reorientations manifest themselves across Himachal's mountains and media. Tracing how the question of "being modern" is framed, answered, and embodied discloses much more than investigating how "local culture" is portrayed in global media or the persistence of religion in "secular" cities. I will demonstrate how each of the actors in this story embodies, and thus theorizes, religion, media, and the city. And perhaps most surprisingly, I will provide a glimpse, if only in flashes, of why a stable definition of religion continues to elude social scientists while simultaneously being self-evident for those who mobilize its powers. To further illuminate my argument, the following three stories show just how complicated this process has become.

BECOMING RELIGIOUS IN LIGHT OF DEVELOPMENT, CAPITALISM, AND HASHISH

In the upper Kullu Valley, there is a small temple dedicated to a goddess identified as Gāyatri Devī. This temple and another smaller *śikhara*-style temple are located in a small village called Jagat Sukh.[13] The history of Jagat Sukh (which was originally called Nast) is extraordinarily interesting. In the earliest period of Kullu's recorded history, this small village was the center of economic and political life in the valley. The kings ruled much of the land surrounding this village for at least twelve generations. All of the stories associated with Kullu's earliest history, including its foundational myth, took place in or around this village.

In this story, as told by Hutchinson and Vogel[14] and thenceforth repeated for decades across languages and media, the founder of Kullu, Behangamani Pal, is recognized as a Rajput and a man who would rule the region. When he is on his way to a fair, Jajoli Jatra, he passes an old woman who asks him to carry her to the festival. He agrees. In oral versions of this story that are now current in this area, he carries her for miles up impossibly steep hills. After he proves his strength and dedication, the woman jumps off his back and tells Behangamai to jump on hers. This is when he realizes that he has been carrying a goddess. In the official chronicle version of the tale, she is Haḍimbā, although some versions say she was a different goddess. She then bestows her grace on

Behangamai, and he soon conquers much of the surrounding area. After taking control of some of the surrounding valleys, he sets up his kingdom in Jagat Sukh. Clear dates for this establishment are not certain, though it appears to have occurred in the early centuries of the Common Era.

As the empire grew and became stronger, the early Pal rulers consolidated their power in Jagat Sukh before they were finally able to overtake the rulers at Naggar and establish themselves as sovereign. There are two impressive monuments from this early period (which have been dated to around the seventh or eighth centuries, although there were numerous later additions). The first is an impressive *śikhara*-style temple dedicated to Śiva.[15] In addition to the main image, there is also a fine image of Mahiṣāsura, which Penelope Chetwode describes in her characteristically dramatic prose: "She is four-armed and carries triśula (trident) in one of her right hands, which she is sticking into Mahisha the buffalo demon, whose tail she grasps in one of her left hands.... Sculpturally speaking this is one of the most rhythmically pleasing images of the goddess in Kulu, and reminiscent of the best work on the Kailasa at Ellora."[16] The other temple in that courtyard is dedicated to Sandhyā (Gāyatri) Devī. An inscription on the temple records that it was built in 1428.[17] However, it has built the past into itself in rich layers. There are carvings and small shrines datable to the seventh century[18] and a new marble floor that the temple priest told me had been built in the previous year. It is a palimpsest of Kullu history.

This same priest, a woman, related the origin of the temple not to the foundation of the valley kingdom but to the rescue of the Pāṇḍav brothers famously chronicled in the *Mahābhārata*. Thus, the temple is intimately connected to some of the most important people and events of Kullu's past. One would expect this site to be not only an important pilgrimage site but also a major tourist destination. In fact, there is a sign on the adjacent road announcing it, and many tourist pamphlets have been produced. However, the site suffers from one fatal flaw. It is located on the wrong side of the river. Although there are now roads that run up both sides of the Beas, the road that runs along the left bank is still under construction in many places. The road on the right bank has been the main thoroughfare since paved roads were introduced in the area. This development has had disastrous consequences for the status of Jagat Sukh. In contrast to other sites that are more modern and less important to the valley's history, this village is quietly overlooked by tourists who travel up the other bank and likely equate Kullu and its history with the town of Manali (although Manali has only recently become an important center in the region).

Jagat Sukh is only a few miles from Manali, arguably Himachal's most important tourism center, and many villagers, clearly aware of the village's noble past, can feel the seduction of tourism. For decades now, tourism has been touted as a social and economic salve. It is the one resource that the state could easily develop and that could benefit the entire populace with little change. The Department of Tourism and its allied forces promised benefits to areas that seemed to offer potential. Jagat Sukh was one such place. However, even though tourism to the region has exploded, and everyone from farmers to pan vendors on the right bank of the Beas has benefited, many on the left bank remain impoverished. This poverty is compounded by the harsh winters that keep villagers inside for three to five months each year. Money must be earned in the summer to sustain families throughout the winter. When they don't earn enough, people go hungry.

Many of the villagers I spoke to, and the priests (all women) in particular, explained the situation in Jagat Sukh in a way that had much in common with what James Ferguson describes as "abjection and the aftermath of modernism" in Zambia. In the early years of Zambian independence, the new government promised a "first class" world of comfort and prosperity, "complete with up-to-date attractive airline hostesses."[19] Ferguson describes the postcolonial situation in Zambia as a process of abjection. By "abjection," he means the process of being prohibited from something that was promised, which still lies just beyond grasp:

The experience of abjection here was not a matter of being merely excluded from a status to which one had never has a claim but of being expelled, cast-out-and-down from that status by the formation of a new (or newly impermeable) boundary. It is an experience that has left in its wake both a profound feeling of loss as well as the gnawing sense of a continuing affective attachment to that which lies on the other side of the boundary. When copperbelt workers of an older generation spoke to me with such feeling of having once, long ago, owned a fine tuxedo or attended a concert by the Ink Spots or eaten T-bone steak at a restaurant, they were registering a connection to the 'first class' that they had lost many years before but still felt, like the phantom pains from a limb long ago amputated.[20]

This feeling of having lost a limb became clear to me when I interviewed the *pujārī* at the Gāyatri temple. After having interviewed all types of people associated with temples in village and urban settings, I had grown accustomed to what I felt was a normal range of reactions, from cold disdain to exhausting enthusiasm. However, there was something different about this woman, something tragic. When I reached the temple, she ushered us in with a wealthy couple from Punjab. We sat behind them and listened as she told the story of how the goddess Gāyatri saved the Pāṇḍav brothers. When she was done, she asked the couple for money. They handed her a one-hundred-rupee note, which I thought was exceptionally generous, but she demanded more and kept demanding until the couple left, confused and angry. We sat for a while longer, and two young women from a nearby village entered the temple. They held their heads low and petitioned the goddess. Each of the women placed a single rupee in the bowl. The priest scowled and pulled her wool shawl over her ample body. "Is that all?" she asked sharply. "You don't expect any help for that kind of money." The women turned and left, seemingly accustomed to such abuse. As they left, she turned to us, as if in anticipation of our departure, and said: "People these days have no faith. They think only of themselves." When we left, we were treated similarly to the others. Even after presenting the priest with a Polaroid photograph—a gift that almost never failed to soothe the most difficult of cultural misunderstandings—and a small contribution, she abused us as we left.

I have spent a long time thinking about this woman and returned to her and Jagat Sukh on several occasions. Initially, I thought she was a money-hungry temple official like many in Mathura or Varanasi. I thought of her simply as a victim of commodification and accumulated wealth. However, I have come to see her as something altogether more tragic, the flotsam of development that did not move in a straight line. Development and modernization are not unilinear progressive forces. They move in fits and starts along different and often conflicting paths. While many in Himachal have benefited from tourism—from the wealth it has brought, the infrastructure it has created, and the opportunities it has fostered—for others, such as that priest, this promise was a poison.

But I do not simply want to vilify tourism along with development and modernity. These nouns are too abstract for me; they cloud more than they clarify. There are many other cases where the opposite has occurred, where a site has been elevated to extraordinary heights and those families traditionally associated with the site have benefited greatly. One such site is only a few miles away, in Manali.

In contrast to the palpable sense of despair and abjection in Jagat Sukh, a few miles up the road is another world. One immediately gets the sense of prosperity, hope, and plenitude when walking around Manali. In the summer months, when India's northern plains are baked and barren, people from across the nation travel to rest and relax. The majority of those who come to the Western Himalayas stay in Manali, which has historically been a major stopping point for traffic between Ladakh, Kashmir, Tibet, and the South Asian plains. For both national and international tourists, Manali is the center of tourism in the Western Himalayas. Not only does it have a fine climate and spectacular views, it has also been advertised as an ancient religious center and is now one of the primary pilgrimage destinations in the Western Himalayas.

Adjacent to Manali is a small village called Dungri. In this village, there is a striking pent-roofed temple often referred to as one of the most beautiful in the Kullu Valley. Though the structure that stands there now is not of extreme antiquity, the legends associated with the site's goddess are. However, there is considerable ambiguity regarding the early origin and character of the goddess. As mentioned above, the earliest ruler of the valley is said to have met a goddess on his way to a festival. This goddess then blessed him and his family with control of the valley. This association is confirmed not only in the genealogical records of the state and by popular memory but also by the fact that she is still referred to as "grandmother" by the royal family. What is not at all clear is her precise identity. She has many names. Most commonly, she is called Hirma Devī. Hirma Devī is a goddess with several shrines throughout the Western Himalayas, including in Kinnaur and Mandi. In one of the early colonial sources, Alfred Frederick Pollock Harcourt's *The Himalayan Districts of Kooloo, Lahoul and Spiti,* she is called Hurimba. In addition to offering a story about the builder of the temple, who was said to have cut off his hand after the project so that he could not build a temple so beautiful again, Harcourt tells us that the goddess was said to have lived in "Purus Ram's time" and received human sacrifice.[21]

The astute reader may hear echoes in the name "Hurimba" of a more widely known goddess. The great historians Hutchinson and Vogel certainly did. In their seminal *History of the Punjab Hill States,* they made a leap that would forever change the character of the area. Drawing on a story told in Harcourt's book, they forged the following assertion, which I quote in full so that readers can make their own conclusions:

> Captain Harcourt thus relates the tradition: "A chief or, as the people call him, a demon, by the name Tandee, fixed his abode on the Kooloo side of the Rohtung pass, and with him lived his sister, Hurimba, whose temple is now at Doongree, near Menalee, in the Upper Bias Valley. Bhaem Sen, the Pandu, next appears on the scene, his mission being to clear Kooloo of all the demons in it, but in this instance he contented himself with running off with Hurimba; and Tandee, aggrieved at this, fought with Bhaem Sen and was in the conflict slain."[22]

Harcourt goes on to relate stories about the children of this union, Makarsa and Bhot, which Hutchinson and Vogel later interpreted as a local story accounting for the different geographic origins of the valley in Kullu (Makarsa) and in Tibet (Bhot). However, Hutchinson and Vogel make another, more important, association, one that continues to inflect practices at the site to this day. In explaining the assertion, they argue that the above version is the form in which the legend has come down from early times in Kullu, but in reality, it is a garbled version of a very ancient legend or myth regarding Bhīma the second of the wife of the Pāṇḍav brothers, found in the *Mahābhārata* (first canto, chapters 152–156). There, Haḍimbā is a *rakshasi* (man-eating demoness), in whom we recognize the goddess Hirma, or Hirimba, of the Kullu Valley. Her brother, called Hiḍimba in the epic and Tandi in the Kullu legend, was killed by Bhimasena. Haḍimbā is probably a goddess who was worshipped from very remote times, and her worship, which was attended with human sacrifices, was non-Aryan.

They appear to be basing their conclusion on two things: the similarity to the name of the goddess and the connection to Bhimasena. I want to point out a few things. First, the association between the goddess of the temple in Dungri and the *Mahābhārata* does not appear to be one that villagers were making before it was asserted by Hutchinson and Vogel. Other great historians of the colonial era, such as Alfred Frederick Pollock Harcourt, Horace Arthur Rose, and William Moorcroft, all fail to mention any such association. It is possible that they simply missed the association, and this is a likely explanation, at least in the case of Moorcroft. However, for the other two writers, this hypothesis cannot hold. They each spent years in this area collecting information. They were, moreover, just as eager as Hutchinson and Vogel to associate local shrines with Brahmanical paradigms. Second, it seems important to note that the story, as it is told in the *Mahābhārata*, does not share that many similarities with the version given by Hutchinson and Vogel. In the *Mahābhārata* version of the story, Haḍimbā arrives early on when the exiled Pāṇḍav brothers are traveling in the forest controlled by Hiḍimba, her demon brother. Hungry for human flesh, Hiḍimba sends his sister to bring him the brothers for his breakfast. However, as soon as she sees the beauty of Bhīma (one of the brothers), Haḍimbā immediately falls in love, turns herself into a beautiful woman, and proposes to him. He initially refuses her so that he can protect his brothers and his mother. When he becomes tired of waiting, Hiḍimba comes to kill the Pāṇḍav brothers himself. When he arrives, he discovers his sister, possessed with lust, and threatens to kill her too. Bhīma stands up for Haḍimbā and fights the demon, ultimately slaying him. Haḍimbā then confesses her love for Bhīma to Yudhiṣṭira, and he agrees to marry them, so long as she returns Bhīma to his family every night. They are married and make love all across the earth and in the heavens. She then gives birth to a demon boy, Ghaṭotkaca ("he who shines like a pot"), who becomes a favorite with the Pāṇḍav family. In the end, Haḍimbā and her son finally leave them, although Ghaṭotkaca promises to return whenever he is needed.

Even though, as Johannes van Buitenen asserted in the introduction to his translation of the *Mahābhārata*, this particular tale is not part of the main story of the epic, it has become an important reference point for the people of Kullu Valley. As we can see, the connections between the story related by Harcourt and that recorded in the *Mahābhārata* are not exact, although there are numerous points of contact. There is in fact a shrine dedicated to Ghaṭotkaca at Dungri, although it is a small tree shrine that appears to be quite recent.

In pointing out the potential disconnection between Haḍimbā and the story as it is related in the *Mahābhārata*, I am not arguing against a connection between the story of the *Mahābhārata* and the local goddess at Dungri. There is indeed substantial evidence to suggest such an association. However, I want to suggest that this connection is not timeless and unchanging. On the contrary, it appears the connection has been reinvented by the writings of Hutchinson and Vogel. This reinterpreted connection has, in turn, been picked up by vernacular ethnohistorians and the Department of Tourism and deployed at the site itself.

This rethinking has had a number of important consequences both in the way the shrine is imagined and in its actual practices.

In the manner in which it has been envisioned, the connection of the temple with the epic has set up a highly ambiguous relationship with the cultural traditions of South Asia. On the one hand, the association with the text authorizes a translocal connection. On the other hand, that association is highly compromised by the content of the text, which casts Haḍimbā as a demon and not a goddess. Thus, the Department of Tourism promotes the temple as an important pilgrimage site of the "Great Goddess." An often-reproduced pamphlet advertises the temple as follows: "This temple constructed in pagoda style displays the finest example of wood carvings on it. This sanctuary is built over a rocky crevice that is worshipped as a manifestation of Durgā an image of the Goddess is also enshrined here." This association with the pan-Indian goddess Durgā allows the Department of Tourism and others associated with tourism to advertise this temple as an ancient pilgrimage site of the Great Goddess sanctioned by the *Mahābhārata*. In many of the pamphlets describing the scene related above, Haḍimbā is described as having been later recognized as a goddess. No mention is ever made of her being a demon. In the words of the prolific Raja Bhasin: "According to legend, Bhīma slew the demon Hadimb and married his sister Haḍimbā who was subsequently elevated to the status of a goddess—an episode from the epic, Mahābhārata."[23]

Grammatical ambiguity notwithstanding, some have seized upon the potentially problematic character of the deity. In conversations I had at the site with Bengali pilgrims and members of the temple administration, it became clear that many of the more orthodox Bengali Brahmins do not in fact consider Haḍimbā to be an authentic goddess but rather recognize her as a demon. In an effort to purge the site of all of its "demonic" associations, the Department of Tourism, the temple committee, and the Archaeological Survey of India (ASI) have placed tight regulations on religious practices at the site.

As is suggested in the scene from the *Mahābhārata,* Haḍimbā and her brother ate human flesh. Like so many of the other local deities in the Western Himalayas, her character is intimately connected to sacrifice. In fact, while most of the early colonial authorities do not connect Haḍimbā to the *Mahābhārata,* none of them fail to mention the intimate connection between her and sacrifice. Many scholars, including Hutchinson and Vogel, even connect her to forms of human sacrifice. Penelope Chetwode, who traveled through the Western Himalayas in the postcolonial period, related her first experience in the temple as follows: "The interior of the temple is dark and mysterious and as your eyes become accustomed to the dim light you see a rope hanging from the ceiling over large natural boulders enclosed by the four walls. One of the boulders partly overhangs the sacrificial stone which is smooth and slopes down to the right and has a dip in the middle into which the blood of animals flows, the goats and the buffaloes which are offered up to the demon goddess, as a described to me by Princess Kiran."[24]

This scene was confirmed by Harcourt in the late nineteenth century: "In the interior there are large rocks, and a rope hangs from the roof, to which, legends have it, human victims were, in old times, suspended by the hands after death and swung to and fro over the goddess."[25] Having spent a fair amount of time inside this shrine myself, I can confirm the presence of the stones. However, the ropes both authors spoke of are notably absent, and this speaks to an important lacuna in the daily practices of the temple.

The temple is at the center of a bureaucratic web. Part of it is controlled by the ASI, part by the local temple committee, part by the Kullu district administration, and part by the Department of Tourism. As is clear from this list, one constituency is notably absent: the people of Dungri. This has led to the implementation of policies that meet the demands of the four parties in control but not those of the people of Dungri. Consequently, a certain standard of practice has been established at the site. Most noticeable is the complete absence of animal sacrifice at or near the temple and the ascendancy of *darśan* as the mode of ritual interaction. While Haḍimbā has historically been a goddess who was propitiated with blood and who satisfied desires and demands in relation to sacrifices given, these practices have now stopped. As if in direct correlation, local patronage to the temple has almost completely stopped. One of the presidents (*pradhān*) of the temple committee (priests rotate quarterly) put it this way: "The people who come here, they are just tourists looking at old things. They do not have any faith [*śraddhā*]. The local people don't come here daily like they used to."[26] Many other things have changed at the site. The temple is now open to all people, regardless of caste or background. The one exception to this rule is the gūr, a man of low caste who speaks on behalf of the goddess. The irony of this situation is that the man who is traditionally closest to the deity is now the only individual not allowed to enter the shrine. I have spent hours inside the shrine and watched local drunks and stoned Israelis visit the site while the one person who actually communicates the will of the deity was sitting outside.

The changes that have taken place are part of an induction into a broader set of styles and practices. These are the styles more traditionally associated with temple Hinduism. They include lines for *darśan*, the offering of flowers and sweets, and relations characterized by devotion. These are, by all estimate, not characteristic of ritual practices common in the upper Western Himalayas, although they are becoming more so. The more common practices of ritual possession, animal sacrifice, questioning (*pūchnā*), and deity mobility (*rāth yātrā*) are waning. These changes are intimately, if not causally, related to the growth of tourism in the upper Beas Valley.

While the same may be said for the shrine at Jagat Sukh, what distinguishes these two sites is the relative "success" of the Haḍimbā shrine in contrast with the Gāyatri temple. What I want to emphasize here is how the creation of a new index can validate the "success" or "failure" of these sites. By this, I mean the way that the efficacy and power of the deity is changing in relation to the tourism industry and its accompanying discourses. Now, the power of these deities is measured in relation to the number of tourists they draw and the amount of money they extract both from tourists and governmental aid agencies. This shifting index is rewriting the constitution of local deities and also the way that individuals conceive themselves.

According to recent estimates, only two students in the village of Malana have matriculated in the past several years. Attendance rates at the local school are abysmal, and nearly all children are expected to drop out. By contrast, the state as a whole has one of the highest literacy rates in the country, and its excellent education system is providing teaching to people in even the most remote of villages. Who or what is to blame for the situation in Malana? Although Malana is a remote village without a connecting road, the lack of graduates is not connected to its isolation. It is, however, intimately intertwined with tourism and a local deity. Malana is the home of Himachal's most lucrative cash crop, high-end hashish. According to many, Malana, because of its high elevation, good soils, and pure air, produces what is widely considered the best hashish in the world. Known as Malana Cream, it began to gain worldwide recognition in the 1980s, when rumors spread in Amsterdam and London about a new type of hashish from India's Himalayas made by a secret ancient culture that was historically linked to Alexander the Great.

From there, things took off rapidly, and Malana became a coveted source of hash across South Asia and beyond. It is located at the center of a very lucrative, if dangerous, drug trade that connects places as distant as Goa, Tel Aviv, Paris, Tokyo, New York, and more recently Moscow. Although the Kullu Valley police and regional officials have attempted to curb the cultivation and sale of these drugs, it continues largely unabated. The district officials have little control in this distant village. They have attempted to educate villagers, to build schools and roads, and to help them plant crops such as potatoes and pulses. However, these crops are manually intensive and need water and fertilizer that is sometimes difficult to obtain. Cannabis plants, on the other hand,

Figure 23. Malana village. Photo by author.

grow everywhere in the area without water, fertilizer, or even the simplest attention. Consequently, cultivation of other crops has virtually disappeared.

The presence of an illicit cash crop in an area, however, does not immediately preclude education. So why is it that Malana has had so few graduates, even though it has a middle school, a steady stream of curious Western tourists, a telephone exchange, and a health center? In short, there are two interconnected reasons, one biological and the other religious. The first is that the hands of children have more pores than those of adults. As a result, when they rub the ripe stalks of cannabis, they are able to produce more hashish from one plant than an older villager can. So in the harvest season (July to October), children are in high demand to work making hashish. A recent newspaper article reported that children can earn as much as five hundred rupees per day rolling the leaves of cannabis plants between their palms.[27]Given that this is likely more than ten times what they could expect to make as adult workers, it is a job that is tough to turn down. Additionally, there is no negative stigma attached to this production in the village. In fact, the job is authorized and sanctioned by the leader of the local community—the organizer of all action in the region and the ultimate judge of all, Jamlu, Malana's deity. Malana's social and political worlds are tied to the agency of its local deity and the individuals who speak in his name. In this case, it is clear that the local economy is tied to the deity. As with all things in the village, nothing is done without the authorization of the deity. Many scholars and travelers have argued that Malana was the world's first democracy, precisely because the populace has been allowed a voice in local administration for as far back as we know. However, ultimate authority lies in Jamlu and the gūr who speaks in his name. As one villager explained: "Unless Jamlu tells us to grow other crops, we will grow only cannabis." In this case, there is a synergy between the market demands of tourists, the will of the deity, and the community. Moreover, this is all being done in the name of cultural preservation. Education and road construction are said by many to "pollute the culture."

Let us, then, think for a second about the logic of these moves. This is an exclusive community, isolated from the turmoil of the plains, that is understood to be participating in "ancient cultural practices" that have remained unchanged over the centuries. All action originates from and is sanctioned by Jamlu, just as it did hundreds of years ago. However, during the past twenty years, contact with tourists and the dissemination of a particular substance have led to the growth of a lucrative transnational industry. As a result, these seemingly opposing forces have been synergistically combined to produce a robust influx of money. People in this community can work less, they have better supplies to make it through the winter, and their houses are better made and insulated. In short, the material standard of living has increased considerably, although no one would argue that the community is wealthy. At the same time, Jamlu has prohibited the construction of a road to the village and discouraged children from attending schools and integrating with other local communities.

I offer no answers to this conundrum. However, I find it exceptionally interesting that this case establishes a deep conflict between two
unquestioned goods: the cultural preservation of a community and the
education of children. What does this say about our conceptions of
development, economic progress, the preservation of deity systems,
and the cultivation and sale of illicit substances? One clear message
from Malana is that no community, no matter how distant, how isolated, or how strong its desire is to remain distant, can remain a world
unto itself. While it is arguable whether Malana and other communities like it were ever autonomous (most evidence suggests that they
weren't), it is clear that Malana is as influenced by hashish demand in
Amsterdam and the availability of Nepali migrant labor (Nepali
migrants tend most of the village's food crops) as it is by the ancient will
of Jamlu.

Chapter 5 began the examination of the ethical dimensions of
becoming religious by looking at the contemporary circulation of religion. The chapter focused on two interrelated processes: the production and maintenance of norms and the production of normalization.
Put another way, it examined the scope and shape of a normative version of religion as presented in three different cases. The picture that
emerged is characteristic of a normative understanding of religion. It
went on to explore how this normative incarnation of religion became
the very substance through which individuals were seduced and/or
coerced to recognize themselves as subject to this normative religion.
Whereas this chapter focused on the ways that normative conceptions
of religion bear down on individuals within the process of becoming
religious, chapter 6 will take up a different, if deeply interrelated, process: the styles and means by which individuals use this new practice of
becoming religious in their own practices of self-cultivation. That is, it
will explore the dynamism of becoming religious as an ongoing process
of negotiation wherein the developing concept of religion constrains
how people think about themselves and their pasts while those same

people work in many different ways to creatively influence this concept. This ongoing process is precisely what I call "becoming religious," and in the final chapter, I will explore how it works by examining the debate over animal sacrifice, as it is in this debate that Himachalis are becoming religious.

CHAPTER SIX

Cultivating Religion amid the Conflicting Desires of Goats, Gods, and Government

SACRIFICE BECOMES A "PROBLEM"

Rita prepared an offering of flowers, sweets, and prayers—as she had every morning and evening—to honor her family deity, who had enabled the family's financial prosperity in the last twelve months. Rita's daughters were singing sweet devotional songs when they heard the parade approach. Standing in the doorway, Rita, proud and thankful, held her head high, welcoming the deity to her doorstep. She waved sandalwood incense in front of her offering, but she was abruptly interrupted before she could finish her prayer. Initially, the procession seemed to be an indistinguishable mass of traditional Kulvi hats, coarse wool jackets, and cheap bus-stand shoes. Then, suddenly, one of the men was seized by a violent force. His body convulsed, his arms shook, and his head jerked backward, sending his hat flying and revealing his long hair. This man was the deity's gūr; the deity had arrived and was ready to speak. Unblinking, with fire in his eyes, the gūr rendered his judgment on Rita and her family. The news was not good.

"You have neglected your duty. You have failed to fulfill your promise, and now you will be punished," he screeched.

Rita was stunned. Perplexed and noticeably angry, she protested: "But I have remembered you every morning and evening. Daily, I give thanks for your miracle [*pratyakṣa*]."

But the deity considered her pleas to be vapid excuses for unjustifiable behavior; they only increased his anger. A year before, the deity performed a series of interventions that brought financial prosperity to her home. Both parties agreed on this fact, but they disagreed about the payment. The deity had demanded a large feast of sacrificed goats, but Rita thought her constant attention and prayers would be more pleasing. She was wrong. The deity was hungry.

Early records from the region show that animal sacrifice has long been a common compulsory component of local rites. As recently as the early 1960s, there was virtually no debate about blood sacrifice as a contentious issue. Local publications from the period commonly showed photographs of these rites and described the rites in detail. Sacrifice was mentioned simply as part of a factual recording of events (e.g., "a certain family offered twenty goats"). This kind of casual disclosure is unthinkable now. Following Himachal's attainment of statehood in 1971, animal sacrifice became the most critical debate for Himachalis struggling to define themselves, their relations with their pasts, and their relations with Indian national culture. To state it more directly, in today's Himachal, animal sacrifice is a problem.[1] The existence of animal sacrifice can no longer be taken for granted. Whether one is in favor of it or against it, one must take a position in relation to it. I argue that animal sacrifice develops into a problem through the emergence of a new category of religion, which determines what is allowed and what is prohibited. Because this category of religion is new in the region and the belief and practices that constitute it are so undefined, it is emotions, anxieties, and passions that animate the debate over animal sacrifice and the shaping of religion. For this reason, the production of religion, the fight over animal sacrifice, and related issues mentioned throughout the book are tied to profound emotional shifts. These issues turn on how different individuals *feel* about religion, the way it strikes them deep in the gut.[2]

Figure 24. Haḍimbā temple. Photo by author.

I call this process the labor of religion. The labor of religion is the force exerted by emergent (and disputed) conceptions of religion combined with the efforts of specific actors to define and delimit the scope of religion.[3] The genitive ambiguity in the phrase "labor of religion" captures the complexity of the process at work in Himachal. It suggests an irresolvable dialectic energized by both the conscious labor of particular actors to define religion and the conceptual labor exerted by religion on the population more generally. Stated differently, when I talk about the labor of religion, I am talking about both the things people do to shape and cultivate religion and the force exerted on these people by normative conceptions of religion—the power of the concept to shape people and of people to shape the concept.

In this respect, the labor of religion is not unlike the labor of the state as discussed in Timothy Mitchell's classic study of relations between state and society, "The Limits of State: Beyond Statist Approaches and Their Critics."[4] Mitchell begins his essay by addressing a paradox at the heart of political science that is very similar to the problem I identify at the heart of the study of religion: while the field of political science is devoted to the study and explanation of "the state," no one has been able to define "the state" precisely. While scholars have long recognized this problem, Mitchell reorients the question. Traditionally, disagreement turned on whether scholars defined the state in narrow terms around specific components of the state apparatus or whether they understood the boundaries between state and society as more porous. For scholars of religion, this is a formula that is very familiar, whether it is phrased in the classic terms of the sacred and the profane or the more contemporary terms of religion and the secular. Mitchell suggests that theorists turn away from concerns about the precise boundaries of the state and toward the formation of these boundaries and their effects. What matters to Mitchell is not so much defining, once and for all, the state's boundaries but rather studying how and why such boundaries are created and the effects of any particular formulation.

This chapter, and the book more generally, extends Mitchell's analysis to the category of religion.[5] This book makes a fairly radical argument: that "religion" is a verb. The boundaries between religion and its others (such as the secular, the political, and the economic) are continually being reset by the people employing the category. This dynamic process is not without consequences, as particular formulations are internalized, normalized, or critiqued. This process is the engine of religion's labor. In this chapter, I will track religion's labor through a series of ethnographic vignettes.

THE NEW ARBITERS OF CULTURAL AUTHENTICITY

My longtime assistant and I were traveling to Pujarli, a village in one of Himachal Pradesh's most remote valleys.[6] The road was long and dangerous. The late monsoon rains had transformed the dusty, potholed dirt track into a surface slicker than oiled ice, and our normally trusty Enfield Bullet was not exactly the ideal transport. Several local historians had encouraged us to attend a rare reestablishment ceremony (*pratiṣṭhā*) in the village, which they said would be "more authentic than any we had ever seen." They expected several hundred animal sacrifices. We would have the chance to see the "real Himachal."

Wet, muddy, and cold, we finally arrived at a tiny cluster of houses at the end of the road. Ecstatic to be off the motorcycle, we began searching for a place to stay. Our relief quickly faded as we faced a very hostile group of young men. Normally, when we reached settlements this far from the circuits traveled by pilgrims and tourists, villagers greeted us with great enthusiasm, offering chai, roti, and a dry place to sleep, but these folks were less than hospitable. There were no offers of chai, water, or even a place to sit outside of the rain. A colleague (a regional development officer in the Department of Language and Culture) who lives in Shimla had given us the name of a local contact and informed him we would be visiting, but as we searched for the contact, the villagers' distrust of us grew even stronger. No one had heard of this man.

We spent the next couple of hours explaining why we were visiting the village and why we could be trusted. It was not that they were skeptical of foreigners. They thought we were working for the government and had arrived to collect back taxes or to solicit bribes. The bags of strange electronics (recording equipment, cameras, computers, and GPS system) we were carrying did not help inspire trust.

Finally, after expressing our own distrust of state officials, reciting the origin stories of two local deities, and offering each man a Polaroid photo, we were introduced to Ashok Sharma. According to the villagers, Sharma was a great historian of the valley. If anyone could help us, he was our man. Sharma invited us to stay in his home for the night, and after a warm dinner of lentils and roti, we sat in his study discussing our work. Despite the street chatter, Sharma was not a historian. He was a conservation biologist interested in the medicinal properties of local plants. In connection with that work, he had done some research in villages nearby, collecting stories about healing and herbal practices. Somewhat perplexed, I asked him why his neighbors thought he was a historian of theological culture (*devīdevatā saṇskṛti*). Eager to appear modern and scientific, he explained that he did not believe in the power of local deities but that he considered himself a very religious man. He was a member of the Radhasoami reform movement, which advocates vegetarianism and meditation practices designed to unify the soul with universal sonic energies (*suratsabdhayoga*).[7]

Intrigued by this disjunction, I asked him what he thought of some of the most influential contemporary historians of Himachal, including one man who is an MLA for a nearby valley. While he had heard of most of them, he confessed that he had read none of their work. The gap in understanding between Sharma and the villagers is a telling example of religion's labor within the process of becoming religious. For the villagers, there was no distinction between religion and *devīdevatā saṇskṛti*, the two were simply synonyms for the same object. Yet Sharma defined religion precisely in opposition to these local traditions.

Early the next morning, my assistant and I began the ascent to our real destination: a tiny village, alleged to be less than an hour away, where the rites would take place. About three hours and six hundred vertical meters later, the village was nowhere in sight. What I did see made me realize that we were nearing the edge of any form of state control. The valley opened up, and I saw verdant terraces etched into the mountainsides. It was strange to see such extensive terraced agriculture at this elevation (nearly four thousand meters), and I began wondering if there was a large village nearby that had been omitted from governmental maps (common in areas like this that border China). However, approaching the fields, I realized that they did not contain corn, rice, or wheat. They were fields of marijuana. We had arrived at harvest time, and the plants were fully mature. Though marijuana plants are common in this region, they are normally wild or cultivated only in small patches. These large fields were meticulously tended. They were well irrigated, and all the male plants had been removed to inhibit pollination and encourage the females to develop the large buds that produce the strongest hashish. Working in the fields, grandmothers and children alike were busy cutting, stacking, and rubbing the plants.[8] Strangely, broken stalks and rotting plants littered several of the fields. These plants were lying haphazardly, as if cut by an absent-minded demiurge with scissor-hands. On further inspection, I noticed a pattern in the destruction. The terraces were divided into sections, each managed by a different family; each had at least one destroyed area. Perplexed, I sought out some of the young men tending the fields in search of an explanation. Worried they might perceive me as a governmental agent and remain aloof (as commonly happened in these types of interactions), I first sat within their site to prepare a chillum. Offering it to them, I asked, "What happened here? It looks like a giant, crazy water buffalo arrived in deep need of the cream." I like to think their smiles were a reaction to my joke, but I expect their warm response had its source in the other offerings I made. Either way, a torrent of chatter was unleashed from all present.

"Only one week ago, the 'government' [English word used] arrived," said a young man in the group. "They cut our plants and left them to rot. They told us we would be 'fined' [English word used] or imprisoned if we did not destroy the fields immediately."[9]

Knowing this to be a foolish question, but curious how they would respond, I asked, "Do you think that people will stop growing the plants [*caras*] now?"

Coughing out smoke as he burst into laughter, he said, "Of course not [*bilkul nahīṁ*]. This is just a little 'tax' [English word used]. You know? Like *baksheesh* [the universal grease of all governmental transactions]. Look around. What can the government do out here? They have no power. They're just like these little kids here." He gestured to the toddlers rolling buds in their hands. "They just piss all over the place."[10]

"Now we clean it up," he said as they slowly walked back to their work. Shouting over his shoulder, he promised to find me later to "enjoy" (he used the English term)—a promise he fulfilled. Frankly, however, although the goat stew I was treated to at the home of his relatives was initially enjoyable, the amount that I was encouraged to eat made it progressively less so.

In many ways, I had come to the limits of state control. Here, there were no roads, no schools, and no tourists (domestic or otherwise). Governmental efforts to control or even regulate hashish production are intermittent and feeble. Every few years, officials travel here, cut some plants, make a few quickly forgotten promises, and extract bribes. Yet, while I may have passed beyond the border of where state officials can exhort even a modicum of control, as the jovial banter of the conversation above suggested, I soon learned that the labor of religion was not equally bound.

We arrived in the village late that afternoon, just as the reestablishment festival began. Festivals such as this are rare, and villagers had invited guests from throughout the region, luring them with the promise of meat (*prasād*) and all-night dancing (*naṭī*). Accompanied by two other local deities, the primary god approached the village from the valley below, returning from a three-day tour of nearby temples. They snaked their way up the steep slopes, carried by men playing brass horns and smoking cigarettes. As they entered the village, the head of one of the wealthier families sacrificed a goat and threw it over the procession as a welcoming gift.

Quickly, the atmosphere turned from giddy and expectant to tense and conflicted.[11] Not everyone in the crowd welcomed the gift. While goat sacrifice is commonplace in this region, some of the assembled masses protested about its appropriateness. This disagreement precipitated a much larger debate about the remainder of the festival. The festival had not been performed for sixty years; the only people who had seen it were either too young to remember the details or too old to be helpful.[12] The disputants argued over most of the festival's rites, but the greatest disagreements centered on when to fire the guns, when to offer goats, and when and where to offer the pig. No one knew of a textual source for the rite (even though they could have turned to several well-known Sanskrit ritual manuals [*paddhati*]). Temple managers could not remember any customary practice, and the pronouncements from the deities themselves (through their mediums) were conflicting. Though all of these people had opinions and arguments, there was no single person or entity invested with the authority to make a binding decision. Normally in this region, the deity's medium or a government official (such as the local MLA) would settle the dispute, but the villagers seated around me all agreed that the mediums and the MLA were biased. Neither understood the "authentic" or "true" practice; they sought only to strengthen their own positions. The force of these words bore down hard on those gathered for the festival. They all wanted the rite to be authentic, but no one knew what that meant. After hours of intense arguments, darkness began to envelop the village.

Sharma arrived in the twilight with some of his relatives. Finding no one to arbitrate the disputes, the villagers agreed that Sharma was the only person who could decide how they should proceed. They considered his expertise objective, and everyone agreed that he was a pious man, unstained by the local and governmental interests that had been driving the debate all afternoon.[13] In the end, Sharma struck a compromise. He decided that the villagers could offer no sacrifices until it was dark but that the shooting could proceed beforehand. He would allow the pig sacrifice, but festival participants could not watch.[14]

How did it happen that a botanist was the person chosen to adjudicate such an important rite? The decision grew out of two deeply connected, seismic shifts in daily life. Each of these shifts is explored in a separate chapter in this book. The first shift, described in chapter 2, was brought about by the land reform acts of the 1950s, which stripped temples of their land holdings, severing the material ties that had linked deities to their communities for generations. The deities became—as one informant told me—"beggars." The gūrs who spoke for the deities were no longer the authoritative voice of God. Now they had become petitioners, forced to cue in the Secretariat building like any other Himachali in need of governmental support.

The second shift, explored in chapters 3 and 4, is more diffuse. In many temples throughout the state, government officials have molded even the tiniest details of daily temple practice to suit their needs. However, in regions like this one, on the edge of state power, government officials have been less successful in controlling rites. This does not mean, however, that temples there have escaped the transformations of the past several decades. The forces of change in these areas may be subtler, but they are no less transformative.[15] They rely less on the overt actions of government ministers and mid-level functionaries and more on the diffusion of Himachal's theoculture (*devīdevatā saṃskṛti*) and the growing authority of local historians who forged it.

The villagers here knew two things about Sharma: he was pious, and he was a writer. It is therefore understandable that, when he stepped up to intervene in the dispute, he spoke with a deep, objective knowledge of Himachal's theoculture. Regardless of whether his actions were malicious, he did not correct the villagers, and his judgment was accepted by all, not because of his connection to the village, the deity, or governmental mandates but because of his presumed expertise in Himachal's theoculture. Ironically, the villagers felt that this expertise was the only thing that would ensure the objectivity of the decision. Proceeding by slights, missteps, ambition, misunderstanding, and a million tiny human interactions, this is the process of becoming religious rendered in narrative form.

BECOMING RELIGIOUS THROUGH PURIFICATION

The prevalence of animal sacrifice at many popular tourist sites across the region has become a mark for drawing the lines between religion and state. Governmental administrators have passed laws prohibiting animal sacrifice, and reformers draw on long traditions (from Sanskrit literature) to legitimize substituting the offering of intentions for the offering of live animals. These efforts have met wide resistance.[16] Not surprisingly, many villagers resist understanding their family deities as mental abstractions. Ironically, the very individuals who legislated and now "enforce" prohibitions—politicians, police officers, and district administrators—have also inhibited the eradication of animal sacrifice. While advocating the elimination of animal sacrifice in legal codes and administrative policies, many of these officials continue to offer sacrifices in their own homes, usually at night or in times of crisis. This is not because they are morally corrupt or ignorant, as their critics assert.[17] Rather, it is because they are going through the process of becoming religious, of discriminating between what is and is not religion. While this may sound abstract, its effects are not.

Seen in this light, animal sacrifice is problematic not because it violates a timeless prohibition on violence or because it cracks the sheen of neo-Hinduism; rather, the problem lies with incommensurable conceptions of the limit, location, and function of religion.[18] Innumerable daily interactions display this irreconcilability, from the performance of domestic rites to state policy. I will examine one recent, well-publicized incident that remains a touchstone for both sides of the debate.

Since the late 1990s, the *Amar Ujālā*, a Hindi-language daily, has reshaped the landscape of North Indian journalism.[19] The paper's aggressive approach to marketing, distribution, and local news coverage has helped it become the most widely read news daily in the Himalayas. Their success in Himachal is primarily a result of their intimacy with local markets. In contrast with other daily newspapers based in Delhi, Lucknow, and Chandigarh, the *Amar Ujālā* has correspondents in even the remotest villages who can transmit stories and images instantly. However, the lack of locally trained journalists has forced *Amar Ujālā* to recruit reporters from other regions of India. Like Western-trained anthropologists, these visitors sometimes misunderstand the events they report.

Tejpal Negi is an exceptional writer and inquisitive researcher, who rose quickly to local prominence after moving from the neighboring state of Uttaranchal to the remote region of Rampur Bushahar. From the moment he arrived, Negi focused on local issues, giving representation to people the state government had long ignored. In the process, he became a popular public figure, trusted by villagers across the region. However, in the fall of 2001, he gravely overestimated his influence and popular sentiments.

Drought was ravaging Rampur Bushahar. The apple trees, which are the area's financial lifeblood, were emaciated. In such a region, water is everything; without it, the crops fail, and crop failure quickly becomes famine. Because of the importance of rain, the region's numerous snake gods (*nāg devatās*), who control the weather, enjoy great popularity and weather predictions dominate daily chitchat. This particular drought was threatening to destroy even the most productive fields. Meteorologists were predicting no rain, and the snake deities, through their mediums, said they were powerless.

In the years before the drought, the deity Bhīmākālī's temple in Sarahan village had become the center of a tourist circuit. Its photogenic location near the snow-capped ranges of Kinnaur and Western Tibet, and its classic cedar and granite architecture had secured its

Figure 25. Bhīmākālī Temple. Photo by author.

place among the state's most marketable tourism destinations. In 1984, authorities drafted legislation designed to eradicate temple corruption and better manage large temples. As a consequence, Bhīmākālī came under the control of the Department of Language and Culture in 1986.[20] This department is the primary governmental force behind religious modernization and the consolidation of regional difference in the Western Himalayas; it has worked to reform both the financial and ritual practices of the state's most prominent temples and funded a robust community of scholars and writers in the service of the state.[21] In response to complaints by tourists and powerful government ministers, department officials met with the chief minister of Himachal, whose family has controlled the Bhīmākālī temple for at least five hundred years, and they agreed to ban animal sacrifice within the temple complex.

This decision was unprecedented, and it violently shook the temple's conceptual and practical foundations. Adjacent to the main temple, which may have been constructed as long ago as in the seventh or eighth century, is a large sloping well, said to be the home of one of the most vicious deities in the region, Lankara Vīr.[22] Although records of this temple are scanty,[23] contemporary oral narratives and colonial documents identify it as a site of human sacrifice through the early nineteenth century.[24] Although the British abolished human sacrifice at the temple,[25] animal sacrifice remained common until the Department of Language and Culture assumed control of the site. The ban enraged Sarahan's villagers. They protested to local officials but were powerless against the seduction of tourism revenue. Feeling beholden to the demands of Bhīmākālī, they were forced to continue their sacrifices outside the temple and in their homes. One local farmer explained the problem: "The local people think that animal sacrifice must be performed. Now that here [in the temple] sacrifice is prohibited, they go outside. They go to the hills and do the sacrifice.... They ask the goddess to bring rain. They are farmers. How can farmers be successful [*suphal,* meaning "fertile" or "profitable"] without rain? How will they fill the bellies of their families if they are not successful? For this reason, they continue to do sacrifice outside the temple." Yet common villagers were not the only people who continue performing these sacrifices. Birbadra Singh, who was patriarch of the region's royal family and the state's chief minister when this dispute occurred, continued to perform these sacrifices as well. While Singh's understanding of the meaning and cause of the drought is unknown, most of Sarahan's villagers believed that the drought proved the goddess was unhappy that sacrifices were not being offered in her temple compound.

When the drought finally broke late in 2001, the rain was understood as a gift from the goddess. Elated at their good fortune and angry with the government, the villagers planned a large festival to thank the goddess for her kindness. They organized the festival without the oversight of the temple committee to limit exposure to the authorities, but word spread quickly. On the appointed day, hundreds of villagers—including temple officials and local state administrators—arrived with goats, rams, lambs, chickens, pigs, and buffalo. The animals were slaughtered, and people feasted all day on the meat. Through her medium, the goddess expressed her satisfaction. Many others, however, were unhappy.

The next day, Tejpal Negi published an article in the *Amar Ujālā* with the deceptively neutral title, "Animal Sacrifice outside of Bhīmākālī Temple."²⁶ Though Negi continues to claim impartiality, the article is a strongly worded criticism of animal sacrifice and those who perform it. He spares no one. After chronicling the different animals sacrificed and the conditions of the sacrifices, Negi recounts what he considered to be the cruelest (*sabse krur*) sacrifice, that of a water buffalo. The buffalo was mutilated and then chased for a kilometer before villagers killed it with three shots. Shocked by such behavior, Negi suggests complicity between the villagers and government officials, insinuating that the state effectively sanctioned the activities. He argues that they knew of the sacrifices and did nothing to stop them. Imagining himself as a lone rational voice, he closes by confessing his astonishment that "no one raised their voice against [*khilāph*] this barbaric [*barbar*] incident."²⁷

Negi's article highlights a gap between the official policies and the actual practices of state officials, including the chief minister, who tolerate and perform these sacrifices. Its readers did not miss the indictment. Maneka Gandhi, who was educated in Himachal before her marriage to former Prime Minister Sanjay Gandhi, sent a personal letter to the Himachal Pradesh government condemning their inaction and holding them responsible for the incident.²⁸ Because Gandhi was a member of the Nehruvian dynasty and held a parliamentary seat, state officials could not ignore her petition. Response to the letter was swift. The state offices shifted blame to local police officials in Sarahan, who, in turn, translated Gandhi's condemnation into baton bruises meted out to those who participated in the rite. Yet many Sarahan villagers remained unapologetic for continuing the rites of their ancestors, and the anger Negi had incited returned to him, magnified by the national circuit it had traversed. The villagers demanded a public apology, the police threatened to beat him, and the government threatened to expel him. The problem was not the sacrifices, but the article that publicized them. Despite these considerable threats, Negi did not apologize.

Implicit in Negi's article, the villagers' actions, and the responses they elicited are competing theories of ritual efficacy. For the villagers performing this sacrifice, the blood offering is integral to their relationship with Bhīmākālī, sustaining relations of mutual care: the deity provides for the people, and they provide for her. The deities of the villagers are not unknowable concepts beyond human understanding or representation. They are unassailably real, with desires and needs not unlike those of humans. Villagers often compare the special capacities and specific needs of the deities to those of children, naughty adolescents, government ministers, or wise old women.[29] All too aware of the frequency of droughts, diseases, floods, and famines, the villagers dread their deities' harsh reminders of their obligations. Simply put, blood offerings are pragmatic, material transactions. One cannot replace a goat with thought or intention. Doing so, as one villager put it, would be like repaying a loan with smiles.

Negi's position, fast becoming hegemonic in the region, relies on a very different logic of ritual efficacy. These discourses reject the religious materialism on which animal sacrifice relies. Negi and others like him consider these offerings to be barbaric and pernicious delusions. As he told me on several occasions, the offering of meat to the deity is nothing more than a strategy to assuage guilt and legitimate inhumane practices. "Who eats the meat?" he would ask me. "It is not the god. People eat the meat." He believes that communication between deities and people occurs between minds and spirits; its success and intensity are the product of intention (*saṅkalp*) rather than substances like blood or money. In this context, material exchanges are superfluous—only spiritual exchanges matter. As long as one's intentions are pure, he told me, the deity will be pleased. In his opinion, offering internal devotion in good faith is more effective than offering meat without good intentions.[30]

Yet formulations such as this—substituting mental action for physical action—are literally incomprehensible to villagers. Consider, for example, the president (*pradhān*) of the Jākh temple in the Pabbar River valley. In response to a question about substituting prayers for animal sacrifices, he asked me, confused and slightly agitated, "But how will Jākh eat? Like the villagers at this festival, he is hungry. If we do not feed him, he will be angry. Have you not heard the stories of his anger?" I had heard such stories, and they were nothing short of terrifying. Only a few days before, one villager explained to me that a recent monsoon was a product of Jākh's anger. Every few years, the heavy monsoon clouds crash against the steep Himalayan foothills, dropping as much as fifty centimeters of rain in an hour. In 1999, a cloudburst in a village just below the temple caused the river to grow so ferocious that it ripped a new steel bridge from its moorings and erased most signs of human habitation in the lower part of the valley. The burst took everything: roads, bridges, crops, and even lives. Those lucky enough to survive interpreted the event as a miraculous proof (*pratyaksa*) of Jākh's power and the consequences of not carrying out rituals.

These competing formulations of ritual efficacy and their attendant consequences highlight another aspect of the labor of religion. For the president of the Jākh temple, the question of "correct" religious practice simply does not arise. There is only the deity, with his blessings and his pressing demands. Questions about whether a particular rite is or is not religious are inappropriate. He is not concerned with adherence to orthodox standards or with the limits of what is or is not "properly" Hindu or an acceptable component of Himachal's theoculture. Yet for Negi and the cluster of critics who coalesced around him, the legitimacy of these rites was always a question to be determined in relation to religion. Negi and most other critics of animal sacrifice in the region do not reject the existence and operation of gods; they are not atheists. Rather, they reject the idea that gods are like people— subject to hunger, anger, and bribes. For them, God is beyond the capriciousness of daily life; droughts and cloudbursts are meteorological events produced by storms, geography, and the laws of nature.[31] Accordingly, deities cannot be influenced by blood sacrifices or five-hundred-rupee notes. Faith is the only offering appropriate to a divinity.

These antithetical approaches to the logic of ritual highlight one of the most powerful effects of religion's labor in contemporary Himachal. Increasingly, Himachalis are coming to understand interactions with their local deities and the festivals that punctuate the year's rhythm in relation to religion, and as they do this, the incredibly diverse modes of interacting with local gods are being flattened and superseded by the seductive simplicity of faith (*viśvās*). Faith, as a unifying concept, first appeared and then rapidly expanded in Himachal in the years following India's independence from colonial rule.[32] It became the central concept used to frame the region's polytheism, understand its ritual transactions, and distinguish the region from other parts of South Asia. This expansion parallels two concurrent developments: the growth of vernacular ethnomedia and the increasing autonomy of the region within India's federalist system. These connections are not accidental, since faith really gained currency through the writings and political efforts of the region's first chief minister, Y. S. Parmar.

These developments have become so pervasive that it is now common to hear villagers explaining the power and effectiveness of all ritual in terms of faith. When I asked villagers to explain how a deity was able to expel a demon—for example, to cure a child's ailment or produce very fertile fields—the most common response by far was, *Yah to viśvās kī bat haiṇ* (literally, "It's a faith thing").[33] This often-repeated formula draws on a powerful ambiguity. For some, the phrase meant that their faith was literally the agent producing the desired result. For others, it meant that the rite's efficient cause was beyond the discriminating capacities of the human mind. In the face of God's sovereignty, faith is our only recourse.

The growth of faith within Himachali discourses has had an enormous impact on everything from ritual reform to self-transformation. Nowhere are these changes more apparent than in the reproduction of Himachali identity, both as a personal ideal and as a normative, state-authored agenda. It is the equation of faith with religion that facilitates the evolution of these festivals into symbols of regional unity. Thus, in Himachal, we see not so much, as Émile Durkheim would have it, that "religion is eminently social" but that the historical labor of religion creates a new object that is symbolic of the social.

METONYMY, MEANING, AND THE SEMANTIC WORK OF BECOMING RELIGIOUS

The most famous festival in contemporary Himachal Pradesh is Kullu Daśaharā. It is one of the few regional events that enjoy national media coverage on an annual basis, and people come from across the country to participate. Some believe this festival has its origin in the time of the *Mahābhārata*, yet the current national status of the festival is a very recent phenomenon. Before the 1970s, it was a local festival for local people. An 1871 account of the ritual by Colonel Harcourt (one of the region's most important early colonial administrators) describes it as a weeklong event that drew seventy or eighty deities from the Kullu valley to the town of Kullu to pay their respects—and their debts—to the valley's most important deity.[34] Harcourt understood the festival as a periodic display of royal power organized to consolidate the kingdom. It was an opportunity for the king to reassert allegiance in a region riven with political, linguistic, and theistic differences and for the British to perform and maintain their relations with the king. As Harcourt explained it, the festival renewed tenuous social bonds: the mediums of local deities predicted the blessings and difficulties of the coming year, and villagers received guidance or repaid debts. All of these transactions were sealed with the offering of animal sacrifices.

In the decades following Harcourt's description, numerous travelers, administrators, and local writers also described the festival, but neither the specific ritual activities nor the meanings ascribed to them differed significantly from Harcourt's original description. It is therefore all the more revealing that both the content and the meaning of the festival began changing in the years following India's independence. The dissolution of the remaining royal power, a series of socialist land-reform measures, and the absence of a unified governing administration in the period from 1947 through the late 1960s nearly led to the extinction of the festival. Having been stripped of their land revenues, temple authorities could no longer afford to send deities and their attendants to the festival. The royal family had neither the money nor the inclination to finance their travels. In these years, only the people from the immediate area visited the famous Kullu meeting grounds (*maidan*). The festival's abandonment was prevented only after the emerging state government recognized the importance of regional theoculture to their fight for independent state status.

Governmental awareness of how important fairs and festivals were in the fight to attain statehood emerged as a byproduct of the 1961 census. In 1961, the Indian national census began publishing supplements to their statistical data on the fairs and festivals of each state. In some states, administrators treated these publications as mere distractions, and the publications were quickly forgotten, but in Himachal Pradesh, the project became integral to the struggle for state independence. Researchers, writers, and photographers were employed throughout the state to collect and present an authoritative archive of the region's innumerable fairs and festivals. The resultant publication is a hodgepodge of personal memoirs, thoughtful reconstructive summaries, undigested lists, modernist fantasies, and nationalist polemics. Despite the volume's uneven quality and clarity, it was effectively the first attempt by Himachalis to formulate a canon of the region's cultural practices, and it rapidly became an index for assessing both authenticity and innovation. The details of its reports were used to formulate most of the state's basic policies on festival management. The descriptions of rituals, processions, and practices have been copied and repeated by scholars, journalists, and advertisers. Despite the volume's authoritative status and the consistent repetition of the festivals detailed therein, many contemporary festivals differ in one significant detail from those described in the 1961 volume: they eliminate or hide animal sacrifice.

In the 1961 volume, animal sacrifice appears matter-of-factly along-side the other details of the rituals. Writers exhibit no need to problem-atize the ritual, explain it, criticize it, lament it, or celebrate it as a unique facet of local ritual practice. Perhaps most striking in this vol-ume are the numerous color photographs of the ritual in all of its vari-ous stages. There are photographs of goats being paraded to their slaughter, action shots moments before decapitation, and images of the blood offered to the deity. For these authors and the editorial board who compiled the volume, animal sacrifice was simply a component of local ritual practice that needed to be represented. It was on equal foot-ing with deities' origin stories, local dances, and the timing and attend-ance of the festival. The ritual had not yet come to signify anything other than itself.

The 1961 volume unified disparate materials into an authoritative whole. It thereby facilitated the interaction between the specific and the general—between specific fairs and festivals and the newly "uni-fied" Himachali theoculture. In this way, each festival became a symbol of the category it was associated with. Transformed into symbols, they assumed their place in the "standing reserve" of the state.[35] Now, the daily and periodic interactions between villagers and their deities mean something beyond the interactions themselves.[36]

Whereas the rites represented in the 1961 volume characterized most interactions with deities as pragmatic transactions aimed at securing a desired result (rain, the alleviation of suffering, general prosperity, immortality, etc.), it is now much more common to understand an offer-ing as a sign of devotion or a festival as a cultural performance.[37] It now becomes possible for the first time to see a local deity or rite more gen-erally as a symbol (*pratīk*) of natural, psychological, or social forces.[38]

In 1978, the state-run newspaper *Girirāj* announced the culmination of religion's labor in Kullu: "After the formation of Viśāl Himachal [the complete state of Himachal] there has been a refinement of the form of Kullu Daśaharā.... This festival is now understood as an international festival.... This festival has really now been made into a symbol of the mutual citizenship and refined unity of the state."[39] How was the festival "refined"? In recognition of the strategic importance of Kullu Daśaharā and similar festivals, the new state government expanded its support for the Department of Language and Culture, specifically promising to fund the travel of deities and their delegations to the festival. As the festival's financial backer, it made a series of important changes to the traditional festival. The central five-fold sacrifices—which had disturbed orthodox Hindus and sensitive travelers like Penelope Chetwode for generations—were removed.[40] The government department assumed control of much of the festival's organization, including its timing and its financing. Finally, they began promoting the festival as part of their tourism development strategy. In the wake of these changes, the festival quickly became a spectacle of regional unity.

While the festival now attracts hundreds of deities, most have become little more than bystanders. The mediums, who once spoke the will of god, have become one of the festival's sideshows. Festival participants no longer need deities to predict the future, to heal children, or resolve disputes. They no longer need to offer goats and pigs to their gods. They need only arrive to enjoy the cultural unity. Now that the festival is, as another *Girirāj* article's headline announced, a "Symbol of Ancient Culture,"[41] they need only bear witness to the evidence of Himachal's ancient religion (*devīdevatā saṇskṛti*). To argue that this symbolization has only recently become possible is not to argue that rituals were meaningless in the past or that rites did not perform a social function. The difference now is that the second-order work of connecting the rite to a larger abstract has transformed the rite itself. Now, when one attends the festival in Kullu, one is participating in the best example of Himachal's *devīdevatā saṇskṛti*. The vast majority of people who attend the festival do not go to ask the deity a question or to heal their child. They go to participate in Himachali religion. Here, religion's labor proceeds by stripping local practices of their specificity and redefining the logic and purpose of the festival. Ironically, in order to become an exemplar of Himachal's unique religion, the festival was transformed into a state-organized gathering, indistinguishable from innumerable other festivals, such as those in Madhya Pradesh or Tamil Nadu.

Afterword

Religion Is a Verb

ON LISTENING

When I was nineteen, I stumbled upon a well-thumbed collection of essays and talks by Jiddu Krishnamurti in a used-book store. It contained a short essay entitled "On Listening," and the words of this piece have haunted me ever since that strange afternoon. They return to me time and time again and in many ways, and they are the creative spark behind both the research for this book and the book itself. Perhaps the questions Krishnamurti raises are less than profound. Had I come across the essay two years earlier or two years later, they might have faded into the land of forgotten things. But as it is, they provide me with ballast. In the essay, Krishnamurti asks: "Why are you here listening to me? Have you ever considered why you listen to people at all? And what does listening to somebody mean? All of you here are sitting in front of one who is speaking. Are you listening to hear something that will confirm, tally with your own thoughts, or are you listening to find out?"[1] These questions ring as true to me today as they did so many years ago. While they do not contain theses or theorems to orient the study of religion, they do articulate a form of engagement that underpins both *Becoming Religious in a Secular Age* and my teaching.

Becoming Religious in a Secular Age is the result of my listening in the manner that Krishnamurti describes, and I hope that readers will approach it ready to do the same. There is no substitute for listening like this; in this sense, this book has nothing to teach. It does not offer any theory to abstract and test. It is not a collection of facts to be archived. It is, however, the result of my listening; it reveals a way of paying attention. In the introduction, I told a story about a young villager named Vijay and my struggle to understand what he was trying to convey. I understood his words, and I even understood their meaning, but I also knew I was missing something. I kept returning to that moment until I realized that I had not actually *heard* Vijay. I had only projected my understanding onto his words. Listening was the only thing that helped me understand that Vijay's words sounded simple solely because I couldn't hear the process of becoming religious that animated them. I could not hear the discovery that animated his words because I was too stuffed with knowledge to discover anything.

In my listening, this project of writing this book has taken many forms, but the curiosity on which the book is founded remains as vital today as when I began writing more than a decade ago. Time and again, I return to these questions: How has "religion" shaped the very horizon of what we understand as interesting and intelligible? How is our understanding of ourselves, our goals, our knowledge, and our obligations indebted to certain conceptions of religion? It is impossible to see one's own face in the mirror, and so I turned outward. The unique way that Himachal had developed in the twentieth century seemed to make it an exceptionally fertile environment in which to ask these questions. This particular situation would allow me to construct what Michel Foucault would have called a historical ontology of religion. This would be the name of a field of study that examines the "truth through which we constitute ourselves as objects of knowledge," the "power through which we constitute ourselves as subjects acting on others," and the "ethics through which we constitute ourselves as moral agents."[2] In order to understand the process of becoming religious in a secular age, I needed to understand how the concept of religion developed in relation to new forms of power and organization, both externally (at the level of politics and economy) and internally (in terms of a new sense of selfhood). I also needed to understand how, in this new environment, religion had become an object of knowledge and administration and how it was shaped by the logics of social science and the prerogatives of development. Finally, I needed to understand how these transformations became the basis by which Himachalis distinguished themselves as moral agents, marking certain activities as ethical and others and prohibited.

WHAT IS SO BECOMING ABOUT BECOMING?

In many ways, the title of this book, *Becoming Religious in a Secular Age*, suggests the work's primary contribution to the study of religion. As a whole, the work offers—to use a phrase taken from the late works of Michel Foucault—a historical ontology of religion. The "becoming" at the heart of this book is a necessarily twofold process. Even as the people of Himachal Pradesh increasingly recognize themselves as becoming religious, the target of their becoming is itself becoming. This confusing, convoluted, and creative process is the historical ontology of religion, but it is important to be clear about the ends of this becoming. Becoming religious is a process without end. This book is not to be understood as the story of the struggle by which a people became religious—that they struggled until they attained a particular state. Becoming religious *is* that state. To give this a Heideggerian bent, we might say that their being *is* their becoming.

What does all this mean? How might it alter the study of religion? How does someone go about studying religion from this perspective, and how is it different from other approaches? Stated more proactively: if I take the primary task of a scholar of religion to be within the provenance of creative and critical reason (i.e., the primary task of a scholar of religion is to help students of religion see differently), then the genealogical task of understanding how particular instantiations of religion came into being is simultaneously the task of seeing how they could have been otherwise.

What differentiates *Becoming Religious in a Secular Ages* from the work of Eliade or Freud? These two men provided answers to the question of religion. By contrast, this book turns us from the seduction of answers to the endless formulation of questions—from asserting to listening. The difference is easy to understand if we return to a concept borrowed from evolutionary biology. For decades following the publication of *On the Origin of Species* (1859), specialists and the public alike commonly understood what Darwin called "preadaptations" as traits designed for a future environment. The traits that would later give rise to feathers were "preadapted" to become feathers; they had a telos, a reason that would reveal itself later. The quest for a theory of religion, which was so central to the development of the social scientific study of religion, shared much with this understanding of preadaptive traits. Scholars like Eliade, Freud, and Tylor sought to, in Durkheim's words, "peel back the overgrowth" to reveal religion's raison d'être. By contrast, *Becoming Religious in a Secular Age* is motivated by a different telos. Rather than attempting to understand what religion is, it endeavors to understand how religiosity and becoming are inextricably bound to one another. This approach does not seek to arbitrate claims or to establish the validity of a particular instantiation of religion. To do so would be to understand religion as a bounded object—as, grammatically, a noun. This book operates in a different mode. The difference turns on the meaning of the word *is*. Or rather, if most scholarship in the study of religion is predicated on the assumption that religion is one object among others, the goal of which is to understand what religion *is*, then *Becoming Religious in a Secular Age* is predicated on an understanding of religion that is attendant to becoming—to understand religion as a verb.

This book opened with several strong critiques of classical approaches to the study of religion. Having arrived at the work's end, the reader might reasonably question whether it offers anything substantially different from those approaches. The book omits the detailed theoretical elaborations that lie behind each of the chapters. Here, I offer a short explanation of the theoretical infrastructure on which the book is built. The afterword, like the book itself, is an enactment—as opposed to a defense—of the contribution of *Becoming Religious in a Secular Age*. This shift from explanation to performance is not sophistry. While deeply engaged with theories of religion, *Becoming Religious in a Secular Age* is not itself a theory of religion. It cannot be used to explain the Kaula reforms or Incan death practices. This book is not an answer to the "problem" of religion. More productively, it offers a style of interrogation, an approach to thinking about religion in the present, freed from assumptions about religion as a static object without a future.

Part I explores the emergence of Himachali religion as it has developed in relation to underlying shifts in the organization and administration of the region. Himachali religion could only emerge once there was a thing to be recognized as Himachal and a people to identify with it. The very possibility of this emergence was inextricably tied to the institution of modern, secular forms of power that took hold in the mid-twentieth century. This transformation can be seen as structurally analogous to the environmental shifts that facilitate the preadaptations familiar to evolutionary biologists. This changing of underlying conditions made possible a new object of identification and elaboration: Himachal and its people. As such, it shares certain logical parallels with a pursuit that dominated the early study of religion: the search for origins.

In the early decades of the twentieth century, when scholars of religion abandoned the critiques of David Hume and Georg Feuerbach, they developed the social scientific study of religion, the foundation of which required articulating the origins of religion. To have a theory of religion was to have a theory about the origin of religion. Some of the most interesting and creative thinking about religion concerns itself with its origins. While many of the conclusions proposed by these scholars may strike contemporary readers as strange, tangential, or simplistic, I believe that we abandon something vital if we laugh away Freud's primal fantasy or Marx's sedative. Origins are important. But it is just as important not to mistake *an* origin for *the* origin. Durkheim knew this, even if he sometimes forgot. The approach articulated in the first two chapters of this book offers a way to engage with the question of origins without collapsing all social and historical difference.

Part 2 describes the process through which Himachali religion becomes an object. Himachali religion is not a natural object. It is not a species that will "breed true." It is an object that has become naturalized, and in doing so it can be identified as an object of reflection and study. In short, it becomes an object of scientific knowledge. The objectification of this knowledge has profound historical, epistemological, and ethical consequences. Taken together, =these consequences may be called the labor of religion. This labor gives rise to new forms of expertise—normalized understandings of Himachali pasts and futures. These, in turn, become functional components of the administration of daily life in Himachal. This part of the book is deeply influenced by scholarship on the history of science as practiced by Arnold Davidson and Ian Hacking, but it is attuned to the particularities of the scientific study of religion. More specifically, attending to the historical ontology of religion in this manner allows scholars of religion to attend to the concerns central to the phenomenology of religion without reducing religion to an immutable essence. In the case of HSV, such an approach allows us to understand the rhetorical power of religion without making ontological assertions.

In one of the many thoughtful summations of his work, Foucault says that he has always been interested in how certain fundamental experiences (of sexuality or madness) that are often imagined as "natural" have in fact emerged from particular configurations of power and knowledge."[3] The final section of *Becoming Religious in a Secular Age* builds on the previous four chapters, which described how shifts in power and knowledge enabled the emergence of Himachali religion, the historical ontology of religion in Himachal.[4]

While parts 1 and 2 strove to articulate how Himachali religion emerged and developed, part 3 looks more directly at the formation of religious experience. More precisely, it examines the ethical effects of religion's naturalization. Such naturalization does not mark the end of "becoming" and the arrival of "being." Rather, it marks the beginning of a full-throated debate about the nature, scope, and function of religion—the basis for ethical discrimination. Having become an object, religion is now an opening where self-definition and self-understanding take place. It is no longer only a placeholder in the restructuring of the state, as it was in part 1. It is more than an object of academic reflection and governmental management, as it was in part 2. Having become an object separated from its others (state, economy, politics, etc.), defined and organized by a science of religion, and regulated and managed by the state, it now circulates as an object of desire, of revitalization, of cultivation. At this moment, the question is no longer *whether* one can relate to religion or whether it is known or knowable; rather, the question becomes *how* one relates to religion and how it does or should inform one's thoughts and actions. Is animal sacrifice a religious act? How is personal authenticity tied to religiosity? Is scientific knowledge a threat to or an asset of religiosity? Seen from this vantage, certain aspects of the study of religion emerge in stark relief. Do we seek answers to these questions? Or, as Krishnamurti does, might we more profitably listen to the questions themselves to discover what we seek?

Notes

INTRODUCTION

1. On religion as neurosis, see Sigmund Freud, *On Creativity and the Unconscious: Papers on the Psychology of Art, Literature, Love, Religion* (New York: Harper, 1958). On religion as compensation for fate, see Freud, *The Future of an Illusion* (Mansfield Center, CT: Martino, 2010). On religion as the social, see Émile Durkheim, *The Elementary Forms of the Religious Life* (London: Allen and Unwin, 1976).

2. Timothy Fitzgerald, *The Ideology of Religious Studies* (New York: Oxford University Press, 2000), 4.

3. The word *khelnā* has many meanings. Literally, it means "to play," and I extend this idea to include a form of play with and as a deity.

4. This concept lies at the heart of *Becoming Religious*. Seen from one angle, the book is a genealogy of the concept. As such, negotiations over the meaning, scope, and importance of the concept are vital, ongoing components of Himachali life. Throughout the book, I will offer several different translations of *devīdevatā saṃskṛti*. They are not mutually exclusive. More commonly, in spite of ongoing negotiations, the semantic variations entrench the concept ever deeper.

5. S.J. Gould, *The Structure of Evolutionary Theory* (Cambridge, MA: Harvard University Press, 2002).

6. Two works suggest the range of such positions: Vinayak Damodar Savarkar, *Hindutva: Who Is a Hindu?*, 5th ed. (New Delhi: Hindi Sahitya Sadan, 2003); and Ashis Nandy, "The Politics of Secularism and the Recovery of Religious

Tolerance," in *Secularism and Its Critics,* ed. Rajeev Bhargava (Delhi: Oxford University Press, 1998), 321–344.

7. Logically, one might understand religion as an a priori human category while still recognizing that a new understanding of religion has developed in the past two hundred years.

8. Ian Hacking, *The Social Construction of What?* (Cambridge, MA: Harvard University Press, 1999); Arnold I. Davidson, *The Emergence of Sexuality: Historical Epistemology and the Formation of Concepts* (Cambridge, MA: Harvard University Press, 2001).

9. René Girard, *The Scapegoat,* Johns Hopkins Paperbacks ed. (Baltimore: Johns Hopkins University Press, 1989).

10. There is a large body of ethnographically oriented scholarship on ethics in South Asia that has informed this entire section. Among the most influential for my work are Leela Prasad, *Poetics of Conduct: Oral Narrative and Moral Being in a South Indian Town* (New York: Columbia University Press, 2007); Anand Pandian, *Crooked Stalks: Cultivating Virtue in South India* (Durham: Duke University Press, 2009); Anand Pandian and Daud Ali, *Ethical Life in South Asia* (Bloomington: Indiana University Press, 2010); Akhil Gupta, "Blurred Boundaries: The Discourse of Corruption, the Culture of Politics and the Imagined State," *American Ethnologist* 22, no. 2 (1995): 375–402; and Gupta, *Postcolonial Developments: Agriculture in the Making of Modern India* (Durham: Duke University Press, 1998).

11. Cheryl Strayed, *Tiny Beautiful Things: Advice on Love and Life from Dear Sugar* (New York: Vintage, 2012).

12. Friedrich Nietzsche, *The Will to Power,* trans. Walter Kaufmann (New York: Random House, 1967), 550.

13. Willi Braun and Russell T. McCutcheon, *Guide to the Study of Religion* (London: Cassell, 2000).

14. S.R. Chandel, "Letter to the President, General Secretary and Members of the Standing Committee of All India States Peoples Conference" (Nehru Memorial Library Archives, 1948).

CHAPTER 1

1. Jawaharlal Nehru, *Selected Works of Jawaharlal Nehru,* vol. 26 (New Delhi: Jawaharlal Nehru Memorial Fund, 1984), 134.

2. R. Boswel Smith, *Life of Lord Lawrence,* vol. 2 (London: Smith, Elder and Co., 1883), 426.

3. Carlo Ginzburg, Martin H. Ryle, and Kate Soper, *Wooden Eyes: Nine Reflections on Distance* (New York: Columbia University Press, 2001).

4. Pahāṛī, literally "of the mountains," refers loosely to the people who inhabit the Western Himalayas. It is also used the denote a diverse group of dialects. There was extensive debate in the late nineteenth century and in the 1960s and 1970s over its proper designation as a language.

5. Charles Montesquieu, *The Spirit of Laws*, vol. II (Colonial Press, 1899), 224.

6. Fanny Parks, *Wanderings of a Pilgrim in Search of the Picturesque* (London: Oxford University Press, 1975), 259.

7. See Ginzburg, Ryle, and Soper, *Wooden Eyes*.

8. James Baillie Fraser, *The Himala Mountains* (Delhi: Neraj Publishing House, 1982), 65.

9. However, this distinction was not supported by everyone in the earliest periods. In particular, travelers from other countries did not subscribe to this theory. Victor Jacquemont, a French naturalist who traveled throughout the Western Himalayas just after Fraser, had a radically different opinion of the Bushahari people. On his trip up the Satluj into Tibet, he stayed in Sarāhan with the king of Bushahar, whom he recognized as a legitimate king. He described him as quite wealthy, earning "a revenue of a hundred and fifty thousand francs a year, without pressing on his subjects, who are the most wretched in the world." Victor Jacquemont, *Letters from India: Describing a Journey in the British Dominions of India, Tibet, Lahore and Cashmere* (Karachi: Oxford University Press, 1979), 252.

10. George Powell Thomas, *Views of Simla* (London: Dickinson, 1846), 66.

11. Stephen Greenblatt, *Marvelous Possessions: The Wonder of the New World* (Chicago: University of Chicago Press, 1992).

12. Alice Elizabeth Dracott, *Simla Village Tales; or, Folk Tales from the Himalayas* (London: John Murray, 1906), x.

13. William Howard Russell, *My Diary in India in the Year 1858–59*, vol. 2 (London: Routledge, Warne and Routledge, 1860), 178.

14. Emily Eden, *Up the Country* (London: Virago, 1983).

15. Government of India, Ministry of States, *White Paper on Indian States,* rev. ed. (Delhi: Manager of Publications, 1950); Y.S. Parmar and Himachal Pradesh India, *Himachal Pradesh: Its Proper Shape and Status* (Simla: Directorate of Public Relations, Himachal Pradesh, 1965).

16. Letter from Sardar Patel to Dr. Pattabhi Sitaramayya, March 18, 1948, quoted in Y.S. Parmar, *Himachal Pradesh: Case for Statehood* (Simla: Directorate of Public Relations, 1968), iii.

17. Quoted in H.L. Vaidya, *Those Turbulent Days* (Delhi: Indian Publishers and Distributors, 1999), 55.

18. Ibid., 59.

19. Y.S. Parmar, *Polyandry in the Himalayas* (Delhi: Vikas, 1975), 183.

20. See India, Reorganization Commission, *Report of the States Reorganization Commission, 1955* (New Delhi: Government of India Press, 1955).

21. Tarasankar Banerjee, ed., *Historiography in Modern Indian Languages, 1800–1947: Report of the National Seminar Held at Santiniketan, from 11th March to 13th March 1985* (Calcutta, India: Naya Prokash, 1987); Bernard S. Cohn, "The Command of Language and the Language of Command," in *Colonialism and Its Forms of Knowledge: The British in India* (Princeton, NJ: Princeton University Press, 1996), 16–56; Robert D. King, *Nehru and the Language Politics of India* (Delhi: Oxford University Press, 1997); Thomas R. Trautmann, *Languages and Nations: The Dravidian Proof in Colonial Madras* (Berkeley: University of California Press, 2006).

22. Fear of Punjab had been a constant concern for Himachali politicians earliest struggles for Himachali statehood. The advisory committee of Himachal Pradesh issued the following statement on October 4, 1948:

> Some of the neighbors who had been looking for the exploitation of those backward people and who were ignorant of our peculiar habits, customs, traditions, culture and language had not looked favorably to the emergence of this new Province. It was true we were backward—educationally as well as economically—but we had a proud heritage of our own and the people of the hills were determined to grow according to their own traditions and culture. Before trying to spread their tentacles it would be more conducive to the interest of their people if the could set their own house in order. We had a colossal task confronting us and if they could not lighten our burden let them not add to our difficulties, but permit us to develop according to our own light. We had good words for every one and a strong desire and urge not only to use our newly won freedom in the interests of our hill people but for the solidification and strengthening of our Motherland. (Quoted in Vaidya, *Turbulent Days*, 47.)

23. The role of Bilaspur in the dam project at Govind Sagar has yet to be adequately investigated. For an initial attempt at understanding the situation, see Paramjit S. Judge, "Responses to Dams and Displacement in Two Indian States," *Asian Survey* 37, no. 9 (1997), 840–851.

24. Parmar explicitly says as much. See Parmar, *Case for Statehood*, 2.

25. There is nothing new about this kind of definitional enterprise. It is repeated in countless other places across centuries.

26. Some might reasonably argue that I have not adequately addressed the so-called language debates, since battles for state autonomy were commonly

articulated on precisely these grounds. There can be little doubt that language politics dominated several important debates over regional autonomy in the early decades of Indian independence. Furthermore, the diminution of these debates should not fool us into assuming that the decrease in language-related violence was indicative of the disappearance of tensions smoldering just beneath the surface. That said, Himachal's argument for autonomy was articulated on the basis of religion, not language. As will become clear in later chapters, the fact that language was not used as a basis for regional autonomy should in no way suggest that the use, transformations, and manipulations of Pahāṛī dialects, trader-Hindi, and even English are not critical to the emerging discourse on Himachali religion. In fact, the words chosen and the grammar employed by a given speaker and the historical references such choices reveal are often the very heart of ongoing negotiations over Himachali religion.

27. Kashmir Singh, "Selected Speeches on the Floor of the Vidhān Sabhā, Discussion of the States Re-Organization Bill, Reprint from the Debates, April 3–5, 1956," *Vidhānmālā* 9, no. 1–2 (2002): 229–231.

28. The construction of Bhakra Dam (the so-called temple of modernity) figured centrally in this debate.

29. K. Singh, "Selected Speeches," 256.

30. A recent popular book opens: "Away from the plains of Punjab, Kullu—the Valley of Village Gods—nestled in the Pir Panjal range of the Western Himalayas.... Having lived for centuries in remoteness and seclusion, Kullu people are comparatively simple and submissive to the constituted authority. They are courteous and generous to outsiders who may gain familiarity with them." Dilram Shabab, *Kullu: Himalayan Abode of the Divine* (New Delhi: Indus, 1999), 15–17.

31. Himachal Pradesh Director of Public Relations, *Himachal Pradesh 1971* (Shimla: The Controller, Printing and Stationary, Himachal Pradesh, 1971), 5.

32. Government of India, Ministry of State, *White Paper,* 219.

33. "The Architect of Himachal Pradesh: Dr. Y. S. Parmar," *Commerce,* January 23, 1971, 3.

34. Quoted in ibid.

35. Vaidya, *Turbulent Days,* 30.

36. Parmar, *Case for Statehood,* iii.

37. See, for example, the long poem *Śrigūl Parmar,* which links the popular hill deity Śrigūl to Parmar.

38. Vaidya, *Turbulent Days,* xv.

39. Y. S. Parmar, *Himachal Pradesh: Area and Language* (Simla: Directorate of Public Relations, 1970), 5.

40. Government of Punjab, *The Resurgent Punjab* (Chandigarh: Public Relations Department, 1956) 25.

41. "The tumult of the plains below had left them untouched and they, for ages lived a life their forefathers had lived. Their faiths were unadulterated, their customs deep rooted and their outlook happy." Parmar, *Polyandry*, 178.

42. For a more general look at the role of planning in India, see T. J. Byres, ed., *The State and Development Planning in India* (Delhi: Oxford Universit Press, 1994); and Sukhamoy Chakravarty, *Development Planning: The Indian Experience* (New York: Oxford University Press, 1987).

43. See, for example, Himachal Pradesh (India), Planning and Development Dept., *First Five-Year Plan, 1951–1956* (Simla: The Dept., 1958).

44. Y. S. Parmar, "Economic Potential of Himachal Pradesh," *Commerce*, August 15, 1970, 1.

45. In the first five-year plan created and administered by Parmar, for the years 1951–1956, the development of roads and communication networks was allotted more than 50 percent of the annual state budget. With national recognition of Himachali statehood, focus returned to state development. In 1948, there were barely two hundred kilometers of navigable roads in the entire region. Now, the department of public works reports that there are over twenty-three thousand kilometers of roadway. These roads and the transport operators of the Himachal Road Transport Corporation, who maintain them, are the foundation for communications in the region. In the early periods of development and in the solidification of a Pahārī identity, these roads were essential to the dissemination of ideas about statehood and cultural difference. Analogous to these transportation networks were the development of communications networks and the spread of vernacular media. See Himachal Pradesh (India), Planning and Development Dept., *First Five-Year Plan*; and Himachal Pradesh (India), Planning and Development Dept., *Third Five Year Plan (1961–66): Achievements* (Simla: The Manager, Himachal Pradesh Administration Press, 1961).

46. Y. S. Parmar, *Years of Challenge and Growth* (New Delhi: Rubicon, 1977), 25.

47. Ibid., 34.

48. Parmar, *Polyandry*, 33.

49. Ibid.

50. Ibid., 183.

CHAPTER 2

1. The gūr is the primary means of communication between the community and the deity. The gūr has a special relationship with the deity; he is the means through which the deity communicates to his community and through which the people of the community convey their hopes, demands, and gratitude to the deity. In these communities, the gūr has exceptional power to shape his village. However, while one would expect these individuals to be relaxing on velvet divans and fanned by young, scantily clad women, they are often simple men who resemble other villagers, distinguished on the surface only by their long hair and dietary restrictions.

2. Inscriptions in the Chamba valley, for example, deal extensively with the granting and control of land. See Jean Philippe Vogel and Bahadur Chand Chhabra, *Antiquities of Chamba State,* Memoirs of the Archaeological Survey of India 72 (1911; repr., New Delhi: Archaeological Survey of India, 1994).

3. Nicholas B. Dirks, *The Hollow Crown: Ethnohistory of an Indian Kingdom,* Cambridge South Asian Studies 39 (Cambridge, UK: Cambridge University Press, 1987); D.A. Washbrook, "Law, State and Agrarian Society in Colonial India," *Modern Asian Studies* 15, no. 3 (1981): 649–721.

4. For a list of these settlement reports from the Simla Hill States, see C.L. Datta, *The Raj and the Simla Hill States: Socio-Economic Problems, Agrarian Disturbances and Paramountcy* (Jalandhar: ABS, 1997).

5. B.H. Baden-Powell, *The Land-Systems of British India: Being a Manual of the Land-Tenures and of the Systems of Land-Revenue Administration Prevalent in the Several Provinces* (Oxford: Clarendon Press, 1892), 617.

6. George Carnac Barnes was one of the primary officers in charge of the early settlement in the hills. His work became a model for settlement officers and ethnohistorians alike.

7. George Carnac Barnes, "Report of the Kangra Settlement" (Himachal Pradesh State Archives, 1872), 16.

8. Somewhat later, in his classic summary statement of land systems in British India, Baden-Powell described the situation in the Western Himalayas as follows: "Here, whether we look to Chambá, which is a feudatory State, or to Kángrá, which is British territory, or to the protected States in the Simla hills, we find no 'villages' in the ordinary sense, and consequently, unless they have been created at settlement, no joint-proprietary communities over villages." Baden-Powell, *Land-Systems,* 692.

9. Ramachandra Guha, *The Unquiet Woods: Ecological Change and Peasant Resistance in the Himalaya,* 2nd ed. (New Delhi: Oxford University Press, 2001), 17–20. In support of his argument, Guha offers a wide range of statistical and census data. The reference to Traill comes from G. W. Traill, "Statistical Sketch of Kumaun," *Asiatic Researches* 16 (1828).

10. Guha, *Unquiet Woods.*

11. Barnes, "Report of the Kangra Settlement," 18.

12. For an interesting account of nostalgia, hill stations, and the reconstruction of both England and the people of the Himalayas, see Dane Keith Kennedy, *The Magic Mountains Hill Stations and the British Raj* (Berkeley: University of California Press, 1996).

13. These transformations were not a conscious project on the part of colonial elites. Instead, the changes had much more to do with the elites' understanding of the progress of humanity and their education in British and Continental history.

14. Many of the letters of petition, reports, and personal grievances are collected in an archive of papers held at the Himachal Pradesh State Archives. "Extract from the Inspection Note on Hatkoti Temple" (Himachal Pradesh State Archives in Re-Settlement in Hat Kothi Jagir, September 21, 1941).

15. In general, the more traditional way that land disputes were resolved was through inviting a local deity to the location in question. Once present, the deity would be asked to walk the line between the contested property or to walk the entire perimeter of the property. For many, this method continues to be preferable to more modern systems of resolution. In fact, many of the deities near Hatkothi continue to perform rites such as this. One man from Rohru told me that nowadays, if people want to resolve a land dispute, they call the deity. If, however, they want to prolong the decision for some reason or attempt to permanently stall the case, they pursue the case through the Himachali court system.

16. Rana Sir Bhagat Chandra, "Letter No. G.7–12/31–617 Rana Sir Bhagat Chandra to the Political Agent, Punjab Hill States, Simla" (Himachal Pradesh State Archives in Re-Settlement in Hat Kothi Jagir, June 29, 1942).

17. It is very possible that this allegiance is only as old as the Gurkha rule. The Pabbar valley, in which these fields are situated, was an important location during the rise and fall of Gurkha rule in the Western Himalayas.

18. On the role of princely states in colonial India, see Ian Copland, *The British Raj and the Indian Princes: Paramountcy in Western India, 1857–1930* (Bombay: Orient Longman, 1982); Barbara N. Ramusack, *The Indian Princes and Their*

States (Cambridge, UK: Cambridge University Press, 2004); and Edward John Thompson, *The Making of the Indian Princes* (London: Oxford University Press, H. Milford, 1943).

19. J. L. Hutchinson and J. P. Vogel, *History of the Panjab Hill States*, 2 vols. (Shimla: Department of Language and Culture, 1982).

20. A parallel can be made between the use of *begār* labor in the construction of the Kalka-Shimla Railway and the abuse of Chinese immigrant labor in the construction of the railroad in the Sierra Nevada in the western United States. See, for example, Annian Huang, *The Silent Spikes: Chinese Laborers and the Construction of North American Railroads* (Beijing: China Intercontinental Press, 2006).

21. This system was, as far as I can tell, not widespread in the rest of the subcontinent.

22. "Final Settlement Report of Kullu Sub-Division of District Kangra" (Himachal Pradesh State Archives, 1913).

23. Vogel and Chhabra, *Antiquities of Chamba State.*

24. E. C. Wace, *Final Report on the First Regular Settlement of the Simla District in the Punjab*, vol. HPSA 894–67 (31) (Calcutta: Calcutta Central Press, 1884).

25. There are fairly good records from many of the larger temples (in particular, temples like Jwalamukhi, Jamlu, and Bhīmākālī) that make assessment possible.

26. The assertion that the Western Himalayas was a feudal area—an idea integral to the independence movement in Himachal—is deeply tied to these developments. The idea of an elite class ruling a poor peasantry appears to be a result of colonial projects and princely powers assuming the reins.

27. Quoted in Nicholas B. Dirks, *Castes of Mind: Colonialism and the Making of Modern India* (Princeton, NJ: Princeton University Press, 2001), 149.

28. Richard Gabriel Fox, *Kin, Clan, Raja, and Rule: State Hinterland Relations in Preindustrial India* (Berkeley: University of California Press, 1971); Irfan Habib, *The Agrarian System of Mughal India, 1556–1707*, 2nd ed. (New Delhi: Oxford University Press, 1999); Thomas R. Metcalf, "Landlords without Land: The U.P. Zamindars Today," *Pacific Affairs* 40, no. 1–2 (1967): 5–18; Metcalf, *Land, Landlords and the British Raj: Northern India in the Nineteenth Century* (Berkeley: University of California Press, 1979).

29. Metcalf, *Land, Landlords and the British Raj.*

30. Punjab Government, *Punjab District Gazetteers: Volume XXX, Kangra District*, ed. Sudershan Vashishtha (1917; repr., Shimla: Himachal Pradesh Academy of Arts, Culture and Language, 2003).

31. "Final Settlement Report of Kullu Sub-Division of District Kangra," 16.

32. Suman Chauhan, "Social Organization and Land Control: A Study of the Role of Temples in Kullu and Shimla" (PhD diss., Himachal Pradesh State University, 1997), 196–197.

33. Ibid., 164; A.H. Diack, *Assessment Report of the Plach Tahsil of the Kangra District* (Lahore: Punjab Government Press, 1892), 11.

34. "Final Settlement Report of Kullu Sub-Division of District Kangra," 12.

35. Ibid., 64.

36. Chauhan, "Social Organization," 176–178.

37. There is some dispute on this topic. Particularly, the hereditary priests of the temple in Malana assert that they maintained excellent ties with Mughal emperors. This is evidenced now in popular imaginations as much as it is in classical sources on the regions, such as those by Harcourt and Hutchinson and Vogel.

38. The complexity of the land reforms has been a subject of intense public debate and more than a little legal debate. Much of this debate came to a head with the case of *Vinod Kumar v. State of Himachal Pradesh.* See Vinod Kumar v. State of H.P. (S.R. Das C.J.) Supreme Court, A.I.R. 46, no. 29 (1959) S.C. 223.

39. Jogishwar Singh, *Banks, Gods and Government: Institutional and Informal Credit Structure in a Remote and Tribal Indian District (Kinnaur, Himachal Pradesh), 1960–1985* (Stuttgart: F. Steiner Verlag Wiesbaden, 1989), 112.

40. V. Verma, *The Emergence of Himachal Pradesh: A Survey of Constitutional Developments* (New Delhi: Indus, 1995), 165–166.

41. India, Planning Commission, *The First Five Year Plan: A Draft Outline* (New Delhi: Manager of Publications, 1951), 184.

42. H.C.L. Merillat, *Land and the Constitution in India* (New York: Columbia University Press, 1970).

43. Ibid. See also Puran Chandra Joshi, *Land Reforms in India: Trends and Perspectives* (Bombay: Allied Publishers, 1975).

44. Merillat, *Land and the Constitution.*

45. Ibid., 106.

46. See Puran Chandra Joshi, "Pre-Independence Thinking on Agrarian Policy," *Economic and Political Weekly* 2 (February 1967): 447–456.

47. Merillat, *Land and the Constitution,* 108.

48. India, Planning Commission, *Fourth Five Year Plan, 1969–74: Draft* (Delhi: Manager Publications Branch, 1969), 1313.

49. "The State has been and still continues to be an agriculture-based area. The plight of the tillers of land in the princely states is a long harrowing

tale. There was no security of tenancy, nor any reasonableness in the sharing of crops. The perniciousness of the system lay in the levy of numerous other cesses in cash and in king, including the exaction of compulsory unpaid labor. The abolition of these impositions came to be regarded by the people a sufficient reason for launching agitations. To the Praja Mandal leaders it was the movement's *raison d'etre.*" Verma, *Emergence of Himachal Pradesh,* 163.

50. Himachal Pradesh (India), "Himachal Pradesh Code" (Simla: Himachal Pradesh Govt. Law Dept., 2003).

51. This is evidenced not only in the Vidhān Sabhā debates but also in the budget statements. See Himachal Pradesh Vidhān Sabhā, *Mukhyamantriyoṃ/ Vittamantriyoṃ Ke Bajat Abhibhaṣaṇa* (Shimla: Himachal Pradesh Vidhān Sabhā, 2000).

52. The Himachal Pradesh Vidhān Sabhā library houses a large archive of all of the debates that have taken place on the floor of the legislature. Examination of these volumes provides the primary evidence for the reconstruction of the legislative history of the region. It is also where one can begin to see the development of the particular character of the Himachali public and the role of politics in these forms of circulation.

53. This is a phrase often invoked by proponents of land reform. On the failure of land reforms see, Ronald J. Herring, *Land to the Tiller: The Political Economy of Agrarian Reform in South Asia* (New Haven: Yale University Press, 1983).

54. Himachal Pradesh (India), "Himachal Pradesh Code."

55. Akhil Gupta, *Postcolonial Developments: Agriculture in the Making of Modern India* (Durham: Duke University Press, 1998); Sunil Khilnani, *The Idea of India* (New York: Farrar, Straus Giroux, 1998); Lloyd I. Rudolph and Susanne Hoeber Rudolph, *In Pursuit of Lakshmi: The Political Economy of the Indian State* (Chicago: University of Chicago Press, 1987).

56. Krishnanad Swami, "24-4-1953 Vidhān Sabhā Debates," Vidhān Sabhā Archives, 1953.

57. This is a very different approach than that taken by states that were more suitable for industrial development.

58. Narayan Kotvi, "Himāchal Pradeś Baṛī Zamīndārī Unmūlan Tathā Bhūmi Sudhār Vidheyak (Shimla: Himachal Pradesh Vidhan Sabha 15)," *Vidhān Mālā* 8, no. 1–2 (2001): 155–229.

59. This is Krishnanad Swami's phrase.

60. Speeches, vol. 143, Vidhān Sabhā Archives, Shimla.

61. Speeches, vol. 148, Vidhān Sabhā Archives, Shimla.

62. Krishnanad Swami, "Viśeṣ Ākarṣṇa-III," in *Vidhān Mālā* 8, no. 1–2 (2001): 155–228.

63. Ibid., 159.

64. The transformation of the Vidhān Sabhā was the result of the Himachal Pradesh and Bilaspur New State Act (1954). See Himachal Pradesh (India), "Himachal Pradesh Code."

65. Vinod Kumar v. State of H. P. (S. R. Das C. J.) Supreme Court, A. I. R. 46, no. 29 (1959) S. C. 223.

66. Herring, *Land to the Tiller,* 4.

67. The logic for this collapse is supported by the way that these reforms are conceptualized, and even articulated, now. My evidence comes primarily from the ethnographic present, and I have never heard anyone make a distinction between the early models of land reform and the later models in discussing the ways that their lives have been transformed by land reform. Moreover, while this book is concerned primarily with the restructuring of land that was owned and controlled by temples, which was effected primarily by the transformations associated with the "abolition legislation," this legislation does not even appear in the current land code manual. It is superseded by the ceiling acts. See Himachal Pradesh (India), "Himachal Pradesh Land Code," ed. Himachal Pradesh Revenue Department (Shimla: Financial Commissioner, Himachal Pradesh, 1991).

68. This situation is not unlike that in Benares in the early part of colonial rule. In that case, a newly formed group of Indian administrators associated with the East India Company were able to profit handsomely from the newly created land market and the newly formed administrative structure implemented by the British. See Bernard S. Cohn, *An Anthropologist among the Historians and Other Essays* (Delhi: Oxford University Press, 1987).

69. For figures on land ownership by these deities, see "Final Settlement Report of Kullu Sub-Division of District Kangra"; and Eberhard Fischer, V. C. Ohri, and Vijay Sharma, *The Temple of Devi-Kothi* (Zurich: Artibus Asiae, 2003), 167.

70. It must be admitted that Singh opens the first section of this text by saying that, "traditionally, the Rājā was the owner of all land." Singh, *Banks, Gods and Government,* 97.

71. Ibid., 98.

72. Ibid., 193.

73. Ibid., 289.

74. Ibid. 313–314

75. The deities he is referring to are predominately Bhīmākālī and Kamru.

76. Some excellent evidence comes from songs about the deities. A fairly large body of Hindi literature has grown up around these songs. In addition to almost innumerable articles in journals like *Somasī*, there are two popular volumes of songs and storytelling: Jagdish Sharma, ed., *Himāchal Pradeś Kī Lokgāthāeṃ* (Shimla: Himachal Pradesh Art, Culture, and Language Academy, 2000); and Sudarshan Vashisth, ed., *Himāchal Pradeś Ke Lok Gīt* (Shimla: Himachal Pradesh Sanskriti Bhasa Akademy, n.d.).

77. Singh, *Banks, Gods and Government.*

78. See, for example, Fischer, Ohri, and V. Sharma, *Temple of Devi-Kothi.*

79. Mahesh Sharma, *The Realm of Faith: Subversion, Appropriation and Dominance in the Western Himalaya* (Shimla: Indian Institute of Advanced Study, 2001), 136. For these figures, Sharma draws on the Jamabandi consolidation report of 1956 and patwari records. Sharma also does an excellent job of examining land relations surrounding a Shaivite Dasanammi math (or monastery) in the village of Thor. What he shows is that the math was a major center not just of cultivation but also of credit. He draws upon a set of archival records that document relations between villagers and the math, in particular the lending practice of the math and the manner in which interest and labor were calculated. While I believe that Sharma may go a little far in his caste-based analysis—arguing that the monastery was a means of consolidating Brahmanical power over low-caste villagers—the information he provides is useful insofar as it offers us a detailed sense of the material relations between religious institutions and villagers in the Western Himalayas.

80. Baden-Powell, *Land-Systems of British India,* 694.

CHAPTER 3

1. For a discussion of the way that certain fields of knowledge become visible to the state, see James C. Scott, *Seeing Like a State: How Certain Schemes to Improve the Human Condition Have Failed* (New Haven: Yale University Press, 1998).

2. It has become very common for scholars to lament the blurry boundary between state and society. Sudipta Kaviraj offers a deft retort: "It is a tiresomely standard procedure in political analysis to investigate between state and society.... It sometimes appears from the absentminded use of these concepts in modern social analysis that state and society are transcendent ideas, applicable without difficulty to all times and spaces, similar to the culturally

neutral descriptive terms of natural science." Kaviraj, "The Modern State in India," in *Dynamics of State Formation: India and Europe Compared*, ed. Sudipta Kaviraj and Martin Doornbos (New Delhi: Sage, 1997), 225. See also Nicholas B. Dirks, "Annals of the Archive: Ethnographic Notes on the Sources of History," in *Historical Anthropology and Its Futures: From the Margins*, ed. Brian Keith Axel (Durham: Duke University Press, 2002), 47–65; and P. Padmanabha, *Indian Census and Anthropological Investigations* (New Delhi: Registrar General and Census Commissioner India, 1978).

3. Quoted in Partha Chatterjee, *The Nation and Its Fragments: Colonial and Postcolonial Histories* (Princeton, NJ: Princeton University Press, 1993), 77.

4. It is also connected to the work of other departments within the growing state apparatus. Those that are most important in the context of this book are the Department of Public Relations, the state library, and the archival services at the Secretariat and the government press. In particular, I am thinking of the work of people such as Mian Goverdhan Singh and Keshav Nārāyaṇa.

5. Indeed, Parmar was regularly cast as a folk hero from the 1970s onward. He now stands as an almost superhuman figure at the state's foundation. There is a poem that circulates in Sirmaur, and even amongst some state officials, called "Śrigul Parmar," which analogizes Parmar with the popular Sirmauri deity Śrigul.

6. Nicholas Dirks summarizes nicely: "British colonialism played a critical role in both the identification and the production of Indian 'tradition.' Current debates about modernity and tradition fail to appreciate the extent to which the congeries of beliefs, customs, practice, and convictions that have been designated as traditional are in fact the complicated by products of colonial history." Nicholas B. Dirks, *Castes of Mind: Colonialism and the Making of Modern India* (Princeton, NJ: Princeton University Press, 2001).

7. Nicholas B. Dirks, "Annals of the Archive: Ethnographic Notes on the Sources of History," in *Historical Anthropology and Its Futures: From the Margins*, edited by Brian Keith Axel (Durham: Duke University Press, 2002), 47–65.

8. Dirks, *Castes of Mind*.

9. Interestingly, this logic is not unlike that employed much later in the postcolonial period. So, for example, the earliest attempts by the state to manage cultural differences and interact with newly acquired territories was based on land and the abolition of big landed estates. This was, in fact, one of the first acts of the legislation, and its centrality in the early years before full rec-

ognition of state hood is evidenced in many places, including the annual budget speeches of the chief minister and the archives of the Vidhān Sabhā. See Himachal Pradesh Vidhān Sabhā, *Mukhyamaṇtriyoṃ/Vittamaṇtriyoṃ*. See also any of the village studies organized by R. C. Singh for the 1961 census. For example, Ishwar Dayal Gupta, *A Village Survey of Gijari, Theog Tehsil, Mahasu District* (Shimla: Government of India Press, 1961).

10. The specific village surveys are thus part of a broader strategy aimed at the production of local level statistics, using the village as it base. For a broader overview of this process and the place of the Planning Commission in the process of constructing the census, see Shyam Chandra Srivastava, *Indian Census in Perspective* (New Delhi: Office of the Registrar General, India Ministry of Home Affairs, 1983).

11. Padmanabha, *Indian Census,* 12.

12. These words are from a short forward written by Register General Ashok Mitra that accompanies every volume in the series. For example, see Chandra Kumar and Ram Chandra Pal Singh, *A Village Survey of Kothi, Kalpa Subdivision, District Kinnaur* (Shimla: Government of India Press, 1963), i–iii.

13. Although there are reports of thirty-five volumes having been produced, I have only been able to see twenty-seven of them. It is not clear whether the other volumes were produced.

14. India, Office of the Registrar General, Ram Chandra Pal Singh, and India, Superintendent of Census Operations Himachal Pradesh, *Himachal Pradesh: Fairs and Festivals* (Delhi: Manager of Publications, 1967).

15. Timothy Mitchell, *Rule of Experts: Egypt, Techno-Politics, Modernity* (Berkeley: University of California Press, 2002), 80–119.

16. Ibid., 86.

17. Ibid., 116.

18. B. S. Ojha, Gurdev Singh Pabla, and Janak Raj Vashistha, *Tandi: A Village in Lahaul and Spiti District of Punjab,* Village Survey Monographs of Punjab 1 (New Delhi: Indian Publications Trading Corp, 1951), v.

19. The separation between culture and economy has its roots in the land reforms of the mid-twentieth century.

20. Jag Mohan and Ram Chandra Pal Singh, *A Village Survey of Shakrori, Seoni Sub-Tehsil, Mahasu District* (Shimla: Government of India Press, 1963).

21. I. D. Gupta, *Village Survey of Gijari.*

22. Mohan Lal Gupta and Ram Chandra Pal Singh, *A Village Survey of Chergaon, Rohro Tehsil, Mahasu District* (Shimla: Government of India Press, 1965), 73.

23. Mohan and C.P. Singh, *Village Survey of Shakrori*, 37.

24. On this point, the authors are very uneven. The authors of the studies of Shakrori, Gijari, and Chirgaon, for example, all present "superstitions" just like any other aspect they were measuring.

25. Charam Pal Kapur, Rikhi Ram Sharma, and Ram Chandra Pal Singh, *Brahmaur: A Village Survey of Brahmaur Sub-Tehsil, Chamba District* (Shimla: Government of India Press, 1963), 56.

26. An interesting study could be made on the direct influence of Western sociological theory on Himachal's elite. Parmar, for example, definitely read his Marx, Weber, and Durkheim.

27. M.L. Gupta and R.C.P. Singh, *Village Survey of Chergaon*, 73.

28. This type of staged, almost Hegelian, logic is present throughout the studies.

29. Chuni lal Sharma, *Shathka: A Village Survey of Kumarasain Sub-Tehsil, Mahasu District* (Shimla: Government of India Press, 1966), 50.

30. These studies are not, and probably never were, widely available. In the United States, I have only been able to locate one institution that has them. In India, they are only slightly more readily available.

31. R.C. Pal Singh, *Census of India, 1961*, vol. 5, *Himachal Pradesh* (New Delhi: Manager of Publications, 1961).

32. Satyapal Sehgal, "In Himachal Fiction Writing Is Up and Up," *Tribune* (Chandigarh), October 14, 2001.

33. See Akhil Gupta's discussion of the multi-sited character of the state, "Blurred Boundaries." Particularly useful is his discussion of the way the state is constituted both in public culture and in local personal relations.

34. See Dirks, *Castes of Mind*.

35. See, for example, the articles in *Somasī* 3, no. 4 (1978).

36. See, for example, many of M.R. Thakur's first editorials, written in the early 1980s.

37. Anna Lowenhaupt Tsing, *In the Realm of the Diamond Queen: Marginality in an Out-of-the-Way Place* (Princeton, NJ: Princeton University Press, 1993).

38. Michael Taussig, *The Magic of the State* (New York: Routledge, 1997).

39. Ibid., 99–108.

40. Walter Benjamin, "On the Mimetic Faculty," in *Reflections: Essays, Aphorisms, Autobiographical Writings*, ed. Peter Demetz (New York: Harcourt Brace Jovanovich, 1978), 333.

41. This is not an orientalist slur. It is a reference to the history of the arrival of the modern state in India and the enchantment that accompanied it.

Sudipta Kaviraj argues that the arrival of the modern state was embraced wholeheartedly by the Indian populace, in late colonial and postcolonial times, because the ascendancy of the state, and the territorial stability it entailed, was not accompanied by an intellectual discourse that criticized the potentially negative power of the state, as was the case in the West, with the work of people like Hobbes and Locke. See Kaviraj, "On the Enchantment of the State: Indian Thought on the Role of the State in the Narrative of Modernity," *European Journal of Sociology* 46, no. 02 (August 2005): 263–296.

42. Mian Goverdhan Singh, *Festivals, Fairs and Customs of Himachal Pradesh* (New Delhi: Indus, 1992), 9.

43. Ibid., 13.

44. Heinrich von Stientencron, "Charisma and Canon: The Dynamics of Legitimization and Innovation in Indian Religions," in *Charisma and Canon: Essays on the Religious History of the Indian Subcontinent*, ed. Vasudha Dalmia, Angelika Malinar, and Martin Christof (New Delhi: Oxford University Press, 2001), 14.

45. Jonathan Z. Smith, *Imagining Religion: From Babylon to Jonestown* (Chicago: University of Chicago Press, 1982), 52.

46. Ibid.

47. Molu Ram Thakur, *Myths, Rituals, and Beliefs in Himachal Pradesh* (New Delhi: Indus, 1997), 5.

48. Molu Ram Thakur, *Himāchal Meṃ Pūjit Devī-Devatā* (New Delhi: Rshabhacarana Jaina evam Santati, 1981), 9.

49. Ibid., 50.

50. Ibid., 59.

51. Thakur, *Myths, Rituals, and Beliefs*, 65.

52. Ibid., 130.

53. Ibid., 5.

54. Ibid., 3.

55. Deepak Sharma, in discussion with the author, digital audio interview, March 13, 2003.

56. Deepak Sharma, in discussion with the author, digital audio interview, March 11, 2003.

57. Deepak Sharma, in discussion with the author, digital audio interview, February 2, 2003.

58. Pushpa Bindra, "Memorial Stones in Himachal," in *Memorial Stones: A Study of Their Origin, Significance and Variety*, ed. Gunther Sontheimer and S. Settar (Heidelberg: South Asia Institute, 1982), 175–182.

59. Deepak Sharma, in discussion with the author, digital audio interview, March 22, 2003.

60. Deepak Sharma, in discussion with the author, digital audio interview, March 22, 2003.

CHAPTER 4

1. My business card and Polaroid camera were arguably the two most important pieces of equipment when I was conducting fieldwork in rural South Asia. The card provided access to otherwise inaccessible realms, and the camera assured that everyone was smiling when I left.

2. This is not the position taken by many early nationalist leaders and members of the Constituent Assembly, for whom the question was not the impossibility of translation but the adequacy of it.

3. This debate has carried on through the rise of the Hindu Right, particularly in debates over the quasi-secular practices of Congress policy.

4. See Partha Chatterjee, "Secularism and Tolerance," in *Secularism and Its Critics,* ed. Rajeev Bhavargava (Delhi: Oxford University Press, 1998), 297–320; J. Duncan M. Derrett, *Religion, Law and the State in India,* Law in India Series (Delhi: Oxford University Press, 1999); J. Duncan M. Derrett and India, *Hindu Law, Past and Present: Being an Account of the Controversy which Preceded the Enactment of the Hindu Code, the Text of the Code as Enacted, and Some Comments Thereon* (Calcutta: A. Mukherjee, 1957); Franklin A. Presler, *Religion under Bureaucracy: Policy Administration for Hindu Temples in South India* (Cambridge, UK: Cambridge University Press, 1987); Donald Eugene Smith, *India as a Secular State* (Princeton, NJ: Princeton University Press, 1963); and Chandra Y. Mudaliar, *The Secular State and Religious Institutions in India: A Study of the Administration of Hindu Public Religious Trusts in Madras* (Wiesbaden: Fritz Steiner Verlag, 1974).

5. Chatterjee, "Secularism and Tolerance," 350.

6. See, for example, Bernard S. Cohn, *Colonialism and Its Forms of Knowledge: The British in India* (Princeton, NJ: Princeton University Press, 1996).

7. Ibid., 5.

8. Ibid.

9. For a discussion of the way that pragmatic consideration drove policy formulation, see Eric Stokes, *The English Utilitarians and India* (Oxford: Clarendon Press, 1959); and Mitchell, *Rule of Experts.*

10. The argument that I am pursing here is indebted to the work of Timothy Mitchell and his examination of the seeds of incalculability that reside in

even the most rigorous of systems of calculability and control. See his excellent collection of essays, *Rule of Experts: Egypt, Techno-Politics, Modernity.*

11. For a short overview on Prathi's life and his ascendancy to the Vidhān Sabhā and his ministerial roles, see Gautan Vyathit, *Lal Chand Prarthi* (Shimla: Himachal Pradesh Academy of Art, Culture, Language, 1994).

12. Other important early figures include M. R. Thakur, Sudharshan Vashisth, B. R. Sharma, and many others.

13. Himachal Pradesh Academy of Arts, Culture, and Languages, *Pahāṛī-Hindī Śabdakośa* (Shimla: Himachal Pradesh Academy of Arts, Culture, and Languages, 1989).

14. Prem Sharma, in discussion with the author, digital audio interview, September 3, 2004.

15. These are the characters of Akhil Gupta's ethnography of the state. See A. Gupta, "Blurred Boundaries."

16. I have not included this informant's name or district in order to protect her.

17. Personal interview, digital video recording, May 2003.

18. Ibid.

19. For example, see M. S. Ahluwalia, *History of Himachal Pradesh* (New Delhi: Intellectual, 1988); and Mian Goverdhan Singh, *Himāchal Pradeś: Itihās, Saṃskṛti Evan Ārthik Avasthā,* trans. Caman Lal Gupta (Shimla: Minerva Book House, 1999).

20. On resisting the seductions of the nation as the subject of history, see the thought provoking work by Prasenjit Duara, *Rescuing History from the Nation: Questioning Narratives in China* (Chicago: University of Chicago Press, 1997).

21. See Lawrence A. Babb, *The Divine Hierarchy: Popular Hinduism in Central India* (New York: Columbia University Press, 1975); David Mandelbaum, "Transcendental and Pragmatic Aspects of Religion," *American Anthropologist* 68 (October 1966): 1175–1191; McKim Marriott and Alan R. Beals, *Village India: Studies in the Little Community,* Comparative Studies of Cultures and Civilizations (Chicago: University of Chicago Press, 1967); Milton B. Singer, *When a Great Tradition Modernizes: An Anthropological Approach to Indian Civilization* (London: Pall Mall, 1972); and Mysore Narasimhachar Srinivas et al., *Dimensions of Social Change in India* (Columbia, MO: South Asia Books, 1978).

22. I am thinking here of the work of people like Gandhi and Ambedkar.

23. See, for example, Dirks, *Castes of Mind;* and Robert Eric Frykenberg, "The Construction of Hinduism as 'Public' Religion: Looking Again at the Religious Roots of Company Raj in South India," in *Religion and Public Culture:*

Encounters and Identities in Modern South India, ed. Keith Yandell and John Paul (Richmond: Curzon Press, 2000), 82–107.

24. This is, however, not to say that Brahmins per se have been absent from the modernization process. A quick glance at this book's bibliography reveals more than a few Sharmas. What I mean to indicate is that the changes that have happened have not been a product of and not been dictated by caste-based identities.

25. Tika Ram Joshi, "Ethnography of Bushahr State," *Journal of the Asiatic Society of Bengal* 7, no. 9 (September 1911): 525–613.

26. M. G. Singh, *Festivals, Fairs and Customs.*

27. Ibid.

28. On this concept, see the discussion of symbols in chapter 5.

29. This is the case with Banar Devatā in the Pabbar River valley.

30. There are logical parallels here with the practices of Garhwal at Nanda Devī. See William Sturman Sax, *Mountain Goddess: Gender and Politics in a Himalayan Pilgrimage* (New York: Oxford University Press, 1991), 13.

31. See Himachal Pradesh Vidhān Sabhā, *Mukhyamantriyoṃ/Vittamantriyoṃ.*

32. A common interpretation of the rite is that these deities travel to Indralok in order to renew their energies. Throughout the year, their energies are slowly depleted, and they need to return to the realm of Indralok in order to, as many people put it, "charge their batteries." The metaphor of electricity is common in explanations of the power of deities. Many describe the ritual possession of the gūr in terms of being shocked or getting plugged in. These metaphors culminate in a major deity of the Kullu valley, Bijli Mahādev, who is the deity of electricity and power. His temple is located at the top of a large ridge and is known for its ability to attract lightning, which is channeled down a long pole onto a pile of butter that is supposed to melt from the heat.

33. See Giorgio Agamben, *Remnants of Auschwitz: The Witness and the Archive* (New York: Zone Books, 2000).

34. Almost without exception, the past is remembered as a colder time with more snow. Every person I asked attributed the change in climatic conditions to rapid deforestation.

35. The rite is also called *gharit mā* or *strain.*

36. "Heaven" is a fair translation of the word *svarg.* It adequately covers the range of meanings associated with it. In my description of *indralok yātrā,* the unsystematic usage of *svarg* and Indralok might seem to equate the two realms, when, in fact, they cannot be exactly equated. However, I have tried to stay as

close to my transcripts as possible, using the terms where they are used in the everyday vernacular. In this case, the equation between *svarg* and *indralok yātrā* is clearly made.

37. Deepak Sharma, in discussion with the author, digital audio interview, April 5, 2003.

38. There are numerous other games that are related to significant ritual activity. This is clearest in the two rites that involve or have involved human sacrifice: Bhunda and Kaikai.

39. Personal interview, digital audio recording, April 8, 2003

40. See Mary Poovey, *A History of the Modern Fact: Problems of Knowledge in the Sciences of Wealth and Society* (Chicago: University of Chicago Press, 1998).

41. Ranajit Guha, *Dominance with Hegemony: History and Power in Colonial India* (Delhi: Oxford University Press, 1998).

42. For descriptions from other parts of India, see J. Bruce Long, "Mahāśivarātri: The Śaiva Festival of Repentence," in *Religious Festivals in South India and Sri Lanka*, ed. Guy Richard Welbon and Glenn E. Yokum Welbon (New Delhi: Manohar, 1982), 189–217; and Oscar Lewis, "The Festival Cycle in a North Indian Jat Village," *Proceedings of the American Philosophical Society* 100, no. 3 (1956), 168–196. Long's analysis was influenced by V. Raghavan, under whom he studied. On the influence of Raghavan and the making of the "Great Tradition," see Mary Hancock, "Unmaking the 'Great Tradition': Ethnography, National Culture and Area Studies," *Identities* 4, no. 3–4 (1998), 343–388; and V. Raghavan, *Festivals, Sports, and Pastimes of India* (Ahmedabad: B.J. Institute of Learning and Research, 1979). See also, P. V. Kane, *History of Dharmaśāstra*, vol. 5 (Poona: Bhandarkar Oriental Research Institute, 1962), 225–236.

43. See, Long, "Mahāśivarātri."

44. There are some who suggest that the rite did not begin until the late eighteenth century, although there is little evidence to support such a position. This is a theory I heard in Mandi. It is also referred many times in the annual reporting on the festival by *Girirāj*.

45. In 1527, Ajbar Sen acquired the land rights to the left bank of the Beas (as recorded in a copper plate inscription) and built a palace and temple. See J. L. Hutchinson and J. P. Vogel, *History of the Panjab Hill States*, 2 vols. (Shimla: Department of Language and culture, 1933).

46. There are many examples of this story. See, for example, Hemendra Vaidya, "Etihāsik Paripreksya Mem Maṇḍī Kī Śivarātri," *Girirāj*, March 12, 1986, 8.

47. Hutchinson and Vogel, *Panjab Hill States*, 385. See also Sudershan Vashisth, ed., *Maṇḍī Dev Milan* (Shimla: Himachal Pradesh Academy of Art, Culture and Language, 1997).

48. Shashi Kanta Sharma, "Śiva Aur Śikārī," *Girirāj*, February 21, 1979.

49. This is an important theme in the annual articles of *Girirāj*. See, for example, Lalani K. Kapur, "Maṇḍī Kā Prasiddha Va Pārampark Śivarātri Melā," *Girirāj*, February 13, 1980, 13; and Satish Kashyap, "Prāchin Parmparāoṃ Kā Anūṭhā Saṅgam Maṇḍī Śivarātri Melā," *Girirāj*, February 14, 2001, 7.

50. Kashyap, "Prāchin Parmparāoṃ."

51. Kapil Sharma, "Devī-Devatāoṃ Kā Saṅgam Hai Maṇḍī Śivarātri," *Girirāj*, February 24, 1993.

52. Sudershan Vashishtha, "Dev Samāgam Kā Parv Maṇḍi Śivarātri," *Girirāj*, March 1, 1994.

53. Ram Singh, in discussion with the author, digital audio interview, March 3, 2003.

54. Granville Austin, *The Indian Constitution: Cornerstone of a Nation* (Oxford: Claredon Press, 1966).

55. These rooms are a common feature of houses in the Western Himalayas. They are public spaces where people of various castes and genders are allowed to sit. They are the most public of domestic spaces, and as such, things that families want to highlight are exhibited in them. Often on display are photos of deceased relatives, childhood photographs, and calendar art. For more about these type of representations, see Kajri Jain, "More Than Meets the Eye: The Circulation of Images and the Embodiment of Values," *Contributions to Indian Sociology* 36, no. 1 (2002): 33–70; Jain, "Producing the Sacred: The Subjects of Calendar Art," *Journal of Art and Ideas* 30–31 (1997): 63–88; Christopher Pinney, *Camera Indica: The Social Life of Indian Photographs* (Chicago: University of Chicago Press, 1997); and Pinney, *Photos of the Gods: The Printed Image and Political Struggle in India* (New Delhi: Oxford University Press, 2004).

56. In fact, while this man is one of the most respected figures in any of the adjacent valleys, he continues his quest for understanding and purification. Often, very early in the morning, I would cross his path in the hills as I was going out to photograph sunrises and he was returning from meditation or collecting herbs.

57. The multiple valences of the word *pratyakṣa* (literally, "in front of the eyes") are extremely important here. The gūr was playing on the ambiguity between the words "revelation," "seeing," "miracle," and "cure." He was well aware of the ambiguity and used the word carefully in formal and informal conversations. He considers a gūr to be special because he is the one that has

access to the power that is the most important function of the deity, the power to reveal and conceal, and with this power, he can remove pain, suffering, and ignorance. As the privileged recipient and medium (*madhyam*) of this, he too participates in this miracle (*pratyakṣa*).

58. Personal interview, digital audio recording, April 16, 2003.

59. Gunther Sontheimer, *Essays of Religion, Literature and Law* (Delhi: Manohar, 2004).

60. Nick Dirks and David Scott are not the only ones to make this point. Long before Foucault, Eric Stokes articulated a subtle change in the political rationale of colonialism in the movement from the reforms of Cornwallis and Munro, which were conservative and defense, seeking to insert English ideas "here and there" while focusing on the extraction of resources and maintaining the mercantilist colonial logic, to the liberal utilitarian reforms which focused on, as Scott summarizes, "the systematic redefinition and transformation of the terrain on which the life of the colonized was lived." David Scott, "Colonial Governmentality," *Social Text* 43 (Autumn 1995): 205. See also Stokes, *English Utilitarians.*

CHAPTER 5

1. The turn here is not from truth to beauty or from economy to expenditure. It is toward understanding concepts (such as truth, beauty, economy, excess, healthy virtue, madness, etc.) as necessarily contingent and rooted in specific configurations of power and knowledge.

2. Jeremy R. Carrette and Richard King, *Selling Spirituality: The Silent Takeover of Religion* (New York: Routledge, 2004).

3. This VCD is typical of many festival recordings. Those of Bhunda, Śant, Fagli, and Buddi Diwali festivals are the most common.

4. I translate *devīdevatā saṃskṛti* literally here because, although the speaker used the term, he did not mean to invoke the Pan-Indian context suggested by the Sanskrit term. Moreover, he did not intend to convey, as many do, the logical harmony I invoke in sometimes translating the concept as "theological culture." He meant simply, "our way of relating to gods and goddesses."

5. On calendar art, see Kajri, Jain, "When the Gods Go to Market: The Ritual Management of Desire in Indian 'Bazaar Art,'" *Communal/Plural: Journal of Transnational and Crosscultural Studies* 6, no. 2 (1998): 187–204; and Christopher Pinney, *Photos of the Gods: The Printed Image and Political Struggle in India* (New Delhi: Oxford University Press, 2004).

6. Simon C.R. Weightman, and S.M. Pandey, "The Semantic Fields of *Dharm* and *Kartavy* in Modern Hindi," in *The Concept of Duty in South Asia*, ed. Wendy Doniger-O'Flaherty and J. Duncan M. Derrett (Columbia, MO: South Asia Books, 1978), 217–227.

7. Sarasvati Dayananda, Prasad Durga, Vaidyanath Shastri, Jagdish Vidyarthi, and Bharatendra Nath, *An English Translation of the Satyarth Prakash: Literally, Expose of Right Sense (of Vedic Religion) of Maharshi Swami Dayanand Saraswati, "the Luther of India," Being a Guide to Vedic Hermeneutics*, 2nd ed. (New Delhi: Jan Gyan Prakashan, 1970).

8. Birbal Sharma, "Himāchal Darśan" (Mandi: Birbal Sharma, 1997).

9. Diana Eck, *Darshan: Seeing the Divine in India* (Chambersburg: Anima, 1981).

10. Personal interview, May 2003.

11. Robert A. Orsi, *Gods of the City: Religion and the American Urban Landscape* (Bloomington: Indiana University Press, 1999).

12. See Charles Hirschkind, "The Ethics of Listening: Cassette-Sermon Audition in Contemporary Cairo," *American Ethnologist* 28, no. 3 (2001): 623–649.

13. Jagat Sukh was Sir Alexander Cunningham's base for all of his tours into the upper Himalayas. His house, built in the 1880s, still stands in the village.

14. Vogel and Chhabra, *Antiquities of Chamba State*, 429–433.

15. Dedications such as this one are common both in popular recollections and in more academic accounts of older temples. I have noticed throughout the discussion of precolonial temples—and, in particular, temples without explicit records and those that are not explicitly female—that the default association is Śiva. In villages from Hatkoti to Jagat Sukh, any temple with a stone in the center is immediately associated with iconographic traditions of Śiva. However, these associations are highly dubious and more than a little disingenuous. If contemporary traditions are any clue, and they may not be, it is more probable that these temples were not originally dedicated to the great Śiva but rather to a particular local divinity. And, as I mentioned in chapter 3, it is highly likely that the image at the center of the temple is a stone found by either a herder or a farmer, just as in most local temples in the region.

16. Penelope Chetwode, *Kulu: The End of the Habitable World* (New Delhi: Times Books International, 1989), 167.

17. Laxman S. Thakur, *The Architectural Heritage of Himachal Pradesh: Origin and Development of Temple Styles* (New Delhi: Munshiram Manohar, 1996), 95.

18. Ibid.

19. James Ferguson, *Expectations of Modernity: Myths and Meanings of Urban Life on the Zambian Copperbelt* (Berkeley: University of California Press, 1999), 235.

20. Ibid., 237–238.

21. Alfred Frederick Pollock Harcourt, *The Himalayan Districts of Kooloo, Lahoul and Spiti* (1871; repr., Delhi: Vivek Publishing House, 1972), 99.

22. Hutchinson and Vogel, *History of the Panjab Hill States*, 2:426.

23. Raja Bhasin and Himachal Tourism, *Himachal Pradesh, India: A Himalayan Experience* (Shimla: Department of Tourism, Government of Himachal Pradesh, n.d.), 32.

24. Penelope Chetwode, *Kulu: The End of the Habitable World* (Delhi: Times Books International, 1989), 172.

25. Harcourt, *Kooloo, Lahoul and Spiti*, 98.

26. Interview with temple committee president, May 30, 2003.

27. Chauhan Kuldeep, "Where Devta Tells Them to Grow Cannabis," *Tribune* (Chandigarh), July 2, 2004.

CHAPTER 6

1. On this usage of "problem," see Michel Foucault and Paul Rabinow, *Ethics: Subjectivity and Truth* (London: Allen Lane, 1997); and Partha Chatterjee, *The Nation and Its Fragments: Colonial and Postcolonial Histories* (Princeton, NJ: Princeton University Press, 1993).

2. *Becoming Religious* develops a line of analysis suggested by Talal Asad's criticism of his important work, *Formations of the Secular*. In a 2006 interview with David Scott, Asad discussed how secularism (as a political and social project) and the secular (as an epistemic space) are set within a progressive narrative (secularization): "I think I should have stressed something that I didn't in the final chapter [of *Formations of the Secular*]: how different ('modern') feelings, experiences, helped to define altered conceptions of 'the real'—of reality that was knowable by *legitimate* methods—and how that contributed to the need for particular kinds of 'reform,' because feelings always come charged with emotion, and *that* makes one desire to maintain or to eliminate their cause. But the notion of *legitimate* methods of knowing tends to render some desires valid and some invalid—as distortions, illusion, sickness." David Scott and Charles Hirschkind, *Powers of the Secular Modern: Talal Asad and His Interlocutors*, Cultural Memory in the Present (Stanford: Stanford University Press, 2006).

3. To be clear, when I use the phrase "labor of religion," I am referring exclusively to the discursive machinations of religion. I do not attribute any metaphysical agency to the concept or its purported objects. Additionally, the primary term that I am translating as "religion" here is not the more customary *dharma*. This word is more commonly used throughout the subcontinent to designate the English word "religion"; however, in Himachal, the word is not used to discuss what happens in temples and between villagers and their local deities. For this, the primary expression is *devīdevatā saṇskṛti*—literally, "god-goddess culture."

4. Timothy Mitchell, "The Limits of State: Beyond Statist Approaches and Their Critics," *American Political Science Review* 85, no. 1 (1991): 77–96.

5. Talal Asad, *Genealogies of Religion: Discipline and Reasons of Power in Christianity and Islam* (Baltimore: Johns Hopkins University Press, 1993).

6. Because of the potentially sensitive nature of this story, I have used a pseudonym for the village's name. Pujarli is the name of many villages in the Western Himalayas.

7. Lawrence A. Babb, *Redemptive Encounters: Three Modern Styles in the Hindu Tradition* (Berkeley: University of California Press, 1986); Mark Juergensmeyer, *Radhasoami Reality: The Logic of a Modern Faith* (Princeton, NJ: Princeton University Press, 1991).

8. Villagers believe that children's hands are best for producing the hash, as the resin in the plants adheres more easily to their soft skin.

9. This conversation was conducted in the Hindi most Himachalis use when interacting with Himachalis from different regions. While this simple Hindi provided the grammatical backbone of our conversation, it was pierced with the local Pahāṛī dialect (Kulvi), which I was eager to show off, and several English words were employed as if they were as natural to their lexicon as any others. However, the words that were taken from English were far from random.

10. The wording of this phrase would be familiar to anyone with even a passing knowledge of the subtle art of "giving" *gālī*.

11. Skeptical readers may reasonably ask whether villagers staged this debate for a curious ethnographer. In my defense, I can say that no one ever asked my opinion. No one explained their rationale afterward, and at no point during the debate did anyone even seem to notice me as I mingled among other visitors.

12. Actually, the number of years since the festival was last performed is unknown. The people who had seen the seen the rite, who were at this point

all in their seventies and eighties, disagreed on when it was last held, giving estimates of anywhere from forty to a hundred years ago.

13. For an interesting look at the production of experts and the role of experts in the transformation of society, see Mitchell, *Rule of Expertse.*

14. I witnessed similar forms of arbitration on a number of occasions while traveling or working with local ethnohistorians and government ministers tasked with managing Himachal's "cultural traditions."

15. This dispute and its resolution show the development of new methods for distinguishing truth from falsehood (objectivity) and new forms of expertise (on religion). All available historical evidence (oral histories, colonial records, textual fragments, and other archival sources) suggests that, in previous centuries, authority was located in local deities and their functionaries; the expertise for distinguishing truth from falsehood developed in relation to these deities. It flowed directly from them through the medium of the gūrs. In the decades that followed Indian independence, land reforms redistributed temple property to peasants, robbing the temples of their economic base and forcing the government to assume greater control of temple management and festival organization. This shift in power has produced a deep resentment between local temple communities and state government. For many, the fight over cultural heritage is between the government and local officials. Yet this story highlights how the labor of religion often moves most powerfully beneath the overt debates between the government and temple officials. The authority that once resided in local temples and that the state government seeks to manage can sometimes escape the control of both.

16. On this form of counterculture, see Michel Foucault, Michel Senellart, and Arnold Ira Davidson, *Security, Territory, Population: Lectures at the Collège de France, 1977–1978* (New York: Palgrave Macmillan, 2007), lecture 8.

17. For examples of these criticisms, see the editorial pages of the *Amar Ujālā* and the *Tribune* (Chandigarh).

18. On the long history of such attempts and failures, see Wilhelm Halbfass, *Tradition and Reflection: Explorations in Indian Thought* (Delhi: Sri Satguru, 1992).

19. See the paper's website, www.amarujala.com.

20. The Department of Language and Culture assumed management of the temple on October 6, 1986. See Department of Language and Culture, ed., "Schedule 1: Temples Administered under Srno Hindu Public Religious Institutions of Charitable Endowments Act, 1984," internal publication, n.d.

21. Currently, twenty-two temples come under the direct control of the state government, according to the provision of the Hindu Public Religious

Institutions of Charitable Endowments Act of 1984. See Department of Language and Culture, "Schedule 1."

22. Informants, particularly at this temple, often asserted that this deity was actually a form of the ubiquitous, if underappreciated, Bhairav.

23. The Nepalese burned most of the records in the early nineteenth century as they retreated in defeat. The current patriarch of the region's royal family, Birbadra Singh, controls the remaining records.

24. R. H. Deuster and Himachal Pradesh Academy of Arts, Culture, and Languages, *Kanawar*, Rare Book Publication 1 (Shimla: Himachal Pradesh Academy of Arts, Culture, and Languages, 1996).

25. Padam Dev Singh facilitated many of these reforms.

26. Tejpal Negi, "Bhīmākālī Maṇdir Ke Bāhar Paśuoṃ Ki Bali," *Amar Ujālā*, November 7, 2001.

27. Ibid.

28. Maneka Gandhi married into the Nehruvian dynasty. Since the death of her husband, Sanjay Gandhi, in 1980, she has become a powerful political force in her own right. She has been a member of the Lok Sabha since 1989.

29. For examples of these stories, see Molu Ram Thakur, *Myths, Rituals, and Beliefs in Himachal Pradesh* (New Delhi: Indus, 1997). During my fieldwork, I collected the origin stories of more than five hundred deities, which amply document this assertion. I hope to make many of them available online in the near future.

30. See Martin Luther, *Preface to the Letter of St. Paul to the Romans* (Grand Rapids: Christian Classics Ethereal Library, 2010).

31. Importantly, when Negi discusses these issues, he uses the singular *bhagavan* rather than the specific names of individual gods or the collective word for gods and goddesses (*devīdevatā*).

32. The interventions of Y. S. Parmar were critical in this regard. Also of interest are the extracts collected in the 1961 census, which describe the fairs and festival of Himachal. These extracts come from administrators all across the state and give us a good idea of the way that English-speaking state officials conceived their traditions. See India, Office of the Registrar General, R. C. P. Singh, and India, Superintendent of Census Operations Himachal Pradesh, *Fairs and Festivals*.

33. There was a strong correspondence between the people who offered such formulations and the rejection of animal sacrifice.

34. Alfred Frederick Pollock Harcourt, *The Himalayan Districts of Kooloo, Lahoul and Spiti* (1871; repr., Delhi: Vivek Publishing House, 1871).

35. On the concept of a "standing reserve," see Martin Heidegger, *The Question Concerning Technology, and Other Essays*, trans. William Lovitt (New York: Harper and Row, 1977).

36. The most common Hindi word used for rituals in Himachal is *rītīrivāj*, which R. S. McGregor glosses as "manners, customs, ways; observances." It is also commonly called simply *rivāj*, which McGregor defines as both "currency, usual occurrence," and "custom, practice." R. S. McGregor, *The Oxford Hindi-English Dictionary* (New Delhi: Oxford University Press, 1993), 865–866.

37. The most interesting evidence for this transformation comes from the annals of the region's vernacular authors, as preserved in the periodicals *Somasī, Girirāj,* and *Himaprastha.*

38. The change is not only a product of modernity or colonialism, as it has happened at other times in South Asia. One of the most interesting of these cases is the semanticization of ritual that occurred in Kashmir with the formulation of high Hindu Tantra in the adept hands of Abhinavagupta. See Alexis Sanderson, "Purity and Power among the Brahmans of Kashmir," in *The Category of the Person,* ed. S. Collins and S. Lukes M. Carrithers (Cambridge, UK: Oxford University Press, 1985), 190–210; and Sanderson, "Meaning in Tantric Ritual," in *Essais sur le rituel III: Colloque du Centenaire de la Section des Sciences religieuses de l'École Pratique des Hautes Études,* ed. Anne-Marie Blondeau and Kristopher Schipper (Louvain: Peeters, 1995), 15–95.

39. "Bhāvātmak Ekatā Kā Pratīk Kullū Daśaharā," *Girirāj,* October 11, 1978, 9.

40. Penelope Chetwode, *Kulu: The End of the Habitable World* (New Delhi: Times Books International, 1989).

41. "Bhāvātmak Ekatā Kā Pratīk Kullū Daśaharā," *Girirāj,* October 11, 1978.

AFTERWORD

1. Jiddu Krishnamurti, *Think on These Things* (New York: HarperOne, 1989), 27.

2. Michel Foucault, "What Is Enlightenment?" in *The Foucault Reader,* ed. Paul Rabinow (New York: Pantheon Books, 1984), 32–50. See also Ian Hacking, *Historical Ontology* (Cambridge, MA: Harvard University Press, 2002), 2.

3. Michel Foucault and Paul Rabinow, *Ethics: Subjectivity and Truth* (London: Allen Lane, 1997).

4. Hacking, *Historical Ontology.*

Bibliography

Agamben, Giorgio. *Remnants of Auschwitz: The Witness and the Archive.* New York: Zone Books, 2000.

Ahluwalia, M.S. *History of Himachal Pradesh.* New Delhi: Intellectual, 1988.

"The Architect of Himachal Pradesh: Dr. Y.S. Parmar." *Commerce,* January 23, 1971, 3.

Asad, Talal. *Genealogies of Religion: Discipline and Reasons of Power in Christianity and Islam.* Baltimore: Johns Hopkins University Press, 1993.

Austin, Granville. *The Indian Constitution: Cornerstone of a Nation.* Oxford: Clarendon Press, 1966.

Babb, Lawrence A. *The Divine Hierarchy: Popular Hinduism in Central India.* New York: Columbia University Press, 1975.

———. *Redemptive Encounters: Three Modern Styles in the Hindu Tradition.* Berkeley: University of California Press, 1986.

Baden-Powell, B.H. *The Land-Systems of British India: Being a Manual of the Land-Tenures and of the Systems of Land-Revenue Administration Prevalent in the Several Provinces.* Oxford: Clarendon Press, 1892.

Banerjee, Tarasankar, ed. *Historiography in Modern Indian Languages, 1800–1947: Report of the National Seminar Held at Santiniketan, from 11th March to 13th March 1985.* Calcutta, India: Naya Prokash, 1987.

Barnes, George Carnac. "Report of the Kangra Settlement." Himachal Pradesh State Archives, 1872.

Benjamin, Walter. "On the Mimetic Faculty." In *Reflections: Essays, Aphorisms, Autobiographical Writings,* edited by Peter Demetz, 333–336. New York: Harcourt Brace Jovanovich, 1978.

Bhasin, Raja, and Himachal Tourism. *Himachal Pradesh, India: A Himalayan Experience.* Shimla: Department of Tourism, Government of Himachal Pradesh, n.d.

Bindra, Pushpa. "Memorial Stones in Himachal." In *Memorial Stones: A Study of Their Origin, Significance and Variety,* edited by Gunther Sontheimer and S. Settar, 175–182. Heidelberg: South Asia Institute, 1982.

Braun, Willi, and Russell T. McCutcheon. *Guide to the Study of Religion.* London: Cassell, 2000.

Byres, T.J., ed. *The State and Development Planning in India.* Delhi: Oxford University Press, 1994.

Byrne, Peter. *Natural Religion and the Nature of Religion: The Legacy of Deism.* Routledge Religious Studies. London: Routledge, 1989.

Carrette, Jeremy R., and Richard King. *Selling Spirituality: The Silent Takeover of Religion.* New York: Routledge, 2004.

Chakravarty, Sukhamoy. *Development Planning: The Indian Experience.* New York: Oxford University Press, 1987.

Chandra, Rana Sir Bhagat. "Letter No. G.7–12/31–617 Rana Sir Bhagat Chandra to the Political Agent, Punjab Hill States, Simla." Himachal Pradesh State Archives in Re-Settlement in Hat Kothi Jagir, June 29, 1942.

Chatterjee, Partha. *The Nation and Its Fragments: Colonial and Postcolonial Histories.* Princeton, NJ: Princeton University Press, 1993.

————. "Secularism and Tolerance." In *Secularism and Its Critics,* edited by Rajeev Bhavargava, 345–379. Delhi: Oxford University Press, 1998.

Chauhan, Suman. "Social Organization and Land Control: A Study of the Role of Temples in Kullu and Shimla." PhD diss., Himachal Pradesh State University, 1997.

Chetwode, Penelope. *Kulu: The End of the Habitable World.* New Delhi: Times Books International, 1989.

Cohn, Bernard S. *An Anthropologist among the Historians and Other Essays.* Delhi: Oxford University Press, 1987.

————. *Colonialism and Its Forms of Knowledge: The British in India.* Princeton, NJ: Princeton University Press, 1996.

————. "The Command of Language and the Language of Command." In *Colonialism and Its Forms of Knowledge: The British in India,* 16–56. Princeton, NJ: Princeton University Press, 1996.

Copland, Ian. *The British Raj and the Indian Princes: Paramountcy in Western India, 1857–1930.* Bombay: Orient Longman, 1982.

Datta, C.L. *The Raj and the Simla Hill States: Socio-Economic Problems, Agrarian Disturbances and Paramountcy.* Jalandhar: ABS, 1997.

Datta, S.K. *The History of the Forman Christian College: Selections from the Records of the College, 1869–1936.* Lahore: Chas. Wollen, 1936.

Davidson, Arnold I. *The Emergence of Sexuality: Historical Epistemology and the Formation of Concepts.* Cambridge, MA: Harvard University Press, 2001.

Dayananda, Sarasvati, Prasad Durga, Vaidyanath Shastri, Jagdish Vidyarthi, and Bharatendra Nath. *An English Translation of the Satyarth Prakash: Literally, Expose of Right Sense (of Vedic Religion) of Maharshi Swami Dayanand Saraswati, "the Luther of India," Being a Guide to Vedic Hermeneutics.* 2nd ed. New Delhi: Jan Gyan Prakashan, 1970.

Department of Language and Culture, ed. "Schedule 1: Temples Administered under Srno Hindu Public Religious Institutions of Charitable Endowments Act, 1984." Internal publication, n.d.

Derrett, J. Duncan M. *Religion, Law and the State in India.* Law in India Series. Delhi: Oxford University Press, 1999.

Derrett, J. Duncan M. *Hindu Law, Past and Present: Being an Account of the Controversy which Preceded the Enactment of the Hindu Code, the Text of the Code as Enacted, and Some Comments Thereon.* Calcutta: A. Mukherjee, 1957.

Derrida, Jacques. "Faith and Knowledge: The Two Sources of 'Religion' at the Limits of Reason Alone." In *Religion,* edited by Gianni Vattimo and Jacques Derrida, 1–78. Stanford: Stanford University Press, 1996.

Deuster, R.H., and Himachal Pradesh Academy of Arts, Culture, and Languages. *Kanawar.* Rare Book Publication 1. Shimla: Himachal Pradesh Academy of Arts, Culture, and Languages, 1996.

Diack, A.H. *Assessment Report of the Plach Tahsil of the Kangra District.* Lahore: Punjab Government Press, 1892.

Dirks, Nicholas B. "Annals of the Archive: Ethnographic Notes on the Sources of History." In *Historical Anthropology and Its Futures: From the Margins,* edited by Brian Keith Axel, 47–65. Durham: Duke University Press, 2002.

———. *Castes of Mind: Colonialism and the Making of Modern India.* Princeton, NJ: Princeton University Press, 2001.

———. *The Hollow Crown: Ethnohistory of an Indian Kingdom.* Cambridge South Asian Studies 39. Cambridge, UK: Cambridge University Press, 1987.

Dracott, Alice Elizabeth. *Simla Village Tales; or, Folk Tales from the Himalayas.* London: John Murray, 1906.

Duara, Prasenjit. *Rescuing History from the Nation: Questioning Narratives in China.* Chicago: University of Chicago Press, 1997.

Eck, Diana. *Darshan: Seeing the Divine in India.* Chambersburg: Anima, 1981.

Eden, Emily. *Up the Country.* London: Virago, 1983.

Ellingson, Terry Jay. *The Myth of the Noble Savage.* Berkeley: University of California Press, 2001.

"Extract from the Inspection Note on Hatkoti Temple." Himachal Pradesh State Archives in Re-Settlement in Hat Kothi Jagir, September 21, 1941.

Ferguson, James. *Expectations of Modernity: Myths and Meanings of Urban Life on the Zambian Copperbelt.* Berkeley: University of California Press, 1999.

"Final Settlement Report of Kullu Sub-Division of District Kangra." Himachal Pradesh State Archives, 1913.

Fischer, Eberhard, V.C. Ohri, and Vijay Sharma. *The Temple of Devi-Kothi.* Zurich: Artibus Asiae, 2003.

Fitzgerald, Timothy. *The Ideology of Religious Studies.* New York: Oxford University Press, 2000.

Foucault, Michel. "What Is Enlightenment?" In *The Foucault Reader,* ed. Paul Rabinow, 32–50. New York: Pantheon Books, 1984.

Foucault, Michel, James D. Faubion, and Robert Hurley. *Power.* New York: New Press, 2000.

Foucault, Michel, Alessandro Fontana, Frédéric Gros, and François Ewald. *The Hermeneutics of the Subject: Lectures at the Collège de France, 1981–1982.* New York: Palgrave Macmillan, 2005.

Foucault, Michel, and Paul Rabinow. *Ethics: Subjectivity and Truth.* London: Allen Lane, 1997.

Foucault, Michel, Michel Senellart, and Arnold Ira Davidson. *Security, Territory, Population: Lectures at the Collège de France, 1977–1978.* New York: Palgrave Macmillan, 2007.

Fox, Richard Gabriel. *Kin, Clan, Raja, and Rule: State Hinterland Relations in Preindustrial India.* Berkeley: University of California Press, 1971.

Fraser, James Baillie. *The Himala Mountains.* Delhi: Neraj Publishing House, 1982.

Frykenberg, Robert Eric. "The Construction of Hinduism as 'Public' Religion: Looking Again at the Religious Roots of Company Raj in South India." In *Religion and Public Culture: Encounters and Identities in Modern South India,* edited by Keith Yandell and John Paul, 3–26. Richmond: Curzon Press, 2000.

Gazetteer of the Kangra District: Part 1; Kangra (1883–1884). 1883–1884. Reprint, New Delhi: Indus, 1994.

Gill, Sam D. *Storytracking: Texts, Stories, and Histories in Central Australia.* New York: Oxford University Press, 1998.

———. "Territory." In *Critical Terms for Religious Studies,* edited by Mark C. Taylor, 298–313. Chicago: University of Chicago Press, 1998.

Ginsburg, Faye D., Lila Abu-Lughod, and Brian Larkin. *Media Worlds: Anthropology on New Terrain.* Berkeley: University of California Press, 2002.

Ginzburg, Carlo, Martin H. Ryle, and Kate Soper. *Wooden Eyes: Nine Reflections on Distance.* New York: Columbia University Press, 2001.

Girard, René. *The Scapegoat.* Johns Hopkins Paperbacks ed. Baltimore: Johns Hopkins University Press, 1989.

Gould, S.J. *The Structure of Evolutionary Theory.* __Cambridge, MA: Harvard University Press, 2002.

Government of India, Ministry of States. *White Paper on Indian States.* Rev. ed. Delhi: Manager of Publications, 1950.

Government of Punjab, *The Resurgent Punjab.* Chandigarh: Public Relations Department, 1956.

Greenblatt, Stephen. *Marvelous Possessions: The Wonder of the New World.* Chicago: University of Chicago Press, 1992.

Guha, Ramachandra. *The Unquiet Woods: Ecological Change and Peasant Resistance in the Himalaya.* 2nd ed. New Delhi: Oxford University Press, 2001.

Guha, Ranajit. *Dominance with Hegemony: History and Power in Colonial India.* Delhi: Oxford University Press, 1998.

Gupta, Akhil. "Blurred Boundaries: The Discourse of Corruption, the Culture of Politics and the Imagined State." *American Ethnologist* 22, no. 2 (May 1995): 375–402.

———. *Postcolonial Developments: Agriculture in the Making of Modern India.* Durham: Duke University Press, 1998.

Gupta, Ghanshyam. "Peep into Himachal Darshan." *Tribune* (Chandigarh), March 24, 2000.

Gupta, Ishwar Dayal. *A Village Survey of Gijari, Theog Tehsil, Mahasu District.* Shimla: Government of India Press, 1961.

Gupta, Mohan Lal, and Ram Chandra Pal Singh. *A Village Survey of Chergaon, Rohro Tehsil, Mahasu District.* Shimla: Government of India Press, 1965.

Habib, Irfan. *The Agrarian System of Mughal India, 1556–1707.* 2nd ed. New Delhi: Oxford University Press, 1999.

Hacking, Ian. *Historical Ontology.* Cambridge, MA: Harvard University Press, 2002.

———. *The Social Construction of What?* Cambridge, MA: Harvard University Press, 1999.

Halbfass, Wilhelm. *India and Europe: An Essay in Understanding.* Albany: State University of New York Press, 1988.

———. *Tradition and Reflection: Explorations in Indian Thought.* Delhi: Sri Satguru, 1992.

Hancock, Mary. "Unmaking the 'Great Tradition': Ethnography, National Culture and Area Studies." *Identities* 4, no. 3–4 (1998): 343–388.

Harcourt, Alfred Frederick Pollock. *The Himalayan Districts of Kooloo, Lahoul and Spiti.* 1871. Reprint, Delhi: Vivek, 1972.

Harrison, Peter. *"Religion" and the Religions in the English Enlightenment.* Cambridge, UK: Cambridge University Press, 1990.

Harvey, David. *A Brief History of Neoliberalism.* New York: Oxford University Press, 2005.

Heidegger, Martin. *Poetry, Language, Thought.* New York: Harper and Row, 1971.

———. *The Question Concerning Technology, and Other Essays.* Translated by William Lovitt. New York: Harper and Row, 1977.

Herring, Ronald J. *Land to the Tiller: The Political Economy of Agrarian Reform in South Asia.* New Haven: Yale University Press, 1983.

Himachal Pradesh Academy of Arts, Culture, and Languages. *Pahāṛī-Hindī Śabdakośa.* Shimla: Himachal Pradesh Academy of Arts, Culture, and Languages, 1989.

Himachal Pradesh (India). "Himachal Pradesh Code." Simla: Himachal Pradesh Govt. Law Dept., 2003.

———. "Himachal Pradesh Land Code." Edited by the Himachal Pradesh Revenue Department. Shimla: Financial Commissioner, Himachal Pradesh, 1991.

Himachal Pradesh (India), Planning and Development Dept. *First Five-Year Plan, 1951–1956.* Simla: The Dept., 1958.

———. *Third Five Year Plan (1961–66): Achievements.* Simla: The Manager, Himachal Pradesh Administration Press, 1961.

Himachal Pradesh Director of Public Relations. *Himachal Pradesh 1971.* Shimla: The Controller, Printing and Stationary, Himachal Pradesh, 1971.

Himachal Pradesh Vidhān Sabhā. *Mukhyamantriyoṃ/Vittamantriyoṃ Ke Bajat Abhibhaṣaṇa.* Shimla: Himachal Pradesh Vidhān Sabhā, 2000.

Hirschkind, Charles. "The Ethics of Listening: Cassette-Sermon Audition in Contemporary Cairo." *American Ethnologist* 28, no. 3 (2001): 623–649.

Huang, Annian. *The Silent Spikes: Chinese Laborers and the Construction of North American Railroads*. Beijing: China Intercontinental Press, 2006.

Hutchinson, J. L., and J. P. Vogel. *History of the Panjab Hill States*. 2 vols. Shimla: Department of Language and Culture, 1933.

India, Office of the Registrar General, Ram Chandra Pal Singh, and India, Superintendent of Census Operations Himachal Pradesh. *Himachal Pradesh: Fairs and Festivals*. Delhi: Manager of Publications, 1967.

India, Planning Commission. *The First Five Year Plan: A Draft Outline*. New Delhi: Manager of Publications, 1951.

————. *Fourth Five Year Plan, 1969–74: Draft*. Delhi: Manager Publications Branch, 1969.

India, Reorganization Commission. *Report of the States Reorganization Commission, 1955*. New Delhi: Government of India Press, 1955.

Jacquemont, Victor. *Letters from India: Describing a Journey in the British Dominions of India, Tibet, Lahore and Cashmere*. Karachi: Oxford University Press, 1979.

Jain, Kajri. "More Than Meets the Eye: The Circulation of Images and the Embodiment of Values." *Contributions to Indian Sociology* 36, no. 1 (2002): 33–70.

————. "Producing the Sacred: The Subjects of Calendar Art." *Journal of Art and Ideas* 30–31 (1997): 63–88.

————. "When the Gods Go to Market: The Ritual Management of Desire in Indian 'Bazaar Art.'" *Communal/Plural: Journal of Transnational and Cross-cultural Studies* 6, no. 2 (1998): 187–204.

Joshi, Puran Chandra. *Land Reforms in India: Trends and Perspectives*. Bombay: Allied Publishers, 1975.

————. "Pre-Independence Thinking on Agrarian Policy." *Economic and Political Weekly* 2 (February 1967): 447–456.

Joshi, Tika Ram. "Ethnography of Bushahr State." *Journal of the Asiatic Society of Bengal* 7, no. 9 (September 1911): 525–613.

Judge, Paramjit S. "Responses to Dams and Displacement in Two Indian States." *Asian Survey* 37, no. 9 (1997): 840–851.

Juergensmeyer, Mark. *Radhasoami Reality: The Logic of a Modern Faith*. Princeton, NJ: Princeton University Press, 1991.

Kane, P. V. *History of Dharmaśāstra*. 5 vols. Poona: Bhandarkar Oriental Research Institute, 1930–1962.

Kapur, Charam Pal, Rikhi Ram Sharma, and Ram Chandra Pal Singh. *Brahmaur: A Village Survey of Brahmaur Sub-Tehsil, Chamba District*. Shimla: Government of India Press, 1963.

Kaviraj, Sudipta. "On the Enchantment of the State: Indian Thought on the Role of the State in the Narrative of Modernity." *European Journal of Sociology* 46, no. 02 (August 2005): 263–296.

―――. "The Modern State in India." In *Dynamics of State Formation: India and Europe Compared,* edited by Sudipta Kaviraj and Martin Doornbos, 225–250. New Delhi: Sage, 1997.

Kennedy, Dane Keith. *The Magic Mountains Hill Stations and the British Raj.* Berkeley: University of California Press, 1996.

Khilnani, Sunil. *The Idea of India.* New York: Farrar, Straus Giroux, 1998.

King, Robert D. *Nehru and the Language Politics of India.* Delhi: Oxford University Press, 1997.

Kotvi, Narayan. "Himāchal Pradeś Baṛī Zamīṇdārī Unmūlan Tathā Bhūmi Sudhār Vidheyak (Shimla· Himachal Pradesh Vidhan Sabha 15)." *Vidhān Mālā* 8, no. 1–2 (2001): 155–229.

Krishnamurti, Jiddu. *Think on These Things.* New York: HarperOne, 1989.

Kumar, Chandra, and Ram Chandra Pal Singh. *A Village Survey of Kothi, Kalpa Subdivision, District Kinnaur.* Shimla: Government of India Press, 1963.

Lacoue-Labarthe, Philippe, and Christopher Fynsk. *Typography: Mimesis, Philosophy, Politics.* Stanford: Stanford University Press, 1998.

Lakoff, George. *Women, Fire, and Dangerous Things: What Categories Reveal about the Mind.* Chicago: University of Chicago Press, 1987.

Lewis, Oscar. "The Festival Cycle in a North Indian Jat Village." *Proceedings of the American Philosophical Society* 100, no. 3 (1956): 168–196.

Long, J. Bruce. "Mahāśivarātri: The Śaiva Festival of Repentence." In *Religious Festivals in South India and Sri Lanka,* edited by Guy Richard Welbon and Glenn E. Yokum Welbon, 189–217. New Delhi: Manohar, 1982.

Luther, Martin. *Preface to the Letter of St. Paul to the Romans.* Grand Rapids: Christian Classics Ethereal Library, 2010.

MacIntyre, Alasdair C. *Whose Justice? Which Rationality?* Notre Dame: University of Notre Dame Press, 1988.

Mandelbaum, David. "Transcendental and Pragmatic Aspects of Religion." *American Anthropologist* 68 (October 1966): 1175–1191.

Marriott, McKim, and Alan R. Beals. *Village India: Studies in the Little Community.* Comparative Studies of Cultures and Civilizations. Chicago: University of Chicago Press, 1967.

Mayo, Katherine. *Mother India.* New York: Jonathan Cape, 1927.

McChesney, Robert W. "Introduction." In *Profit over People: Neoliberalism and Global Order,* edited by Noam Chomsky, 7–19. New York: Seven Stories Press, 1999.

McGregor, R.S. *The Oxford Hindi-English Dictionary.* New Delhi: Oxford University Press, 1993.

Merillat, H.C.L. *Land and the Constitution in India.* New York: Columbia University Press, 1970.

Merleau-Ponty, Maurice. *The Visible and the Invisible.* Translated by Alfonso Lingis. Evanston: Northwestern University Press, 1968.

Metcalf, Thomas R. *Land, Landlords and the British Raj: Northern India in the Nineteenth Century.* Berkeley: University of California Press, 1979.

———. "Landlords without Land: The U.P. Zamindars Today." *Pacific Affairs* 40, no. 1–2 (1967): 5–18

Mishra, Pankaj. *Temptations of the West: How to Be Modern in India, Pakistan, Tibet and Beyond.* New York: Farrar, Straus, and Giroux, 2006.

Mitchell, Timothy. "The Limits of State: Beyond Statist Approaches and Their Critics." *American Political Science Review* 85, no. 1 (1991): 77–96.

———. *Rule of Experts: Egypt, Techno-Politics, Modernity.* Berkeley: University of California Press, 2002.

Mohan, Jag, and Ram Chandra Pal Singh. *A Village Survey of Shakrori, Seoni Sub-Tehsil, Mahasu District.* Shimla: Government of India Press, 1963.

Montesquieu, Charles. *The Spirit of Laws.* Vol. II. Colonial Press, 1899.

Moorcroft, William, George Trebeck, and H.H. Wilson. *Travels in the Himalayan Provinces of Hindustan and the Panjab; in Ladakh and Kashmir; in Peshawar, Kabul, Kunduz, and Bokhara; From 1819 to 1825.* London: J. Murray, 1841.

Mudaliar, Chandra Y. *The Secular State and Religious Institutions in India: A Study of the Administration of Hindu Public Religious Trusts in Madras.* Wiesbaden: Fritz Steiner Verlag, 1974.

Nandy, Ashis. "The Politics of Secularism and the Recovery of Religious Tolerance." In *Secularism and Its Critics,* edited by Rajeev Bhargava, 321–344. Delhi: Oxford University Press, 1998.

Negi, Tejpal. "Bhīmākālī Maṇdir Ke Bāhar Paśuoṃ Ki Bali." *Amar Ujālā,* November 7, 2001.

Nehru, Jawaharlal. *Selected Works of Jawaharlal Nehru.* Vol. 26. New Delhi: Jawaharlal Nehru Memorial Fund, 1984.

Nietzsche, Friedrich. *The Will to Power.* Translated by Walter Kaufmann. New York: Random House, 1967.

Ojha, B. S., Gurdev Singh Pabla, and Janak Raj Vashistha. *Tandi: A Village in Lahaul and Spiti District of Punjab.* Village Survey Monographs of Punjab 1. New Delhi: Indian Publications Trading Corp, 1951.

Olivelle, Patrick. *Language, Texts, and Society: Explorations in Ancient Indian Culture and Religion.* New Delhi: Munshiram Manoharlal, 2005.

Orsi, Robert A. *Gods of the City: Religion and the American Urban Landscape.* Bloomington: Indiana University Press, 1999.

Padmanabha, P. *Indian Census and Anthropological Investigations.* New Delhi: Registrar General and Census Commissioner India, 1978.

Pandian, Anand. *Crooked Stalks: Cultivating Virtue in South India.* Durham: Duke University Press, 2009.

Pandian, Anand, and Daud Ali. *Ethical Life in South Asia.* Bloomington: Indiana University Press, 2010.

Parks, Fanny. *Wanderings of a Pilgrim in Search of the Picturesque.* London: Oxford University Press, 1975.

Parmar, Y. S. "Economic Potential of Himachal Pradesh." *Commerce,* August 15, 1970, 1–3.

———. *Himachal Pradesh: Area and Language.* Simla: Directorate of Public Relations, 1970.

———. *Himachal Pradesh: Case for Statehood.* Simla: Directorate of Public Relations, 1968.

———. *Polyandry in the Himalayas.* Delhi: Vikas, 1975.

———. *Years of Challenge and Growth.* New Delhi: Rubicon, 1977.

Parmar, Y. S., and Himachal Pradesh India. *Himachal Pradesh: Its Proper Shape and Status.* Simla: Directorate of Public Relations, Himachal Pradesh, 1965.

Pinney, Christopher. *Camera Indica: The Social Life of Indian Photographs.* Chicago: University of Chicago Press, 1997.

———. *Photos of the Gods: The Printed Image and Political Struggle in India.* New Delhi: Oxford University Press, 2004.

Poovey, Mary. *A History of the Modern Fact: Problems of Knowledge in the Sciences of Wealth and Society.* Chicago: University of Chicago Press, 1998.

Prasad, Leela. *Poetics of Conduct: Oral Narrative and Moral Being in a South Indian Town.* New York: Columbia University Press, 2007.

Presler, Franklin A. *Religion under Bureaucracy: Policy Administration for Hindu Temples in South India.* Cambridge, UK: Cambridge University Press, 1987.

Punjab Government. *Punjab District Gazetteers: Volume XXX, Kangra District.* Edited by Sudershan Vashishtha. 1917. Reprint, Shimla: Himachal Pradesh Academy of Arts, Culture and Language, 2003.

Radice, William. *Swami Vivekananda and the Modernization of Hinduism.* New York: Oxford University Press, 1998.

Raghavan, V. *Festivals, Sports, and Pastimes of India.* Ahmedabad: B.J. Institute of Learning and Research, 1979.

Ramaswamy, Sumathi. *Passions of the Tongue: Language Devotion in Tamil India, 1891–1970.* Berkeley: University of California Press, 1997.

Ramusack, Barbara N. *The Indian Princes and Their States.* Cambridge, UK: Cambridge University Press, 2004.

Rose, H.A., Denzil Ibbetson, and Edward Maclagan. *A Glossary of the Tribes and Castes of the Punjab and North-West Frontier Province.* 3 vols. New Delhi: Rima, 1985.

Rudolph, Lloyd I., and Susanne Hoeber Rudolph. *In Pursuit of Lakshmi: The Political Economy of the Indian State.* Chicago: University of Chicago Press, 1987.

Russell, William Howard. *My Diary in India in the Year 1858–59.* Vol. 2. London: Routledge, Warne and Routledge, 1860.

Sanderson, Alexis. "Meaning in Tantric Ritual." In *Essais sur le rituel III: Colloque du Centenaire de la Section des Sciences religieuses de l'École Pratique des Hautes Études,* edited by Anne-Marie Blondeau and Kristopher Schipper, 15–95. Louvain: Peeters, 1995.

———. "Purity and Power among the Brahmans of Kashmir." In *The Category of the Person,* edited by S. Collins and S. Lukes M. Carrithers, 190–210. Cambridge, UK: Oxford University Press, 1985.

Savarkar, Vinayak Damodar. *Hindutva: Who Is a Hindu?* 5th ed. New Delhi: Hindi Sahitya Sadan, 2003.

Sax, William Sturman. *Mountain Goddess: Gender and Politics in a Himalayan Pilgrimage.* New York: Oxford University Press, 1991.

Scott, David. "Colonial Governmentality." *Social Text* 43 (Autumn 1995): 191–220.

Scott, David, and Charles Hirschkind, ed. *Powers of the Secular Modern: Talal Asad and His Interlocutors.* Cultural Memory in the Present. Stanford: Stanford University Press, 2006.

Scott, James C. *Seeing Like a State: How Certain Schemes to Improve the Human Condition Have Failed.* New Haven: Yale University Press, 1998.

Sehgal, Satyapal. "In Himachal Fiction Writing Is Up and Up." *Tribune* (Chandigarh), October 14, 2001.

Shabab, Dilram. *Kullu: Himalayan Abode of the Divine.* New Delhi: Indus, 1999.

Sharma, Aradhana, and Akhil Gupta. *The Anthropology of the State: A Reader.* Blackwell Readers in Anthropology. Oxford: Blackwell, 2006.

Sharma, Birbal. "Himāchal Darśan." Mandi: Birbal Sharma, 1997.

Sharma, Chuni lal. *Shathka: A Village Survey of Kumarasain Sub-Tehsil, Mahasu District.* Shimla: Government of India Press, 1966.

Sharma, Jagdish, ed. *Himāchal Pradeś Kī Lokgāthāeṃ.* Shimla: Himachal Pradesh Academy of Art, Culture, and Language, 2000.

Sharma, Mahesh. *The Realm of Faith: Subversion, Appropriation and Dominance in the Western Himalaya.* Shimla: Indian Institute of Advanced Study, 2001.

Singer, Milton B. *When a Great Tradition Modernizes: An Anthropological Approach to Indian Civilization.* London: Pall Mall, 1972.

Singh, Jogishwar. *Banks, Gods and Government: Institutional and Informal Credit Structure in a Remote and Tribal Indian District (Kinnaur, Himachal Pradesh), 1960–1985.* Stuttgart: F. Steiner Verlag Wiesbaden, 1989.

Singh, Kashmir. "Selected Speeches on the Floor of the Vidhān Sabhā, Discussion of the States Re-Organization Bill, Reprint from the Debates, April 3–5, 1956." *Vidhānmālā* 9, no. 1–2 (2002): 208–278.

Singh, Mian Goverdhan. *Festivals, Fairs and Customs of Himachal Pradesh.* New Delhi: Indus, 1992.

———. *Himāchal Pradeś: Itihās, Saṇskṛti Evan Ārthik Avasthā.* Translated by Caman Lal Gupta. Shimla: Minerva Book House, 1999.

Singh, R.C. Pal. *Census of India, 1961.* Vol. 5, *Himachal Pradesh.* New Delhi: Manager of Publications, 1961.

Smith, Donald Eugene. *India as a Secular State.* Princeton, NJ: Princeton University Press, 1963.

Smith, Jonathan Z. *Imagining Religion: From Babylon to Jonestown.* Chicago: University of Chicago Press, 1982.

Smith, R. Boswel. *Life of Lord Lawrence.* Vol. 2. London: Smith, Elder and Co., 1883.

Sontheimer, Gunther. *Essays of Religion, Literature and Law.* Delhi: Manohar, 2004.

Srinivas, Mysore Narasimhachar, S. Seshaiah, V.S. Parthasarathy, Institute for Social and Economic Change, Indian Council of Social Science Research, and Indian Institute of Advanced Study. *Dimensions of Social Change in India.* Columbia, MO: South Asia Books, 1978.

Srivastava, Shyam Chandra. *Indian Census in Perspective.* New Delhi: Office of the Registrar General, India Ministry of Home Affairs, 1983.

Stientencron, Heinrich von. "Charisma and Canon: The Dynamics of Legitimization and Innovation in Indian Religions." In *Charisma and Canon: Essays on the Religious History of the Indian Subcontinent,* edited by Vasudha Dalmia,

Angelika Malinar, and Martin Christof, 14–38. New Delhi: Oxford University Press, 2001.

Stokes, Eric. *The English Utilitarians and India.* Oxford: Clarendon Press, 1959.

Strayed, Cheryl. *Tiny Beautiful Things: Advice on Love and Life from Dear Sugar.* New York: Vintage, 2012.

Swami, Krishnanad. "24–4-1953 Vidhān Sabhā Debates." Vidhān Sabhā Archives, 1953.

———. "Viśeṣ Ākarṣṇa-III." In *Vidhān Mālā* 8, no. 1–2 (2001): 155–228.

Taussig, Michael. *The Magic of the State.* New York: Routledge, 1997.

Thakur, Laxman S. *The Architectural Heritage of Himachal Pradesh: Origin and Development of Temple Styles.* New Delhi: Munshiram Manohar, 1996.

Thakur, Molu Ram. *Himāchal Meṃ Pūjit Devī-Devatā.* New Delhi: Rshabhacarana Jaina evam Santati, 1981.

———. *Myths, Rituals, and Beliefs in Himachal Pradesh.* New Delhi: Indus, 1997.

Thomas, George Powell. *Views of Simla.* London: Dickinson, 1846.

Thompson, Edward John. *The Making of the Indian Princes.* London: Oxford University Press, H. Milford, 1943.

Traill, G. W. "Statistical Sketch of Kumaun." *Asiatic Researches* 16 (1828).

Trautmann, Thomas R. *Languages and Nations: The Dravidian Proof in Colonial Madras.* Berkeley: University of California Press, 2006.

Tsing, Anna Lowenhaupt. *In the Realm of the Diamond Queen: Marginality in an Out-of-the-Way Place.* Princeton, NJ: Princeton University Press, 1993.

Vaidya, H. L. *Those Turbulent Days.* Delhi: Indian Publishers and Distributors, 1999.

Vashisth, Sudarshan, ed. *Himāchal Pradeś Ke Lok Gīt.* Shimla: Himachal Pradesh Sanskriti Bhasa Akademy, n.d.

———, ed. *Maṇḍī Dev Milan.* Shimla: Himachal Pradesh Academy of Art, Culture and Language, 1997.

Verma, V. *The Emergence of Himachal Pradesh: A Survey of Constitutional Developments.* New Delhi: Indus, 1995.

Vogel, Jean Philippe, and Bahadur Chand Chhabra. *Antiquities of Chamba State.* Memoirs of the Archaeological Survey of India 72. 1911. Reprint, New Delhi: Archaeological Survey of India, 1994.

Vyathit, Gautan. *Lal Chand Prarthi.* Shimla: Himachal Pradesh Academy of Art, Culture, Language, 1994.

Wace, E. C. *Final Report on the First Regular Settlement of the Simla District in the Punjab.* Vol. HPSA 894–867 (31). Calcutta: Calcutta Central Press, 1884.

Washbrook, D. A. "Law, State and Agrarian Society in Colonial India." *Modern Asian Studies* 15, no. 3 (1981): 649–721.

Weightman, Simon C. R., and S. M. Pandey. "The Semantic Fields of *Dharm* and *Kartavy* in Modern Hindi." In *The Concept of Duty in South Asia,* edited by Wendy Doniger O'Flaherty and J. Duncan M. Derrett, 217–227. Columbia, MO: South Asia Books, 1978.

Index

abjection, 173, 198–200
Ambika, 25, 74–75
apple, 30, 163, 223
archive, 10, 16, 41, 66, 95, 98–99, 112,
    144–145, 231, 244, 249–251–257, 262,
    273–276, 285
Ārya Samāj, 187
authenticity, 6, 146–148, 162–164, 176,
    180–188, 195, 216, 231, 241

Banar, 150, 162, 262
baṇdhārī, 90
Banjar, 25, 86
Barnes, George Carnac, 63, 249
bāveri, 129
Beas River, 155, 188
becoming, 1–7, 237–241
Bekhali Mata, 75
Bengal, 8, 13, 96, 187, 262, 279
Bengali Renaissance, 8, 13
Benjamin, Walter, 114, 258
Bhairava, 170
Bhakra, 29, 36–37, 247
bhekhal, 182–183
Bhīmākālī, 72, 75, 223–227, 251, 255, 270,
    281
bhunda, 182, 263, 265

Bhuri Singh Museum, 108
Bhutnāth, 155
Bijli Mahadev, 74
Biśu, 119, 125
blood, 17, 100, 134, 192, 205–206, 213,
    227–228, 232
Brahmaur, 29, 106, 258, 279
Buddhism, 22–23, 29, 87, 183
Bushahar, 2, 23, 25, 41, 43, 49, 66–67,
    74–75, 87, 133, 174, 223, 245

calculation, 74, 102, 141, 147
canon, 93, 95, 116–119, 231, 259, 284
capitalism, 7, 179–180, 196
caste, 43, 60, 63, 99, 104, 145–146,
    182–183, 206, 251, 255–256, 275, 283
categorization, 98–99, 139–145
census, 17, 21, 28–29, 99–101, 103–108,
    110, 141, 143, 146, 231, 250, 256–258,
    282, 284
Chamba, 22–25, 27, 67, 70–72, 74–75,
    89–90, 108, 143, 249, 251, 258, 266, 279,
    285
Chamunda, 89
Chand, Sansar, 23
Chandigarh, 28, 58, 96, 163, 223, 248, 258,
    267, 269, 277, 283